Taekwondo

This book provides a comprehensive overview of the historical, political, and technical evolution of taekwondo. Many of the supposedly 'traditional' and 'ancient' Korean cultural elements attached to taekwondo are, in fact, remnants of East Asia's modernization drive, and largely inherited from the Japanese martial arts. The current historical portrayal has created an obstacle to a clear understanding of the history of taekwondo, and presents problems and contradictions in philosophy and training methodology. Using rich empirical data, including interviews with leading figures in the field, this book brings together martial arts philosophy with an analysis of the technical aspects and the development of taekwondo, and provides a detailed comparison of karate and taekwondo techniques. It debunks nationalistic mythology surrounding taekwondo to provide a reinterpretation of taekwondo's evolution.

Udo Moenig is a lecturer in the Department of Taekwondo, Youngsan University, South Korea.

Routledge Research in Sports History

The *Routledge Research in Sports History* series presents leading research in the development and historical significance of modern sport through a collection of historiographical, regional, and thematic studies which span a variety of periods, sports, and geographical areas. Showcasing ground-breaking, cross-disciplinary work from established and emerging sport historians, the series provides a crucial contribution to the wider study of sport and society.

Available in this series:

1 **Representing the Sporting Past in Museums and Halls of Fame**
   Edited by Murray G. Phillips

2 **Physical Culture and Sport in Soviet Society**
   Propaganda, acculturation, and transformation in the 1920s and 1930s
   Susan Grant

3 **A Contemporary History of Women's Sport, Part One**
   Sporting women, 1850–1960
   Jean Williams

4 **Making Sport History**
   Disciplines, identities and the historiography of sport
   Edited by Pascal Delheye

5 **A Social History of Tennis in Britain**
   Robert Lake

6 **Association Football**
   A study in figurational sociology
   Graham Curry and Eric Dunning

7 **Taekwondo**
   From a martial art to a martial sport
   Udo Moenig

Taekwondo
From a martial art to a martial sport

Udo Moenig

LONDON AND NEW YORK

First published 2015
by Routledge
2 Park Square, Milton Park, Abingdon, Oxon, OX14 4RN

and by Routledge
711 Third Avenue, New York, NY 10017

Routledge is an imprint of the Taylor & Francis Group, an informa business

© 2015 Udo Moenig

The right of Udo Moenig to be identified as author of this work has been asserted by him in accordance with the Copyright, Designs and Patent Act 1988.

All rights reserved. No part of this book may be reprinted or reproduced or utilised in any form or by any electronic, mechanical, or other means, now known or hereafter invented, including photocopying and recording, or in any information storage or retrieval system, without permission in writing from the publishers.

Every effort has been made to contact copyright holders for their permission to reprint material in this book. The publishers would be grateful to hear from any copyright holder who is not here acknowledged and will undertake to rectify any errors or omissions in future editions of this book.

Trademark notice: Product or corporate names may be trademarks or registered trademarks, and are used only for identification and explanation without intent to infringe.

British Library Cataloguing in Publication Data
A catalogue record for this book is available from the British Library

Library of Congress Cataloging in Publication Data
Moenig, Udo.
Taekwondo : from a martial art to a martial sport / by Udo Moenig.
pages cm. — (Routledge Studies in Sports History)
1. Tae kwon do—History. 2. Tae kwon do—Training. I. Title.
II. Title: Tae kwon do.
GV1114.9M64 2015
796.815'7—dc23
2014037610

ISBN: 978-1-138-83983-0 (hbk)
ISBN: 978-1-315-73322-7 (ebk)

Typeset in Times New Roman
by FiSH Books Ltd, Enfield

For Greg, the old generation, and Achilles, the new generation of taekwondo fighters

Contents

List of figures xi
List of tables xiii
Acknowledgments xiv

Introduction 1

1 **Early Korean martial arts and *t'aekkyŏn*** 13
   The prevalent portrayal of taekwondo history 13
   Weaponless martial arts in early Korean history 14
   Early existing t'aekkyŏn *records* 18
   T'aekkyŏn in modern times 23
   T'aekkyŏn as an example of the 'invention of tradition' 25
   Summary 26
   Notes 28
   Bibliography 31

2 **The relationship of taekwondo to karate** 34
   Karate in Okinawa and theories regarding its origin 34
   The introduction of karate to Japan (1922) 37
   The introduction of karate to Korea (1944) 39
   Early attempts to renounce the Japanese karate tradition 44
   The emergence of new leaders in the post-Korean War period (1953) 46
   A new name for the art: the dawn of taekwondo (1955) 48
   The formation of modern taekwondo 51
   Summary 55
   Notes 57
   Bibliography 62

viii Contents

3 The significance of forms   66
The origins of forms training in Asian martial arts   66
The origins of taekwondo forms   67
Existing forms and interesting features in early taekwondo manuals   69
Forms training in modern times   78
Summary   80
Notes   80
Bibliography   82

4 The origins of full-contact sparring   84
The introduction of free sparring to karate training   84
The attitudes of Korean leaders toward full-contact sparring   88
The introduction of full-contact sparring to Korea   90
Summary   93
Notes   94
Bibliography   96

5 The origins of taekwondo competition rules   98
The original competition rules   98
Important competition rule changes during the 1960s and 1970s   100
The quest to join the Olympics: competition rule changes during the 1980s and 1990s   101
Comprehensive changes of competition rules after 2000   102
Improvement of scoring transparency   103
Unanticipated outcomes of recent competition rule changes   107
The competition system of the International Taekwondo Federation (ITF)   108
Safety considerations in taekwondo sparring in comparison to other combat sports   109
Summary   110
Notes   112
Bibliography   113

6 The evolution of sparring technique   115
Kicking techniques in early karate and taekwondo   115
Modification and innovation of techniques in early taekwondo full-contact sparring   118
General trends and tendencies in taekwondo sparring history   126
The evolution of specific techniques in sport taekwondo   129

Summary 138
Notes 140
Bibliography 142

7 The philosophical roots of taekwondo 145
The philosophical aspects of East Asian martial arts 149
The philosophical foundations of taekwondo 156
The introduction of a sports character to the East Asian martial arts 161
The inconclusive transformation of taekwondo into a sport 163
The diversification of taekwondo training activities 165
Summary 167
Notes 169
Bibliography 172

8 Forms versus sparring 175
The technical inconsistencies in taekwondo 175
The purpose of forms training 180
The purpose of forms training in taekwondo 181
General training activities in taekwondo schools 183
Summary 183
Notes 184
Bibliography 185

9 Conclusion: the incomplete transformation of taekwondo from a 'martial art' to a 'martial sport' 186
Fact and fiction in Korean martial arts presentations 187
The formation of modern Japanese and Korean martial arts 187
A reinterpretation of taekwondo's origins 189
The origins of taekwondo as a sport 190
The cause of inconsistencies in taekwondo philosophy and training activity 190
The value of taekwondo as a martial art for self-defense 191
The diversification of taekwondo training activities and the arising contradictions 192
Concluding remarks 193
Notes 195
Bibliography 196

Appendix A: Individuals interviewed for this study 197
Appendix B: General classification and terminology of East
  Asian martial arts 199
Appendix C: Martial arts literature in chronological order 202
Appendix D: Forms in early taekwondo manuals 207
Appendix E: General terminology for kicking techniques in
  taekwondo 211

Glossary 213
About the author 224
Index 226

Figures

1.1	The *Muye chepo pŏnyŏk sokchip*, *kwŏnbŏp* instructions	17
1.2	*Taek'wae-do*	19
2.1	Connections of *kwan* or school founders to karate	43
3.1	Timeline for the general use of forms in taekwondo schools	69
3.2	Existing publications of *kwan* founders, their students, and Choi Hong Hi	70
3.3	*Solim Changkwŏn* by Hwang Kee	72
3.4	World Taekwondo Poomsae Championships gold medalist, Noreen Thackery (USA)	79
4.1	Kendo *bōgu* gear	86
4.2	*Bōgu* sparring at Tōyō University in Tokyo, in 1937, at Sensei Motobu Chōki's karate club	87
4.3	Kendo fencing at an agricultural school in Japan during the early twentieth century	90
4.4	1958 demo at presidential mansion square (Seoul, Korea)	91
4.5	1960s-style modified body protector: *hogu* with bamboo stick inserts	92
5.1	First officially recognized electronic body protector by the WTF	105
5.2	The center referee	106
6.1	The contact area of the roundhouse-kick	120
6.2	The instep roundhouse-kick	120
6.3	The evolution of the roundhouse-kick	122
6.4	The evolution of the back-kick	123
6.5	The counter back-kick against a roundhouse-kick attack	124
6.6	The counter spinning-back-kick against an attack	125
6.7	The under-kick against a roundhouse-kick attack	127
6.8	The punch	130
6.9	The push-kick	131
6.10	The axe-kick	132
6.11	The spinning-back-kick	134
6.12	The cut-kick	136
6.13	Reinhard Langer (left) against Ko Chŏng-ho (right) in 1983	137
6.14	Modern taekwondo training for competition	140
7.1	Taekwondo training in Korea (Youngsan University team)	168

8.1	The traditional forward stance	177
8.2	The sparring stance	177
8.3	The traditional punch (I)	178
8.4	The punch in boxing and Thai-boxing	178
8.5	The traditional punch (II)	178
8.6	The punch in taekwondo sparring	178
8.7	The front-kick versus the roundhouse-kick	180
A.1	Foreigners training in Korea at Dongsŏng High School, during the early 1990s	224

Tables

2.1	Terminology used for Chinese *quanfa*	35
2.2	Terminology used for karate (I)	35
2.3	Terminology used for karate (II)	37
2.4	Founders and founding *kwan* of taekwondo	45
3.1	Funakoshi's 13 *Shōrin-ryū* and 6 *Shōrei-ryū kata* in *Karate-dō Kyōhan*	71
5.1	Paper and pencil scoring limitations – losing points	104
5.2	The use of protective equipment in combat sports	110
6.1	Samples of kicking techniques in early karate and taekwondo manuals	117
6.2	General trends in the use of taekwondo sparring techniques	128
6.3	Estimated timeline for the evolution of kicking techniques	139
7.1	The correlation between objectives, values, and training methodologies in martial arts	148
7.2	Time periods for the taekwondo diversification process	167

Appendix B

A.1	General classifications of East Asian martial arts	199

Appendix D

3.2	Forms described and/or illustrated in early taekwondo literature (I)	208
3.3	Forms described and/or illustrated in early taekwondo literature (II)	209
3.4	Forms described and/or illustrated in early taekwondo literature (III)	210

Appendix E

6.4	Terminology used for kicking techniques and punches	211

Acknowledgments

This work could not have been completed without the patient help and support of my wife Pranom, as well as my many colleagues and friends. I would especially like to thank my taekwondo senior, Dr. Gregory S. Kailian, for proofreading the different chapters numerous times, and for making suggestions for improvement.

I have been working on this book for well over six years. Based on my Ph.D. dissertation, "The Incomplete Transformation of Taekwondo from a 'Martial Art' to a 'Martial Sport,'" several chapters previously appeared in various academic journals, some co-authored with friends and colleagues who helped me, or provided me with research material or other kinds of support. Chapter 1 was published in the *Acta Koreana* (Cho, Sungkyun, Udo Moenig, and Dohee Nam. "The Available Evidence Regarding T'aekkyŏn and Its Portrayal as a 'Traditional Korean Martial Art.'" *Acta Koreana*, 15, 2 [2012]: pp. 341–68); Chapter 3 was published in the *Korea Journal* (Moenig, Udo, Sungkyun Cho, and Taek Yong Kwak. "Evidence of Taekwondo's Roots in Karate: An Analysis of the Technical Content of Early 'Taekwondo' Literature." *Korea Journal*, 54, 2 [2014]: pp. 150–178); and, Chapter 5 was published in the *The International Journal of the History of Sport* (Moenig, Udo, Sungkyun Cho, and Hyeongseok Song. "The Modifications of Protective Gear, Rules and Regulations during Taekwondo's Evolution–from Its Obscure Origins to the Olympics." *The International Journal of the History of Sport*, 29, 9 [2012]: 1363–81). Moreover, Chapters 2 and 6 were published solely under my name ("The Influence of Korean Nationalism on the Formational Process of T'aekwŏndo in South Korea." *Archiv Orientalni*, 81 [2013]: 321–44; "The Evolution of Kicking Techniques in Taekwondo." *Journal of Asian Martial Arts*, 20, 1 [2011]: 8–31). This finished book, however, is extensively rewritten and significantly updated.

I would like to express my gratitude to all those who helped me from the initial Ph.D. dissertation research stage to this final publication: Dr. Song Hyeongseok, Dr. Willy Pieter, Dr. Andrew Jackson, Dr. Steven D. Capener, Dr. Kevin Shepard, Cashel Rosier, Dr. Yang Jin Bang, Dr. Cho Sungkyun, Dr. Kwak Taek Yong, Matthew Cullivan, and David Baleanquel.

Peter Bolz, and my good friend Michael Chong-Sok Han, contributed many of the photographs. Additionally, while many of my university students posed for pictures, the photographs without attribution were taken by me.

Special thanks are due to my taekwondo master instructors, Ko Eui Min, and Kim Sei Hyeok, who invited me to work out for many years at Dongsŏng High School in Seoul.

Lastly, thanks to the many friends and training partners, with whom I trained and sparred, over the years; especially the members of the Corona Taekwondo Club, Steven D. Capener, Greg Kailian, Stig Kramer, Bobby Clayton, Andrew Jackson, Mads (Kato) Nielsen, James O'Sullivan, and Dan Harmon, as well as my German friends, Norbert Illmann, Eugen Nefedow, and Georg Streif.

Although this book has taken me over six years to research and write, I remain somewhat unsatisfied with several sections. I am not a native English speaker, and my English writing skills are not what I would wish them to be; nevertheless, I must acknowledge and accept any inadequacies, and flaws. I take full responsibility for mistakes of omission and commission, and readily admit that all errors were mine, alone, and not those of my many sources. Hopefully, critical readers will inform me of problems in grammar, usage, syntax, research, or content.

Udo Moenig

Introduction

Originally, this study intended to be narrow in focus, with a sole concentration on the technical development of taekwondo sparring. I had taken for granted that taekwondo was known to be an offshoot of karate; although, as it turns out, the martial arts 'establishment' is far from agreement on this issue. Therefore, in order to begin the analysis of taekwondo's evolution, I found it necessary to return to the discussion about the origins of taekwondo and its relation to karate, a decision which forced me to considerably broaden my research. Since taekwondo's historical depiction has been greatly distorted over the last fifty to sixty years, objective analysis was difficult to undertake. As a result, this book has turned into a historical research study, with certain philosophical and technical issues addressed in the analysis.

Because I analyze the historical, technical, and philosophical components of taekwondo's evolution, my range and focus may seem, at times, to have been overly broad. However, since these components are closely interrelated, any comprehensive study would need to include all elements to provide an accurate picture. Furthermore, taekwondo's evolution was affected by significant historical, political, and cultural forces which cannot be ignored in any comprehensive analysis.

Martial arts are first and foremost a physical activity, and the essential, fundamental element is practical training. Physical activity is the foundation from which the mental and spiritual aspects of martial arts have their basis. One cannot claim to be a martial artist by merely philosophizing or theorizing about it; the training hall or gymnasium is the foremost place for martial arts education and training, not the study room or meditation chamber. This is not to suggest that mental guidance does not play an important role, but rather to stress that the physical training component in martial arts is the point from which spiritual development begins. The spiritual aspects of martial arts may be the ultimate objective of many practitioners and instructors, but it is not the starting point.

This brings us to, what I consider to be a fundamental division in the general martial arts world: the division between self-styled *traditionalists*, who often emphasize the spiritual characteristics of martial arts, and adhere to the fundamental objectives of self-defense; and *modernists*, who emphasize pragmatic methods associated with sports training. This split is manifested by the different training methodologies followed by the two camps – forms versus sparring. There also exists much conflict and confusion over how to deal with the sporting aspects on a philosophical level. This study will focus on the little understood schism between traditionalists and modernists, which represents the root cause of many of the contradictions, inconsistencies, and problems within the training activities and philosophies of the martial arts in general, and taekwondo in particular.

In reality, taekwondo consists of many different components, loosely consolidated into two main divisions: 'traditional' (forms/self-defense) taekwondo, which is associated with conventional martial arts training, and sparring/competition taekwondo, which is considered a combat sport. The former represents a vestigial legacy from Japanese karate, whereas the latter represents taekwondo free-sparring techniques and methods invented and developed in Korea over the past fifty years.

Despite this clear dichotomy, taekwondo is historically and philosophically still presented as a single entity that seeks common goals, and claims to have compatible, consolidated training activities. Most modern day taekwondo leaders want to preserve this image of unity while, at the same time, encouraging further diversification in the form of *p'umsae* (forms or patterns), board-breaking, and other theatrical competitive events including taekwondo demonstrations, aerobics, dance, creative performances, and gymnastic-style entertainment. As a result, the question naturally arises about which activities accurately define or represent taekwondo, today.

In addition, because of all the many new activities included under the umbrella and name 'taekwondo,' a general lack of direction and consistency seems to have developed. In connection with this, taekwondo leaders are neither able to present a consistent philosophy, nor a consistent training methodology for contemporary taekwondo. The origin of this apparent identity conflict is not very well understood because the portrayal of taekwondo's history has been, at times, disingenuous with a general lack of openness in the discussion. The current historical portrayal has actually become an obstacle to understanding this dilemma and reforming taekwondo. Therefore, taekwondo's early transplantation from Japan, genuine evolution, and subsequent development into a new martial sport, needs to be examined and analyzed in order to more intelligently discuss the current state and better ensure the future growth of taekwondo.

Definitions and linguistic essentials

A bewildering array of general martial arts terminology exists (see Appendix B), especially with reference to taekwondo, which serves to confuse the issues and muddy the waters related to arguments about origins. For those not familiar with Asia and martial arts, it is profoundly important to define and explain essential terminology. Hence, this section touches on definitions used throughout this study.

Romanization of Korean, Japanese, and Chinese terms

The Romanized spelling of Asian terms in general literature is seldom standardized and often arbitrary, thus contributing to the confusion regarding pronunciation, spelling, and the meaning of terms. In this study, the Romanization of words was conducted according to the McCune-Reischauer system for Korean, the Hepburn for Japanese, and the Pinyin (without tone mark indicators) for Chinese. The 'McCune-Reischauer system' was chosen over the 'Revised Romanization of Korean' introduced by the Korean 'Ministry of Culture, Sports and Tourism,' because in most international academic publications the former is customarily used. I did not revise direct quotes or words assimilated in English: for example, taekwondo, judo, or kungfu. I also chose to leave the spelling of names used by well-known individuals and authors. For example, Choi Hong Hi or Hwang Kee, are spelled the way they are known in popular literature, so that it is easier for non-experts in Asian studies to follow the narrative. However, as a result, some persons' names, or terms such as 'taekwondo,' can be seen spelled in a variety of ways in direct quotations throughout this study. Foreign words, which are not assimilated into English, are indicated in italics, with the exception of proper names. I chose not to capitalize 'taekwondo' because the names of other sports are not capitalized either. In the text, Korean and Japanese names are left according to tradition, family names first.

Taekwondo terminology used in this study

The analysis of taekwondo literature can be complicated due to the absence of any uniform language. The terminology of techniques has changed over time; different schools and regions prefer certain different terms, and slang is often used as well. Furthermore, especially for younger readers, some of the older terms used in taekwondo literature might be completely unfamiliar.

Although the Kukkiwon-based, World Taekwondo Academy (WTA),[1] aims to standardize taekwondo language, success has, so far, remained elusive. The WTA has, however, mostly achieved consensus on the terminology regarding forms and related techniques, as well as the formal language of the sparring competition process. With that being said, there was a complete absence of any formal language regarding kicking techniques for sparring until recently, even though this aspect of taekwondo is represented at the International Olympic Games. In 2009, the World Taekwondo Academy finally made an attempt to bring some standardization to this process.[2] However, the result was unsatisfactory because terms were presented in an unstructured and often overly complicated fashion. In addition, the WTA released the terms only in Korean, leaving no standardized English terminology as of yet. Chapter 6 explains in detail many of the techniques and terms used in taekwondo sparring (see also Table 6.4 in Appendix E for English and Korean terminology of kicking techniques). In regards to key terminology used in this study, this book distinguishes between two fundamentally different systems of taekwondo: 'traditional taekwondo' versus 'sport taekwondo.'

Traditional taekwondo

Throughout this study, 'traditional taekwondo,' refers to schools that use training methods which preserve and pursue conventional self-defense oriented martial arts objectives. As a fundamental training methodology, traditional taekwondo stresses the practice of basics, forms, and repetitive patterns and stance postures that tend to be somewhat static in execution. Moreover, training routines and policies tend to be conservative in nature with an emphasis on copying the teacher as closely as possible. While the term includes those traditional elements present in the taekwondo style of the World Taekwondo Federation (WTF), it also embraces other traditional-based taekwondo systems like those of the International Taekwondo Federation (ITF),[3] as well as Hwang Kee's Tang Soo Do style, among myriad others.

Sport taekwondo

In contrast, the full-contact, sparring-based training activities that feature competitions and a sporting character as a central basis, are referred to, at times, as 'sparring taekwondo,' 'sparring/competition taekwondo,' 'sparring/sport taekwondo,' or simply 'sport taekwondo.' However, in this study, these terms refer only to the sparring style practiced by the World Taekwondo Federation, which is recognized as an Olympic sport. Therefore, these terms may not apply to other sparring systems and styles practiced by other taekwondo organizations.

Popular literature also often refers to WTF-style taekwondo as 'Olympic taekwondo' in distinction to all other styles and organizations not recognized by the International Olympic Committee (IOC). I chose not to use this term since the WTF, and all WTF-style commercial taekwondo schools and recreational clubs retain many traditional taekwondo training elements, as well. In addition, WTF-style taekwondo has introduced a variety of new activities such as demonstration taekwondo and aerobics, while 'Olympic-style taekwondo' represents really only the 'sparring/competition element' of the WTF. I also intentionally avoided the term 'competitive taekwondo,' which is used in several American taekwondo publications, because it harbors some nuances regarding 'competitive sports,' in contrast to 'recreational sports.' I want to emphasize that those students who train taekwondo as a recreational sport, nevertheless, can and should engage in sparring and competitions.

I avoided the term 'modern taekwondo' in connection with 'sparring/competition taekwondo,' because 'traditional taekwondo' (according to the definition above) also developed some new training elements and activities in modern times, such as demonstration taekwondo, modern forms contests, and artistic performances. These elements are often loosely related to traditional taekwondo in terms of technique, methodology, and/or spirit. In addition, these elements are often practiced and supported by the same practitioners that regard themselves as followers of traditional taekwondo.

Karate and taekwondo literature

Although many books have been written concerning karate, taekwondo techniques, and training methods, the existing literature focuses primarily on instructional manuals. Very early on, some excellent Japanese karate manuals were published with high-quality content, presentation methods, and illustrations. In contrast, there are only a limited number of (recently published) Korean taekwondo publications that have reached this standard. This literature review introduces not only principal sources, but also presents a general historical overview of karate and taekwondo literature

Early karate manuals

Since taekwondo is a direct descendant of karate, and karate literature predates taekwondo literature, a close investigation of early karate publications is necessary. The Hawaii Karate Museum has an extensive collection of karate books and articles dating back to the late nineteenth century. The first article citing Okinawan karate (at that time under a different name) in this collection was published in 1873.[4] The first comprehensive book written about karate, with full technical illustrations, is generally considered to be *Ryūkū Kempō Tōdi,* published in Japanese in 1922 by the late Okinawan karate master Funakoshi Gichin. The illustrations in this book consist only of drawings, but the 1925 revised and expanded version, *Rentan Goshin Tōdi-jutsu,* displays photographs.[5] Funakoshi was the founder of *Shōtōkan* karate, although he never referred to it as such, instead calling his art *karate-dō*.

The second publication to use photographs was the work of Motobu Chōki, *Okinawa Kenpō Tōdi Jutsu Kumite-Hen* (1926), the following year.[6] Motobu was a well-known pioneer in *kumite* (free fighting), as indicated by his book title. Several self-defense manuals for women, police, and some publications from Tokyo University followed these earliest books. In 1932, Motobu compiled a second work with the title: *Watashi no Karate-Jutsu*.[7] Another influential instructor, Mabuni Kenwa, published a variety of manuals during the 1930s, as well.

During this period, Funakoshi's main work, *Karate-Dō Kyōhan* (1935),[8] was the most influential. Revised and republished in 1957 shortly after his death, the book was translated into English in 1973. Funakoshi's works are interesting for the development of early karate because of his relationship to several of taekwondo's founders.

During the 1930s and 1940s, when the West had little knowledge of karate, dozens of books and articles were written, but only in Japanese. Most consider the first English language book with a karate link to be a work written by James M. Mitose in Hawaii, *What is Self Defense? Kenpo Jiu-Jitsu* (1953).[9] Several English-language karate publications soon followed, the most important among them Ōyama Masutatsu's,[10] 1958 publication, *What is Karate?*. Ōyama started karate training under Funakoshi, studied under several famous masters, and finally sought to establish his own style of karate, *Kyokushin Kaikan*, during the late

1950s. He included techniques from other martial arts, with heavy emphasis on full-contact sparring without any protective padding. However, Ōyama's works are not essential to this study, because he was not related to any of the taekwondo founders, and did not become a prominent figure in karate until the late 1950s.

The most influential book about karate was the classic work of Nishiyama Hidetaka, *Karate Art of Empty Hand Fighting* (co-author Brown), first published in 1960. Nishiyama started learning *Shōtōkan* karate in 1943 in one of Funakoshi's schools, and during the 1950s, he was considered one of the best instructors in Japan. In 1961, he emigrated and became one of the most influential instructors in the United States. His book has been the most-sold book on karate, and is still in print. There also exists a variety of other early karate publications, which could not all be mentioned in this review because of their minor importance; karate publications after this period are considered to be insignificant for this study.

Early Korean martial arts manuals

A brief overview of early exiting Korean martial arts manuals discussed in detail in Chapter 3, follows. Most of the manuals published in Korea are very rare, with only a few copies left in a number of Korean libraries. In 1949 (*Tan'gi* 4282),[11] Hwang Kee, the founder of *Mudŏk Kwan*, published what is thought to be the first modern Korean martial arts book under the title, *Hwasudo textbook* (in Korean only). From early on, he preferred to use Korean names for his art, and the '*hwa*' (花 'flowers') refers to the long ago '*hwa-rang*' (花郎 'flower youth' or 'flower boys'). The book was written in the traditional top to bottom, and right to left direction, and employs extensive use of Chinese characters.

Another very early book, *Kwŏnbŏp textbook* (in Korean only), was published by Ch'oe Song-nam in 1955. Ch'oe was a soldier and a *Ch'ŏngdo Kwan* member.[12] However, Ch'oe was not a key figure in the process of the development and formation of taekwondo.

In his second book, published in 1958 (*Tan'gi* 4291), Hwang Kee uses the title *Tangsudo textbook* (in Korean only). A large part of the book describes, oddly, such various skills as first-aid and how to rescue someone from drowning. In later publications, Hwang also uses the term "Soo Bahk Do" (*subakdo*), which he adapted around the late 1950s, to also describe his art.

Pak Ch'ŏl-hŭi is the author of *Kwŏnbŏp association – Kongsudo textbook* (in Korean only), published in 1958. He was originally a member of the YMCA *Kwŏnbŏp Pu,* but split from the school in 1956 to co-found *Kangdŏk Wŏn*. Park was an influential figure in the formation of taekwondo.

In 1958 (*Tan'gi* 4291), Choi Hong Hi, the founder of *Odo Kwan*, published the first, full-length instructional manual under the name *Taekwondo textbook* (in Korean only), making it the first book using the word 'taekwondo' in its title. Although the Korea Military Academy published around the same time, or possibly earlier, a similar textbook with the same title, using simple drawings instead of photographs. For both books, several *Ch'ŏngdo Kwan* members, among them Nam T'ae-hŭi, reportedly contributed extensively to the content.[13]

Choi's next publication, which was the first English taekwondo manual, followed in 1965 under the title *Taekwondo – The Art of Self-Defence*.[14] This book partly expands on the content of the former Korean publication, using new and better-quality photographs and more detailed explanations. The book was compiled before Choi's break with the Korean taekwondo world, and the South Korean government, during the early 1960s. Considering Choi's status and influence in the formative process to unify taekwondo in Korea, his books are considered representative of general taekwondo activity at that time.

In 1965, a monograph published in English, titled: *Taekwondo: A Way of Life in Korea*, also used the term 'taekwondo' in the title; author Chai Ik Jin stated that his publication pre-dated Choi Hong Hi's by several months.[15] Chai posed for several photographs and most likely advised the American writer, Stanton E. Read, on the content. Chai was first a student at *Ch'angmu Kwan* and later at *Kangdŏk Wŏn*. While not an instructional manual, the book tried to introduce general information about taekwondo to English speaking audiences.

Yi Kyo-yun's manual, titled *Taesudo textbook for the masses* (1965, in Korean only), was the only book published under the name '*taesudo*,' the official name chosen by the martial arts association for the discipline from 1961 to 1965. Yi was originally a member of *Chosŏn Yŏnmu Kwan* but, in 1956, founded *Hanmu Kwan*, which became one of the most important schools. He was an influential leader in early taekwondo.

In 1968, Lee Won Kuk, the founder of *Ch'ŏngdo Kwan*, published, *Taekwondo manual* (in Korean only). Even though, he was the most important and senior figure during the first years of martial arts activity in Korea, he had become largely irrelevant in the Korean taekwondo world by the time of this publication.

Son Duk Sung became the leader of *Ch'ŏngdo Kwan* after Lee Won Kuk fled to Japan. However, during the late 1950s, Son had disagreements with his vice-president and split from the organization. Subsequently, he joined *Kungmu Kwan* and became its leader in 1959.[16] In 1963, Son moved to the United States and several years later, in 1968, he published a book titled *Korean Karate – The Art of Tae Kwon Do* (co-written, Clark). Son was a well-known figure in the Korean taekwondo world and later in the United States.

Sihak Henry Cho, who joined *Jido Kwan* in 1953, was one of the first Korean taekwondo instructors to immigrate to the United States (1958). He wrote several books in English during the late 1960s. In 1968, Cho published first, *Korean Karate – Free Fighting Technique* (1968), and the same year, *Tae Kwon Do – Secrets of Korean Karate*, which presents the same content as his earlier book, but with a different title. Subsequently, he published, *Better Karate for Boys* (1969), and *Self-Defense Karate* (1970). Cho became an influential figure in the American taekwondo world.

Later publications are less important for this study, because that is the time when taekwondo changed substantially and developed distinctively from traditional karate. Despite this fact, one book is worth mentioning because it provides some additional interesting information.

8 *Introduction*

In 1972, as chairman of the technical committee of the Korea Taekwondo Association, Lee Chong Woo published a manual titled *Taekwondo textbook* (in Korean only), which was essentially the first modern taekwondo textbook. Lee was fundamental to the formation and promotion of modern taekwondo while he worked for the Korea Taekwondo Association and the World Taekwondo Federation. He was an original member of *Jido Kwan*, and became its leader in 1967. Subsequently, Lee held the positions of secretary general and vice-president of the World Taekwondo Federation, and vice-president of the Kukkiwon.

Modern taekwondo literature

The era after the 1960s concerns mostly publications regarding sport taekwondo with a focus on sparring and competition. This was the time when sparring technique developed rapidly and separately from traditional technique which stayed largely the same. Therefore, later publications regarding traditional taekwondo are, by and large, not related to this study, with the exception of the presentation of historical and philosophical accounts. On the other hand, sport taekwondo literature helps to explain the technical evolution of sparring technique.

Between the mid-1970s and early 1990s, more than a dozen master's theses at Korean universities and articles in Korean journals were published dealing with the technical aspects and developments in sparring. However, most authors focused on analyzing scoring frequency and kicking patterns in competition. Lee Sung Kook,[17] in particular, contributed to a variety of interesting studies in this field, and some of these articles were helpful in establishing a time-line for the development of kicking techniques.

The first book written about sparring technique is *Taekwondo Wettkampf* (*Taekwondo competition*), 1980, by Ko Eui Min. It was not well-known in Korea because it was published only in German. Ko, the Korean national team coach for the 1975 and 1977 Taekwondo World Championships, moved from Korea to Germany in 1978. All the pictures for this book were taken in Korea, in 1977. Some of the notes for the book about steps and other techniques date back to the early 1970s;[18] therefore, the book provides a good glimpse of the sparring techniques of the 1970s. Many of the models for the pictures were top Korean athletes of that time, including Kim Sei Hyeok (recently retired general director of the Korea Taekwondo Association), Ju Sin-kyu (former head coach of the professional team of the Korea Gas Cooperation during the 1990s, and former national team coach), Ha Sŏk-kwan, and Son Tae-hwan (former world champions). The book shows taekwondo about ten to fifteen years after the introduction of full-contact competitions. Great differences from karate can be seen: Dynamic stances and steps, and especially the existence of direct counterattack kicks; the targets for training (boxing mitts) differ from karate, and in most of the pictures displayed, the body protector (*hogu*) is used to demonstrate technique. The book presents a striking departure from earlier publications, and helps to explain some of the theories discussed in this study. With this publication, taekwondo graduates from being a static, reactive, self-defense oriented physical activity to an exciting, dynamic, pyrotechnical combat sport.

The first book published in Korea about competition taekwondo appeared only in 1988; most likely due to the attention that taekwondo received as a result of its inclusion as a demonstration sport in the Seoul Olympics. The title of the book is *Taekwondo sparring discussion* (in Korean only), by Ch'oe Yŏng-nyŏl. Some years later, Yi Kyŏng-myŏng and Chung Kuk Hyun, the four-time world champion, published a book titled, *Taekwondo sparring* (1994).[19] Unfortunately, however, the quality of pictures is sometimes less than ideal. The manual comprehensively describes the competition system, but many of the aspects, as, for instance, the chapter about rules and regulations, are outdated. For this study, Ch'oe's, and Yi and Chung's books are not of significance, because the technical transformation into modern taekwondo was already completed by that time.

Oddly enough, while English-language publications were leading in quality and quantity in the early years of taekwondo, there have been no books written in English, or translated from Korean into English, exclusively about sparring taekwondo until rather recently. A variety of instructional videos have been published in English about sparring and taekwondo training, but as regards to competition taekwondo, there exists no major original or groundbreaking contribution.

As a result of the many new taekwondo departments at Korean universities, academic publications and research in the field has mushroomed. During the last ten years, many books and articles, as well as master's theses and doctoral dissertations have been published about traditional and sport taekwondo in the fields of science, philosophy, and history. However, critical studies regarding taekwondo's history and development are rare, and it sometimes seems that these fields of inquiry are neither much encouraged nor greatly welcomed as research topics in Korean universities. Instead, many works attempt to reinforce the most commonly accepted popular taekwondo stereotypes, leaving just a few articles critical in nature. The Korean educational establishment does not generally encourage deviation and controversy, preferring, instead, to maintain a polite status quo. And so, because Korean students are integrated into a hierarchical web of relationships and expected behavioral norms, challenges to common views held by the establishment are difficult to find. Perhaps an outsider's perspective is necessary to kindle some degree of critical discussion and debate.

Even though there exist a few critical publications that deal with taekwondo's history and evolution (see Annotation in Appendix C), none of these works relate to taekwondo's contemporary problems: namely the vast diversification of program and training activities in the absence of any consistent philosophy, policy, and direction. Moreover, most of these studies do not suggest any future directions or reforms for taekwondo, at all. The few articles which do include such proposals are now outdated because of the major changes that taekwondo has experienced over the past decade, plus. This book, therefore, will attempt a comprehensive overview and analysis by beginning with an examination of the distant past.

Notes

1 In 1973, the Kukkiwon was established by the South Korean government as the taekwondo headquarters responsible for taekwondo technical matters, policy, and doctrine. It is the home of the World Taekwondo Academy, which is responsible for technical and educational matters, as well as world-wide black belt promotions.
2 See World Taekwondo Academy, [*Research to establish taekwondo terminology*].
3 The International Taekwondo Federation (ITF) split into several organizations after Choi Hong Hi's death in 2002. All of these splinter groups claim to be the official, successor organization.
4 See Hawaii Karate Museum, "Rare Karate Book Collection," (last modified August, 2009). [Retrieved from http://museum.hikari.us/].
5 Noble, "The first Karate books." Funakoshi's *Tōdi arts: Polish your courage for self-defense* (translation of title as in Hawaii Karate Museum) is a reprint of the original Japanese edition. *To-te jitsu* is the title of the English translation. However, the editor of *To-te jitsu* stated that the book was a translation of Funakoshi's 1922 work. In fact, the manual represents a translation of Funkoshi's 1925 book.

'*Tōdi-jutsu*' is an alternative reading of '*karate-jutsu*,' of the two Chinese characters 唐 and 手, and was used by the Okinawans. In this book, Funakoshi still uses the old '*tang*' 唐 character to write 'karate.' In his book from 1935, *Karate-dō kyōhan – The master text*, the character is replaced with the 'empty' 空 character (see a detailed discussion in Chapter 2, pp. 37–8).
6 Reprinted in Koharu, [*Research in early Ryukyu karate*]; an English translation was published in 1995. See Motobu, *Okinawan kempo*. '*Kenpo*' and '*kempo*' are merely different forms of Romanization.
7 Reprinted in Koharu, [*Research in early Ryukyu karate*].
8 Funakoshi's *Karate-dō kyōhan – Master text for the way of the empty-hand* is a translation of the original first edition of 1935. *Karate-dō kyōhan – The master text* is a translation of the second edition of 1957.
9 Noble, "The West learns about the 'empty hand.'"
10 Ōyama was Korean with the birth name Ch'oe Yŏng-ŭi. He went to Japan, learned karate, changed his name and adopted Japanese nationality.
11 '*Tan'gi*' refers to the foundation of the Korean state by the mythical founder Tan-gun. In the Republic of Korea, books were numbered according to this date from 1948–1961.
12 Hŏ, [*Taekwondo's formation history*], p. 43.
13 Kim, "A study on the first taekwondo textbooks."
14 A Korean version exists as well (Choi, [*Taekwondo guide*]), published around the same time.
15 Email correspondence with Chai Ik Jin, October 16, 2013.
16 Hŏ, [*Taekwondo's formation history*], p. 51.
17 Lee Sung Kook (Yi Sŭng-guk) was the coach of the Korean national taekwondo team several times, and later became the president of the Korea National Sport University (한국체육대학교).
18 Ko Eui Min, personal interview, January 13, 2010.
19 An English edition was published in 1999, by Kim *et al.*, *Tae kwon do kyorugi: Olympic-style sparring*.

Bibliography

Cho, Sihak Henry. *Korean karate – Free fighting technique*. Rutland and Tokyo: Charles E. Tuttle Company, 1968.

[Ch'oe Song-nam] (최송남). 拳法敎本 [*Kwŏnbŏp textbook*]. Seoul: Donga Munhwasa, 1955. [In Korean only].

[Ch'oe Yŏng-nyŏl] (최영렬). 태권도 겨루기 論 [Taekwondo *sparring discussion*]. Seoul: Samhak Ch'ulp'ansa, 1988. [In Korean only].
Choi, Hong Hi [Ch'oe Hong-hi] (최홍희). 跆拳道敎本 [*Taekwondo textbook*]. Seoul: Sŏnghwa Munhwasa, 1958. [In Korean only].
_____. *Taekwondo – The art of self-defence*. Seoul: Daeha Publication Company, 1965.
_____. 태권도지침 [*Taekwondo guide*]. Seoul: Chŏngyŏnsa, 1966. [Korean version of *Taekwondo – The art of self-defence*].
Funakoshi, Gichin. 錬膽護身 唐手術 *Rentan goshin tōde-jutsu* (*Tōdi arts: Polish your courage for self defense*). Tokyo: Airyudo, 1996. [In Japanese; original work published 1925].
_____. *To-te jitsu*. Trans. Shingo Ishida. Hamilton: Masters Publication, 1997. [Original work published 1925].
_____. *Karate-dō kyōhan – Master text for the way of the empty hand*. Trans. Harum Suzuki-Johnston. San Diego: Neptune Publications, 2005. [Original work published 1935].
_____. *Karate-dō Kyōhan – The Master Text*. Trans. T. Ohshima. Tokyo: Kondansha International Ltd, 1973. [Translation of revised edition of 1957; first edition published 1935].
[Hŏ In-uk] (허인욱). 태권도형성사 [*Taekwondo's formation history*]. Kyŏngki-Do: Hanguk Haksul Ch'ŏngbo, 2008. [In Korean only].
Hwang, Kee [Hwang Ki] (황기). 花手道敎本 [*Hwasudo textbook*]. Seoul: Chosŏn Munhwa Ch'ulp'ansa, 1949. [In Korean only].
_____. 唐手道敎本 [*Tangsudo textbook*]. Seoul: Kyerang Munhwasa, 1958. [In Korean only].
Kim, Sang H., Kuk H. Chung and Kyung M. Lee. *Tae kwon do kyorugi: Olympic style sparring*. Trans. Wethersfield: Turtle Press, 1999. [Original work published in Korean, 1994, by Yi Kyŏng-myŏng, and Chŏng Kuk-hyŏn].
Kim, Young-Sun [Kim Yŏng-sŏn] (김영선). 태권도 교본에 관한 연구 ("A study on the first taekwondo textbooks"). *Taekwondo Journal of Kukkiwon*, 5, 2 (July 2014): 1–24.
Ko, Eui Min. *Taekwondo Wettkampf* (*Taekwondo competition*). Munich: Schramm Sport, 1980. [In German only].
Koharu, Iwai (ed.). 本部朝基と琉球 カラテ [*Research in early Ryukyu karate*]. Tokyo: Airyudo, 2000. [In Japanese only].
Lee, Chong Woo [Yi Chong-u] (이종우). 태권도교본 [*Taekwondo textbook*]. Seoul: Korean Taekwondo Association Publication, 1972. [In Korean only].
Lee, Won Kuk [Yi Wŏn-guk] (이원국). 跆拳道敎範 [*Taekwondo manual*]. Seoul: Jinsudang, 1968. [In Korean only; the first edition was probably published around 1965].
Motobu, Choki. *Okinawan kempo*. Trans. Hamilton: Masters Publications, 1995. [Originally published in Japanese, 1926].
Nishiyama, Hidetaka, and Richard C. Brown. *Karate the art of "empty hand" fighting*. Vermont and Tokyo: Charles E. Tuttle Company, 1960.
Noble, Graham. "The first karate books." *Fighting Arts International*, 90 (1995): 19–23. [Retrieved from http://seinenkai.com/articles/noble/noble-books1.html].
_____. "The West learns about the 'empty hand.'" *Fighting Arts International*, 93 (1997): 42–48. [Retrieved from http://seinenkai.com/articles/noble/noble books2.html].
[Pak Ch'ŏl-hŭi] (박철희). 破邪拳法 – 空手道敎本 [*Kwŏnbŏp association – Kongsudo textbook*]. Seoul: Kudŏgwŏnsa, 1958. [In Korean only].
Read, Stanton E., and Chai Ik Jin [Ch'oe Ik-chin]. *Taekwondo: A way of life in Korea*. Seoul: America-Korea Friendship Association, 1965.

Son, Duk Sung [Son Tŏk-sŏng], and Robert J. Clark. *Korean karate – The art of tae kwon do*. New York: Prentice-Hall, Inc. Englewood Cliffs, 1968.

World Taekwondo Academy. 태권도 용어정립 연구 [*Research to establish taekwondo terminology*]. Seoul: Kukkiwon, December, 2009. [In Korean only].

[Yi Kyo-yun] (이교윤). 百萬人의 跆手道敎本 [*T'aesudo textbook for the masses*]. Seoul: T'op'ik Ch'ulp'ansa, 1965. [In Korean].

[Yi Kyŏng-myŏng, and Chŏng Kuk-hyŏn] (이경명, 정국현). 태권도 겨루기 [*Taekwondo sparring*]. Seoul: Osŏng Ch'ulp'ansa, 1994.

1 Early Korean martial arts and *t'aekkyŏn*

During its development, taekwondo has been presented in popular literature, and by institutions affiliated with the South Korean government, as an indigenous Korean martial art with a lineage traceable to ancient times. The most common association made is between taekwondo and *t'aekkyŏn*.[1]

T'aekkyŏn has recently received much attention in the South Korean press. After a long effort for acknowledgment, in late 2011, *t'aekkyŏn* was listed, as the 'first martial art,' by UNESCO as an Intangible World Cultural Heritage.[2] Furthermore, its roots are reported as being traceable to the early Korean kingdom of Koguryŏ. Some murals of this era supposedly depict *t'aekkyŏn* or its forerunner, which is often thought to be *subak*.[3] The same murals are also claimed by the World Taekwondo Federation as proof of taekwondo's origin. In addition, the taekwondo establishment maintains that *t'aekkyŏn* is one of its predecessors.[4] On the other hand, *t'aekkyŏn* literature usually does not acknowledge having any relationship to taekwondo, and the Korea Taekkyon Federation (*Taehan T'aekkyŏn Yŏnmaeng*) also denies any link.[5]

This chapter explores early, historical Korean martial arts records in general, and *t'aekkyŏn* documentations in particular. However, at first, it briefly discusses the popular portrayal of taekwondo's history as described in dominant martial arts literature and by the World Taekwondo Federation.

The prevalent portrayal of taekwondo history

Until recently, the majority of martial arts publications consisted of instructional manuals for the application of fighting techniques. However, these manuals also contained an introduction with brief historical accounts and some philosophical and ethical guidelines. The principal historical descriptions of the evolution of East Asian martial arts in ancient times mostly follow the same pattern: originating in sixth-century India, they were brought by the semi-legendary Bodhidharma to China together with Zen Buddhism.[6] Another general theme is the importance of the Shaolin Monastery, although these legends are less pronounced in taekwondo literature. For Korean authors the influence of the ancient *hwarang*[7] is a far more common focal point.[8] Amusingly, however, it seems that most authors simply copied the narratives from one another over the years, confusing mythology with historical fact. When it comes to the question of how taekwondo was transmitted to Korea, however, the narratives begin to unravel.

The most prominent authors of early Korean martial arts books are Hwang Kee and Choi Hong Hi. Generally, Hwang portrayed ancient *hwarangdo* as being the prototype of modern Korean martial arts, while Choi claimed that taekwondo is a fusion of ancient *t'aekkyŏn* and Japanese karate.[9] Oddly enough, the authors gave more content and detail to ancient history than recent history, and all but ignored the post-war period after Korea's liberation from Japan.[10] A variety of different historical accounts were presented at that time, with an 'official' narrative gradually developing over the years.

According to historical accounts presented by the World Taekwondo Federation (WTF, 2013) on its official homepage, the origins of taekwondo are to be found almost two thousand years ago, when it "descended from" the early martial arts of *subak* and *t'aekkyŏn*. During that time, the *hwarang* of Silla are portrayed as important promoters of these martial arts. It is thought that further evidence of the native martial arts of Korea is the existence of the 1790 military manual *Muye tobo t'ongj*. Moreover, the content of the WTF homepage states that during the late Chosŏn Dynasty, martial arts in Korea experienced a decline because of an emphasis on "literary art" over "martial art." As a result, the Korean nation started "neglecting… martial arts."[11] Following the Japanese occupation, the story continues, all martial arts and related activities, including *t'aekkyŏn*, were forbidden by the authorities. Therefore, it was usually practiced in secret. Only after Korea's liberation were the martial arts, formerly known as *subak* and *t'aekkyŏn*, re-established under different names. The modern martial art and sport, known under the name 'taekwondo,' is supposedly the direct result of these events. This 'legend' is, in short, the official account of taekwondo's historical evolution as presented by the WTF.[12] Similar versions have been propagated for the past fifty years in mainstream martial arts literature, and by institutions affiliated in one way or the other with the South Korean government. Although most taekwondo leaders would not acknowledge any formal or technical similarities between karate and taekwondo, evidence in the historical records seems to reflect just the opposite.

Weaponless martial arts in early Korean history

A few murals, depicting two individuals facing each other in fight-like positions, survived from Korea's early Kokuryŏ period (37 BCE-668 CE).[13] While the two antagonists stand, facing one another in a posture typical of hand-to-hand combat, there likely existed no clear distinction between grappling and striking activities at that time. However, the earliest credible reference to the existence of any bare-handed martial art in Korea appeared in the early twelfth century during the Koryŏ Dynasty (918–1392 CE), in the *Koryŏsa* (高麗史 *History of Koryŏ*), which mentions a martial practice called *subak*.[14] It should be added that the *Koryŏsa* was only composed during the reign of King Sejong (r. 1418–1450), after the fall of the Koryŏ Dynasty, and '*su-bak*' (手搏 literally 'hand fighting'; 'Chinese:

'*shoubo*') is a term used for Chinese unarmed contest or boxing. As the name indicates, *subak* emphasized striking with the hands. Kicking techniques, with the possible exception of some low kicks, were probably not used much. The Chinese started using distinct terms for 'grappling' and 'striking' probably during the seventh century; subsequently, Koreans modeled their martial arts after Chinese classifications and terminology.[15] The grappling activity was called, '*kangnyŏk*' (角力 Chinese: '*jueli*') or '*kakchŏ*' (角觝 Chinese: '*jiaodi*'). Over the centuries, a variety of modified terminology appeared in Korean literature, and the modern successor of the wrestling-based arts became *ssirŭm*. In the origin of Korean wrestling, Mongolian descent or at least influence cannot be ruled out either, since modern Mongolian wrestling and *ssirŭm* look very much alike; although many wrestling arts tend to have similar attributes throughout history and region.

Contrary to portrayal in popular movies and pulp fiction novels, weaponless martial arts in ancient militaries were only used for the physical training of soldiers and played no significant role in actual combat.[16] Moreover, wrestling was more suited than striking for this kind of fitness and strength training for soldiers. In this context, the alleged existence of an ancient bare-handed striking art during the latter part of the Silla Dynasty (57 BCE–935 CE), in association with the *hwarang*, a group often portrayed as having practiced a forerunner of taekwondo, is difficult to support, since no specific references to the *hwarang* in connection with any bare-handed martial arts has yet been found. This scenario seems to be largely a comforting myth, propagated during the twentieth century, to foster nationalism and pride,[17] at a critical time in modern Korean history. According to the late Richard Rutt (1925–2011), a devoted scholar-missionary in Korea, the first work that portrayed the *hwarang* as being a group foremost associated with martial arts activities and martial prowess was the *Hwarangdo yŏn'gu* (花郎道研究 *Hwarangdo research*) of Yi Sŏn'-gŭn, published in Seoul, in 1949: "This work is...in the nature of an essay on the spirit of *hwarang* as it appealed at the time of publication to Korea's burgeoning nationalism. Much of the book is frankly speculative about the legacy of *hwarang* ideals."[18] Nevertheless, the myth depicting the *hwarang* as primarily a military group became mainstream in Korean popular literature and propagandistic history descriptions. Likewise, from very early on, the *hwarang* were also linked to unarmed martial arts activities by Korean martial arts enthusiasts who were neither historians nor intellectuals (see also Chapter 2, p. 44).

Following the twelfth century, *subak*, or assumingly *subak*-like martial arts under some different names, were mentioned several times in a variety of documents. According to some references, *subak* was possibly used for physical training by segments of the Korean military at certain times. In addition, by the fourteenth century, *subak* and wrestling exhibition fights became perhaps popular spectator events, among the royals and commoners alike.

Subsequently, during the Chosŏn Dynasty (1392–1910), Confucian values favoring scholarly ideals dominated the Korean aristocracy. Consequently, any interest in martial arts gradually waned among the upper classes. During the Chosŏn period there existed a great time gap without any specific references to weaponless martial arts. Between the mid-fifteenth to the late-eighteenth centuries – a period of about two hundred and fifty years – historical evidence is sparse, apart from a few military combat manuals, which were compiled due to invasions by the Japanese, and later by the Manchu.

The 1598 *Muye chepo* (武藝諸譜 *Illustrated martial arts records*) is the earliest extant Korean martial arts publication (see Figure 1.1). However, it is mainly based on an earlier Chinese military manual and features mostly Chinese weaponry and only a little *'kwŏnbŏp'* (拳法 'fist method,' Chinese: *'quanfa'*) fighting instruction.[19] The *Muye sinpo* (武藝新譜 *New martial arts records*), published in 1759, was based on the *Muye chepo*, but has since been lost. The better-known and much more comprehensive manual, *Muye tobo t'ongji* (武藝圖譜通志 *Comprehensive illustrated manual of martial arts*), 1790, an expanded version of former manuals, also deals with military instructions combined with illustrations of how to use a variety of weapons. One small segment, however, titled, "Kwŏnbŏp po" (拳法譜 'Fist method documentation'), deals with weaponless fighting methods.[20] It is precisely this section that many in the Korean martial arts community often point to as proof of the existence of ancient weaponless martial arts native to Korea,[21] even though the book is mostly a modified copy of an earlier Chinese manual, the *Jixiaoxinshu* (紀效新書 *New book recording effective techniques*). Some alterations in selected sections of the Korean manual regarding fighting with weapons were made, but the section on fist fighting is largely a copy in terms of the illustrations and text.[22] The stances and positions of hands and legs all resemble classic Chinese boxing techniques, and there is little in this manual that resembles modern *t'aekkyŏn*.

Early Korean military martial arts consisted mostly of weapon arts, but also included ancient versions of striking and grappling, likely, strongly influenced by, or of Chinese origin, altogether.[23] Later, during the early Chosŏn Dynasty, traditional martial arts fell into decline; however, because of foreign invasions, Chinese martial arts were reintroduced, only to enjoy a short-lived renaissance. Among a variety of weapon arts was also a weaponless fighting method called *kwŏnbŏp*. Nevertheless, toward the end of the Chosŏn Dynasty, archery was the only popular martial art practiced because it was embraced by the Confucian elite as a leisurely activity, highly regarded for its ritualistic, ceremonial, and spiritual dignity.[24]

In addition to the general distaste of the Korean aristocracy for military activities, the introduction of Western firearms rendered traditional Asian martial arts largely obsolete, leading to an extinction of traditional Korean martial arts activity by the end of the Chosŏn period. However, there endured a game-like activity, popular among farmers, country folk, and commoners, called *t'aekkyŏn*, which, today, has become associated with martial arts. The earliest existing evidence of *t'aekkyŏn* activity dates back to the eighteenth century,[25] with various accounts from a number of sources appearing over the next two hundred years.

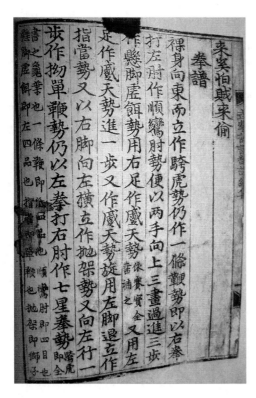

Figure 1.1 The *Muye chepo pŏnyŏk sokchip* of approximately 1610, is a copy of the *Muye chepo*.[26] Cover page, and pages three and two (in reverse order, written in right to left direction), *kwŏnbŏp* instructions

Source: Courtesy of Keimyung University Dongsan Library

Early existing *t'aekkyŏn* records

A common assumption by Korean scholars is that due to the Japanese annexation of Korea in 1910, the two successive Korean nations lost great parts of their history and identity. Moreover, soon after liberation from Japanese colonial rule in 1945, the devastating Korean War (1950–1953) ensued between the North and South, causing extensive destruction. Whatever the reasons or causes, there are few extant, available records regarding the history of *t'aekkyŏn*, which was literally kept alive by just one man, the 'last *t'aekkyŏn* player of the Chosŏn Dynasty,' Song Tŏk-ki (1893–1987).[27] Song was the only person found after Korea's liberation still able to perform the art. To a great extent, his testimonies and instructions have preserved the past and future legacy of *t'aekkyŏn*. Apart from Song, the few existing *t'aekkyŏn* records are references in a variety of literary publications, depictions in paintings, and a single photograph by an early Christian missionary.

According to existing records, '*t'aekkyŏn*' was actually referred to as '*t'akkyŏn*' in older documents. The term *t'aekkyŏn*, spelled 태견 in Korean, was used for the first time in a Korean dictionary compiled by the Korean Language Society in 1933.[28] In 1983, when *t'aekkyŏn* was designated an 'Important Intangible Cultural Asset' by the Korean government, the spelling was changed to 택견. *T'aekkyŏn*, regardless of the spelling, represents a pure Korean word which is not written with Chinese characters, whereas the term *t'akkyŏn* (탁견, 卓見 literally 'high view,'[29] or 托肩 'push shoulder'; both sets of characters were used) possibly has some Chinese roots. Although the meaning might be coincidental, it could simply be the result of representing Korean phonology through Chinese characters, in which meaning and pronunciation was often complicated to parse. Stanley Henning, an expert on Chinese martial arts, believes that the confusion regarding the name could be the result of a "lack of knowledge of the Chinese characters or an attempt to disassociate it from possible foreign [Chinese] origin."[30] Song Tŏk-ki stated that the art had originally been called '*t'akkyŏn*,' but the practitioner '*t'aekkyŏn-kun*.'[31] However, Song seemed to have used *t'akkyŏn* as well as *t'aekkyŏn* interchangeably in some of his correspondences.[32] Some possible reasons for the confusion might include a lack of any formal *t'aekkyŏn* institutions, conventions, and standards. In addition, the low education of commoners, who were the predominant practitioners of *t'aekkyŏn*, possibly combined with different regional dialects, most likely contributed to irregular spellings and different pronunciations.

The first reference to *t'akkyŏn* (or *t'aekkyŏn*) appeared in a book of poems. *Ch'ŏnggu yŏngon* (青丘永言 *Collection of ancient Sijo*),[33] published in 1728, is a collection of poems assumed to have been composed by Kim Ch'ŏn-taek during the end of the Koryŏ period (918–1392 CE). However, exact dates pertaining to when it was written are not known. Poems 253–260 and 741–742 refer to *t'aekkyŏn*, and to a certain Kim Min-sun who had enjoyed practicing *t'aekkyŏn* during his youth, between the age of fifteen and twenty.

The next proof of the existence of *t'aekkyŏn* is in the form of a painting, *Taek'wae-do* (大快圖), by Sin Yun-bok (1758–unknown) created in 1785.[34] The inscription in the painting's upper-right corner reads: "When all kinds of flowers are at the point of blooming, humans who live during such a peaceful reign are painted in a peaceful time."[35] The painting consists of three scenes: The upper part of the picture shows a landscape with some hills and a sedan chair parade. The middle scene represents the center of activity, with a large crowd of commoners and some noblemen, a few of them smoking, in front of a walled compound, watching performances of what is generally assumed to be *ssirŭm* and *t'aekkyŏn*. The lower scene depicts some laughing men drinking and smoking. According to Confucian custom, women are excluded from the activities and only observe from a distance. The painting expresses an element of folk entertainment and cheerful festivity, accompanied by the performances of the games, and also displays down-to-earth aspects of life, fortified by social smoking and drinking. Under the influence of the Chinese fine arts, Sin Yun-bok was one of the leading painters of that time. Therefore, due to the fact that he depicted such a scene, it may be assumed that *t'aekkyŏn* was a fairly popular game and spectator destination during that period.

A replica of the *Taek'wae-do* was painted by Yu Suk (1827–1873) in 1846 (see Figure 1.2). Its inscription says: "When all sorts of flowers came into full bloom, I painted the people playing peacefully in the broad street."[36] It is an almost identical copy of Sin Yun-bok's painting, except for the sedan chair parade in the upper part of the painting.

Figure 1.2 Taek'wae-do. Replica by Yu Suk, the photograph shows the central part of the painting only

Source: Courtesy of Seoul National University Museum

Ssirŭm-like wrestling and an assumed striking performance, identified as being *t'aekkyŏn*, are depicted as distinctive activities in the painting. Most researchers automatically assume that the activities depicted in the image represent *ssirŭm* and *t'aekkyŏn*, despite the absence of written attribution.[37] The assumed *t'aekkyŏn* performance merely portrays two individuals facing each other in a dance-like posture. The *t'aekkyŏn* performers are wearing a *top'o*, which is an overcoat worn only by Confucian scholars. This feature is unusual because in other sources, *t'aekkyŏn* is mostly depicted in association with lower class people. The performance is a public spectator event, but such performances were likely less sport-like according to modern standards. Public games, especially wrestling matches, which have always been popular during festivities among spectators in many societies, were usually related to some broader ritualistic and religious events.[38] Traditional Korean festivities, which centered on agriculture, the change of seasons, and/or ancestral memorials with strong elements of Shamanism and Confucianism, reinforced social cohesion and hierarchy, as well as addressing the divine and spiritual needs of the people. The scene depicted in the painting could be such an event since *yangban* (Korean aristocrats) and commoners alike are present to commemorate the occasion. Even today, during traditional Korean holidays such as *Ch'usŏk* (the Korean harvest festival), *ssirŭm* is still performed, and the competition event is considered to be one of the most important tournaments of the year. Song Tŏk-ki also stated that he performed *t'aekkyŏn* exclusively during times of major festivities, such as *Ch'usŏk* or the *Tano Festival*.[39] He reported competing in a friendly, game-like manner with players from other districts or villages.[40] The teams, coming for instance from Wangsimni or Chongno, were village or district representatives and did not characterize schools or styles, as some have claimed.

Moreover, since *t'aekkyŏn* is portrayed in a similar fashion as the wrestling activity in *Taek'wae-do*, *t'aekkyŏn* likely served some comparable role during certain periods in Korean history, as a ritualistic game related to some social, agricultural, spiritual, and religious festivals. The performance of *t'aekkyŏn* during such events could also explain its ritualistic, dance-like characteristics as an element of playful and enjoyable entertainment. In any case, the *ssirŭm*-like wrestling arts were not considered to be combat 'martial arts,' but merely recreational 'folk game-like activities.'[41] Since *t'aekkyŏn* is depicted together with wrestling, both activities likely had similar attributes and purposes.

The next record about early *t'aekkyŏn*, the *Chaemulpo* (才物譜 *Book of expertise*),[42] presumably written by Yi Man-yŏng in 1798, presents an early type of cultural, historical encyclopedia. For many Korean scholars, it represents the most important source of knowledge about early Korean martial arts.

Among researchers, opinions differ as to the accurate translation of the old text concerning the page on martial arts.[43] The issue with the interpretations is that these scholars are reaching general conclusions based on a small amount of text. In addition, even the exact meaning of the text is controversial. Except for *t'aekkyŏn* and *ssirŭm*, none of the 'martial arts' mentioned have survived to modern times. These arts are known only by their names since no instructional manuals, illustrations, or other technical references exist. Therefore, coming to any definitive conclusions about their nature seems highly speculative, not to mention, premature.

Interestingly, the authors of *Chaemulpo* did not mention Chinese *kwŏnbŏp* in the text. *Kwŏnbŏp* instructions were only introduced during the late sixteenth century from China to Korea with the publication of instructional manuals for the military. The *Chaemulpo* represented a cultural encyclopedia, a collection of folk arts and customs; hence, *kwŏnbŏp* was probably not performed by the general public, but only by the military. However, many analysts of the martial arts seem to have in mind the visual images of the *kwŏnbŏp* illustrations of the *Muye tobo t'ongji* or *Muye chepo* when they try to define the nature of early Korean striking arts. Since those mentioned in the *Chaemulpo* represented folk and not military arts, they might have been much more ritualistic and game-like than generally assumed.

The author of the *Chaemulpo* created a kind of cultural historical encyclopedia and dealt with many aspects of Korean culture and life. He was likely not an expert on martial arts, and the brief descriptions should not be taken as certitude. The most interesting point is that *t'aekkyŏn* is mentioned in the document in connection *with* other martial arts. The author of the document, a layman with regards to martial arts, nevertheless, considered *t'aekkyŏn* to be a martial art. However, he made the same association with the *ssirŭm*-like wrestling arts, which are usually not considered martial arts but athletic games.

The next evidence regarding the existence of *t'aekkyŏn* is a reference in the nineteenth century documentary record called *Namwŏn'gosa* (*History of Namwŏn*),[44] written by an unknown author between 1864 and 1869. The main content of the text consists of a dialogue between prisoners and a guard. The captives were sent to prison for being drunk and disorderly, thereby using *t'aekkyŏn* and *ssirŭm* during brawling. Since the *Namwŏn'gosa* was a crucial documentary record, it can be assumed that *t'aekkyŏn* was fairly common at that time. It also demonstrates that *t'aekkyŏn* and *ssirŭm* were common among the lower classes, and apparently associated with unruly behavior.

The earliest extant photograph of a *t'aekkyŏn* performance was taken by William Arthur Noble (1866–1945), an American Methodist church missionary in 1890. Unfortunately, Noble did not comment on the picture, and he does not describe the activity played by the children as *t'aekkyŏn*. However, since the dance-like positions are particularly characteristic of *t'aekkyŏn*, and the postures of the children resemble those of the modern style, we can safely assume that the activity probably represents *t'aekkyŏn*. Although Noble had been persuaded to teach for some time at a Korean school in Seoul, his main interest was preaching the gospel, which he did for fifteen years. According to Song Tŏk-ki's testimony, it is generally assumed that *t'aekkyŏn* existed toward the end of the Chosŏn Dynasty merely in the vicinity of Seoul.[45] However, Noble had mainly worked in Pyongyang. Thus, the photograph of the children was possibly taken there. This could mean that *t'aekkyŏn* was still more widespread at that time than generally assumed.

An additional Western reference to *t'aekkyŏn* survived from the anthropologist Steward Culin. He was inspired by the Columbian Exposition Fair in 1893 – in which a Korean delegation participated, exhibiting cultural artifacts and customs – to write a book about Korean games in comparison to those found in Japan and China. In the preface, Culin states that he gathered the information for the book's content from his personal collection of games, some museum records, and "from natives of Eastern Asia residing in the United States, the author never having visited the East." He describes *t'aekkyŏn* as follows:

> XXXII. HTAIK-KYEN-HA-KI KICKING (*Fr. Savate*).
> *Htăik-kyen-hă-ki* [*t'aekkyŏn*] is a combat between two players, chiefly with the feet. They take their positions with their feet apart, facing each other, and each endeavors to kick the other's feet from under him. A player may take one step backward with either foot to a third place. His feet, therefore, always stand in one of three positions. One leads with a kick at one of his opponent's legs. He moves that leg back and kicks in turn. A high kick is permitted, and is caught with the hands. The object is to throw the opponent. This game also occurs in Japan, but the Chinese laborers from Canton do not appear to be familiar with it.[46]

In Korean, the suffix '*haki*' (하기) that he also uses to describe "ssi-reum-ha-ki" (*ssirŭm haki*), has the meaning of 'doing.' In his main description, Culin describes and thinks of *t'aekkyŏn* as a game, and not a martial art. On the other hand, he compares *t'aekkyŏn* to French *savate* in the caption, which was probably seen more as a sport or fighting skill at that time. This could mean that Culin found *t'aekkyŏn* difficult to categorize.

Culin's description of *t'aekkyŏn* is uncharacteristically short and lacking in illustrations when compared to his presentation of other Korean games, where he often used drawings as visual or explanatory tools. Thus, he might not have had enough information about *t'aekkyŏn*, or he may not have regarded it as essential. Although the accuracy of his accounts is uncertain because he never visited the Far East, Culin's work is an important source about traditional Korean culture and games. His reference to the existence of a similar game in Japan seems doubtful because no other sources have yet been found to support this report.

Another record about *t'aekkyŏn* is preserved in a series of paintings called *Paekcha-do* (百子圖), also named *Paekdongja* and *Yuhŭi-do*. *Paekcha-do* translates into 'many children's paintings.' '*Baek*' (百) expresses 'abundance' rather than the figurative number 'one hundred.' These images are said to have decorated children's and married women's rooms in order to encourage the growth and prosperity of descendants. They were likely painted during the end of the Chosŏn period, and about twenty still exist, three of them depicting *t'aekkyŏn* as a theme. However, once again, this assumes the activity depicted in the images really represents *t'aekkyŏn*, since there is no mention of *t'aekkyŏn* in these paintings.

Two brief references regarding *t'aekkyŏn* exist in the early twentieth century. In 1919, An Hwak (1886–1946) published *Chosŏn musa yŏngungchŏn*

(朝鮮武士英雄傳 *Chosŏn military heroes*). An wrote that *subak* emphasized hand skills during the Koryŏ time, but transformed to *t'aekkyŏn*, which centers on foot skills, during the Chosŏn era.[47] Given the scarce historical references regarding *t'aekkyŏn*, and the fact that *t'aekkyŏn* was already basically extinct during that time, An's references seem to be entirely speculation. However, An's theory became popular in modern times among a variety of Korean scholars.

Another short reference to *t'aekkyŏn* appeared several years later (1925) in the book called *Haedong chukchi* (海東竹枝 literally *Korean bamboo branch*), a kind of unofficial historical presentation. According to the author, Ch'oe Yŏng-nyŏn, *t'aekkyŏn* was outlawed by the authorities and despised because of its rough nature and connections to undignified (by Confucian standards) activities, like gambling, indolence, and brawling, which eventually contributed to its demise. Ch'oe stated: "*T'aekkyŏn* became a means of exacting revenge for a slight or winning away an opponent's concubine through betting. Due to this, the game was outlawed by the judiciary and eventually disappeared."[48] Modern taekwondo history asserts that *t'aekkyŏn* was forced underground as a result of being outlawed by Japanese colonial authorities. However, Song Tŏk-ki stated that *t'aekkyŏn* eventually disappeared because Japanese colonial authorities did not allow gatherings of crowds larger than ten people.[49] In any case, *t'aekkyŏn* did not vanish because the Japanese felt threatened and regarded it as a 'dangerous martial arts activity.' In all likelihood, *t'aekkyŏn*'s demise was the consequence of earlier Korean authorities' suppression of unruly behavior by commoners and lower class ruffians during King Kojong's reign (r. 1863–1907). During Song's time, according to his own statements, performances were already restricted to his native Seoul only. *T'aekkyŏn* had likely already disappeared in the rest of the country by that time.

T'aekkyŏn in modern times

The scant references and few paintings cited in this study reflect the dearth of existing *t'aekkyŏn* data before the twentieth century. Moreover, at the beginning of the twentieth century, *t'aekkyŏn* performances practically disappeared, altogether. In 1958, Song Tŏk-ki was invited to give an exhibition of the art in honor of the birthday of the first Korean president, Rhee Syngman (Yi Sŭng-man), who still had some memory of *t'aekkyŏn* from his childhood; however, not a single partner for the performance could be located throughout the country.[50] At the time, Song was the only person who kept the memory of *t'aekkyŏn* techniques still alive. Song was also briefly featured in the 1971 motion picture, *Kŭki taekwondo* (*The national sport taekwondo*), in which Song instructs the taekwondo protagonist how to do some low and push-like kicks, in addition to leg blocks.[51] Song's brief appearance in this movie certainly contributed to the popular myth that taekwondo's roots are found in *t'aekkyŏn*.

During that time, a sparse revival of *t'aekkyŏn*, especially with the establishment of some university clubs, was aided by the general restoration of Korean cultural traditions, which was promoted by the newly established Park Chung Hee regime (1961–1979) to foster Korean pride and identity.

In addition to Song, another surviving *t'aekkyŏn* practitioner existed, Sin Han-sŭng (1929–1987). Even though he concentrated in his youth more on *ssirŭm* than on *t'aekkyŏn* practice, Sin claimed that he had learned *t'aekkyŏn* from his granduncle in Wangsimni (which is now a district of Seoul), who was supposedly a *t'aekkyŏn* instructor. Regardless of his background, Sin became essential for promotion and lobbying by modern *t'aekkyŏn* proponents. As a result of his efforts, the Korean government recognized *t'aekkyŏn* as an 'Important Intangible Cultural Asset,' in 1983. Except for Song's and Sin's testimony, examples of past *t'aekkyŏn* instructions are unknown, today. Modern *t'aekkyŏn* techniques and knowledge have descended solely through these two proponents. Several of the founders of taekwondo claimed to have practiced *t'aekkyŏn* during their youth, but these claims are likely exaggerations, given the fact that *t'aekkyŏn* activity was practically extinct during that time.

Song, together with Pak Chong-gwan, published the first *t'aekkyŏn* manual in 1983, but there exists no older detailed records about *t'aekkyŏn* techniques.[52] *T'aekkyŏn* became popular only after the South Korean government designated it as an Important Intangible Cultural Asset that same year. Subsequently, *t'aekkyŏn* adopted a formal organization and structure, and introduced competitions with rules and regulations, in a fashion similar to the already established national Korean martial art – taekwondo.

Most students who started practicing *t'aekkyŏn* had prior knowledge and exposure to taekwondo training, since during that time in Korea, a large majority of boys attended small, local street corner taekwondo gyms during their childhood, or learned it in public schools, and later practiced it as a mandatory activity during compulsory military service.[53] Therefore, modern *t'aekkyŏn* actually adapted many kicking techniques from taekwondo and not the other way around as generally assumed. According to Lee Chong Woo, who was one of the leading figures responsible for the development of taekwondo:

> Taek Kyun has transformed significantly recently. Since people who practiced Taekwondo are learning Taek Kyun, the kick is being transformed into the Taekwondo style... I know well the difference between Taekwondo kicks and Taek Kyun kicks. Taek Kyun kicks upward with a straight foot without bending the knee, and this form is not being performed these days.[54]

Traditionally, *t'aekkyŏn* practitioners applied only push-like kicks and slaps, with the primary aim of just gently striking or knocking down the opponent; players did not execute blows with full force to incapacitate or injure the adversary. The goal was simple contact, not strong impact. Modern *t'aekkyŏn*, in terms of techniques, organization, and formalities, was much more influenced by taekwondo traditions than vice versa.

T'aekkyŏn as an example of the 'invention of tradition'

As historian, Eric Hobsbawm pointed out, cases of invented tradition occur in all societies. Invented traditions are easily recognizable in the "ceremonials" and "symbolism" of authoritarian governments and nations such as Nazi Germany. Yet they also arise commonly in democratic governments and monarchies as, for instance, in Britain. Regimes, ruling classes, and special interest groups typically invent traditions for ideological objectives, propaganda purposes, and social cohesion. While there are countless instances of invented traditions in the realm of politics, it commonly occurs also among non-political groups, institutions, and entities. The aim of these groups or individuals is to project some continuity, by means of "semi-fiction" or outright "fabrication," from the early past to the present. Subsequently, if certain ceremonies and claims are repeated often enough, then, at some point they become "tradition," and, in extreme cases, "history."[55]

The traditional mask dance of Andong would be a specific example of the invention of tradition in Korea. In this case, the tradition was invented by a Korean academic. In order to reconstruct the dance, a university professor was able to locate and interview one elderly man who in his youth participated in such a dance. The professor was accused of asserting his own suggested interpretations and assumed version of the dance into the answers of the individual. Considering the advanced age of the man and the time gap involved, he likely could not have presented such detailed, and presumably accurate accounts. Nevertheless, precisely this version, 'produced' during the interview, was generally accepted as a genuine account of forgotten Korean culture and tradition.[56]

Parallels may be drawn with *t'aekkyŏn*, which also had a single remaining survivor, namely Song Tŏk-ki, the 'last *t'aekkyŏn* player of the Chosŏn era,' whose testimonies and subsequent interpretations by scholars are intended to present an accurate picture of *t'aekkyŏn*'s lineage and tradition. For instance, in 1983, at the advanced age of ninety-one, Song was interviewed by a Korean television crew. During the interview, Song described *t'aekkyŏn* primarily as a game, but also admitted that 'gangsters' (or 'ruffians,' which would be a more appropriate translation considering the Korean culture) were sometimes associated with *t'aekkyŏn* activities. This depiction of *t'aekkyŏn* seems similar to its portrayal in the *Haedong chukchi*. Later, when the interviewer asked whether *t'aekkyŏn* was a form of self-defense, Song hesitated and did not give a clear answer. After the interviewer pressed several times regarding *t'aekkyŏn*'s status as a martial art, Song did not reply, but only gave casual 'yeses,' which might be said to correlate with a rather inconclusive 'nod' in the Korean language. When asked, if *t'aekkyŏn* was practiced by officers in the Korean military at that time, Song nodded as well.[57] However, at the turn of the century, Song was a very young man with the humble background of a commoner; it is highly unlikely that he would have had any knowledge of Korean military affairs, let alone officers' training routines. Moreover, except in the case of Korean wrestling for physical fitness training, no records have been found, so far, documenting the fact that the Korean military of the late Chosŏn Dynasty practiced any unarmed combat drills. During that period, martial arts in general were despised by the aristocracy and only archery was popular.[58] Moreover, by the end of the nineteenth century, Korea was caught in the middle of a geopolitical power struggle with its neighbors. As a result, the Korean armed forces tried to modernize and transform into a Western-style military force by adopting firearms and modern combat methods, because traditional martial arts had long become obsolete. During the meeting with Song, the *t'aekkyŏn* interviewer asserted his own suggested interpretations, which were subsequently presented as 'history.' Even though Song is a much more credible witness than the mask dance observer, the interpretations and suggestions of academics and martial arts 'experts' often exhibit a biased picture.

The initiators of invented traditions were in many cases the authoritarian Korean governments of the recent past. At present, a variety of academics and institutions continue this practice, as in the case of *t'aekkyŏn* and taekwondo. *T'aekkyŏn*'s promotion as a 'martial art' and its inclusion as an Intangible World Cultural Heritage by UNESCO should be considered in this context. Taekwondo was not recognized by UNESCO, but its traditions appear to have been invented and promoted in a similar fashion for the past fifty years, although on a much grander scale.

Summary

The martial art based on stand up striking and often mentioned in early Korean sources is *subak*, which is, at least in name, of Chinese origin. The wrestling-based arts appear to have Chinese influence or predecessors as well. A variety of branches and modified terms for the arts developed over the centuries, but the diversification process is not clear because of the lack of available historical records. *Kwŏnbŏp*, another Chinese martial art based upon striking, was only introduced during the early Chosŏn period for training purposes in the Korean military. However, it seems to have disappeared again after the eighteenth century, since *kwŏnbŏp* is not mentioned in records any longer.

Whether *t'aekkyŏn* evolved from *subak* or any other existing martial art or game from earlier times remains open to speculation and discussion. The interpretation of the issue continues to be disputed because available records remain inconclusive. Considering the existing references, the confirmed history of *t'aekkyŏn* is only about three hundred years old, dating back to the early eighteenth century.

For many Korean scholars, the references in the *Chaemulpo* represent one of the main sources when analyzing the evolution of early Korean martial arts. However, the exact translations and interpretations are uncertain. The *Chaemulpo* mentions a variety of martial arts terminology alongside familiar terms, as well as some names for wrestling arts, which are likely interchangeable with *ssirŭm*. In regards to *t'aekkyŏn*, the *Chaemulpo* seems to be the only document on record before the twentieth century that associates *t'aekkyŏn* with martial arts. However, the authoritative voice that many scholars ascribe to the *Chaemulpo* is questionable, since the author, who was likely not a martial arts expert, simply compiled a cultural encyclopedia. Moreover, none of the activities cited, except for *t'aekkyŏn* and *ssirŭm*, have survived to the present day. It is worth mentioning, though, that *kwŏnbŏp* was not mentioned, since it was introduced more recently to Korea from China, and probably was only used as an exercise by the military and possibly never developed a folk character like the other arts.

T'aekkyŏn may have been a popular and widespread activity during the eighteenth and early nineteenth centuries, since it was depicted in paintings by Sin Yun-bok and Yu Suk, and mentioned in some official records. However, it is generally believed that toward the beginning of the twentieth century, *t'aekkyŏn* had almost vanished.

Depending on the author, *t'aekkyŏn* has been described as a game, a type of folk art, and/or a martial art. Traditional *t'aekkyŏn* certainly does not really fit the general definition of a martial art as we think of martial arts today, because *t'aekkyŏn* had neither association with any esoteric Oriental philosophies or beliefs, nor the organizational structure associated with Asian martial arts. Moreover, *t'aekkyŏn* was certainly not an activity used by the military, criminal groups,[59] or individuals preparing for actual combat or self-defense. However, *t'aekkyŏn* did have a modicum of fighting to it. *T'aekkyŏn*, in association with *ssirŭm*, was mentioned in the *Namwŏn'gosa* and was reportedly used by some lower class individuals in scuffles. *T'aekkyŏn* was likely disliked by the *yangban* (nobles) upper class, since they and commoners had quite different value systems and ways of life at that time. *T'aekkyŏn*'s rough nature eventually contributed to its demise as reported by Ch'oe Yŏng-nyŏn in 1921. *T'aekkyŏn*'s disappearance was almost certainly not the result of a ban by Japanese colonial authorities as generally described in popular literature; it disappeared earlier, likely as a consequence of repression by local Korean authorities impatient with its undesirable characteristics.

In contrast to *t'aekkyŏn*'s association with ruffians, several existing references portray *t'aekkyŏn* as a kind of game. The depiction of 'children playing *t'aekkyŏn*' is a recurring theme. *T'aekkyŏn* certainly contains a strong, folk game-like element, especially by way of its dance-like rhythms. Modern *t'aekkyŏn* performances used to be often accompanied by a band of folk musicians; this likely also happened in the past and could explain its dance-like moves and tempo. *T'aekkyŏn* was mostly performed by lower class practitioners and, similar to the *ssirŭm*-like wrestling games, also connected with cultural, agricultural, or ritualistic festivities. The existing fighting contests performed by commoners were probably more game-like and/or ritualistic, as we think of wrestling today, and not methods for actual fighting and battle.

Most claims and discussions about early Korean martial arts are often unproven assertions and guesswork because of a general lack of concrete, documentary evidence. *T'aekkyŏn*'s portrayal as a 'traditional Korean martial art' shows similarities to the 'mask dance case of Andong' as a case of 'invention of tradition' in Korean culture. Available information about *t'aekkyŏn* is frequently misrepresented and the often-made assertion that *t'aekkyŏn* is 'ancient' is a gross exaggeration.

The first *t'aekkyŏn* manual was only published in 1983, by Song Tŏk-ki (co-author Pak Chong-gwan), the 'last *t'aekkyŏn* player of the *Chosŏn* period.' In his publication, Song acknowledged, that when he started practicing *t'aekkyŏn* in his childhood, *t'aekkyŏn* was perceived as being merely a "folk game" and nobody thought of it as a "martial art."[60] In contrast, first and foremost, the taekwondo establishment has stated that *t'aekkyŏn* was a martial art. Subsequent representatives of *t'aekkyŏn* over the past thirty years, started to embrace the martial arts narrative as well. Moreover, the taekwondo establishment has been claiming that *t'aekkyŏn* is taekwondo's predecessor, an assertion which even the *t'aekkyŏn* establishment never agreed upon.

Much has been said about the supposed historical connection between taekwondo and *t'aekkyŏn*. In actuality, there exists no convincing physical relationship and, contrary to popular belief, modern *t'aekkyŏn* was actually structured and fashioned after the existing Korean martial art – taekwondo. Moreover, in contrast to *t'aekkyŏn*, taekwondo actually has a well-documented history that originates in karate, a history which will be discussed in the following chapter.

Notes

1 A great variety of articles and books have been published on this topic, probably because *t'aekkyŏn* (in addition to *ssirŭm*) is the only surviving, putative 'Korean martial art,' and *t'aekkyŏn* experienced a significant revival during the past decades.
2 See UNESCO Culture Sector – Intangible Heritage – 2003 Convention, "Taekkyeon, a traditional Korean martial art." [Retrieved from www.unesco.org/culture/ich/index.php?lg=en&pg=00011&RL=00452].
3 See for example, "Official site of Korea Tourism Org.: Taekkyeon," (n.d). [Retrieved from http://english.visitkorea.or.kr/enu/CU/CU_EN_8_2_7.jsp].
4 World Taekwondo Federation, "History," 2013.
5 Korea Taekkyon Federation "History of taekkyon," (1999). [Retrieved from www.taekkyon.or.kr/en/]. There are about three major and two minor *t'aekkyŏn* associations.
6 See for example, Funakoshi, *Karate-dō kyōhan – The master text*, p. 7; Hwang, [*Hwasudo textbook*], pp. 24–7; [*Tangsudo textbook*], pp. 10–1; Ch'oe, [*Kwŏnbŏp textbook*], p. 11; Cho, *Korean karate – Free fighting technique*, p. 17; Son, and Clark, *Korean karate – The art of tae kwon do*, pp. 1–2.
7 Most standard literature in Korea presents the *hwarang* of the Silla Dynasty (57 BCE–935 CE) as a youth group with assumed militaristic associations.
8 See for example, Hwang, [*Hwasudo textbook*], pp. 3–7; Choi, *Taekwondo – The art of self-defence*, p. 22; Son, and Clark, *Korean karate – The art of tae kwon do*, p. 3; World Taekwondo Federation, "History."
9 See Choi, *Taekwondo – The art of self-defence*, cover note, p. 22.
10 Of all the Korean martial arts literature of the 1950s and 1960s, only Hwang Kee briefly describes the early *kwan*; see Hwang, [*Tangsudo textbook*], pp. 21–2.
11 World Taekwondo Federation, "History."
12 Ibid.
13 See photographs in Song, [*New history discussion of taekwondo*], pp. 87–91. Song also displays earlier, but similar Chinese depictions.
14 Song, [*Taekwondo history lecture*], pp. 108–109.
15 Henning, "Traditional Korean martial arts," p. 12.
16 Lorge, *Chinese martial arts*, p. 5.

17 Pieter, "Notes on the historical development of Korean martial sports: An addendum to Young's History and development of tae kyon," pp. 82–89; Gu, "Aggression, nationalism and combat sport in East Asia," pp. 44–45.; see also Tikhonov, "Hwarang organization: Its functions and ethics."
18 Rutt, "The flower boys of Silla (hwarang), notes on the sources," p. 1.
19 Illustrated in Sin, [*Collection of martial arts documentations including interpretation*], pp. 2–27.
20 Illustrated in Pak, [*Recorded documents of martial arts illustrations and commentary*], pp. 413–428; see also Kim, *Muye dobo tongji – The comprehensive illustrated manual of martial arts of ancient Korea*.
21 See for example, World Taekwondo Federation, "History." Click "Modern times."
22 Pratt, "Change and continuity in Chosŏn military techniques during the later Chosŏn period," pp. 31–48. However, several versions of the manual exist. According to Henning ("Traditional Korean martial arts," p. 11), a few "escape and seizing techniques" were added.
23 Henning, "Traditional Korean martial arts," p. 12.
24 See Kim Ki-hoon, "The archery tradition of Korea," unpublished presentation paper, (2003). [Retrieved from http://ktarchery.com/sites/default/files/what%20is%20KTA/korean%20traditional%20archery%20presentation%20paper.pdf].
25 Song, [*Taekwondo history lecture*], p. 168.
26 The *Muye chepo pŏnyŏk sokchip* (武藝諸譜翻譯續集 *Series of illustrated martial arts records*) was produced by Ch'oe Ki-nam, a government official, because of re-invasion by foreign enemies. It was published around 1610, and provides also information on the Japanese army. The book is the last surviving copy of the *Muye chepo* in Korea. It is in the collection of the Keimyung University Dongsan Library.
27 Capener, "Problems in the identity and philosophy of *t'aegwondo* and their historical causes," p. 84; Yi, *T'aekkyŏn*, p. 15.
28 The Korean language dictionary (한글맞춤법통일안) was compiled by the Korean Language Society (조선어학회) in 1933.
29 This pair of characters (卓見 'high view') was likely a product of the '*idu* script,' which was an old writing system representing Korean phonology through Chinese characters. The characters were merely picked for their sound and not for meaning. When translated, they do not make any sense.
30 Henning, "Traditional Korean martial arts," p. 10.
31 '-*kun*' ('mister' or 'sir') is an archaic term used to respectfully address a man.
32 Cho, "Ethnographic approach to the initiation type of taekgyeon and its meaning [sic]," pp. 51–67.
33 Kim's *Ch'ŏnggu yŏngŏn* is in the collection of the 'National Central Library of Korea.'
34 The *Taek'wae-do* is in the collection of the National Museum of Korea.
35 工巳萬花方 時節擊壤世人寫於康衢煙月 蕙園
36 丙午萬花方暢時節 擊壤世人 寫於康衢煙月
37 See for example, Kim, and Hŏ, ["Past records on the etymology of *t'aekkyŏn*"], pp. 195–203; Chŏng, *A characteristic of taekgyeon as a traditional martial arts* [sic], p. 75; Song, [*New history discussion of taekwondo*], p. 123.
38 For example, wrestling and '*pankration*' contests ('all powers'), a kind of ancient mixed martial art, with ritualistic and religious overtones were performed in the ancient Olympics in Greece. See Poliakoff, *Combat sports in the ancient world*, pp. 90–1.
39 The *Tano Festival* is a Korean traditional holiday that falls on the fifth day of the fifth month of the lunar calendar.
40 See Song's interview, retrieved from http://taekkyon.de/download/song_interview_translation_EN_DE.pdf. Original interview http://mov.taekkyonkorea.com/tkkorea/data/pds/2001/tk2001061713.asf; translation retrieved from www.youtube.com/watch?v=gWCLMmEH_88. During the *Tano Festival*, a

tournament called *Kyŏllyŏn*, which included *t'aekkyŏn*, *ssirŭm* and other activities, took place.

41 Nowadays, *ssirŭm* is generally considered to be a modern competition sport, but it was only introduced in 1912 as such. However, wrestling contests, often under different names, were popular for centuries during Korean holidays. See for example, Korea Taekkyon Federation (Taehan T'aekkyŏn Yŏnmaeng, 1999). [Retrieved from www.taekkyon.or.kr/en/].

42 Yi's *Chaemulpo* is in the collection of the 'Kyujanggak Institute for Korean Studies at Seoul National University.'

43 Important points of the *Chaemulpo*:
- 角觝　漢武帝始作著牛頭俱相當角力　The document states that *kakchŏ* (角觝) and *kangnyŏk* (角力) represent similar wrestling arts. The terms were known since the (Chinese) *Han Dynasty* (206 BCE-220 CE).
- 梓校 씨름 迭校・還校　仝　The document states that *chaegyo* (梓校), *chilgyo* (迭校), and *hwan'gyo* (還校) are *ssirŭm*-like wrestling arts. They refer to 'contests of strength [between adversaries].' Furthermore, all these arts originated from, or are similar to older China-based arts.

The interpretation of the following sentences is disputed:
- 卞　手搏爲卞角力爲武若今之탁견
- 庳博　梓校之類亦탁견
- 手搏　仝・今之 슈벽維與此不同而當用此字

One possible interpretation is that the martial arts of *subak* (手搏), *kangnyŏk* (角力), *t'akkyŏn* (탁견), *sibak* (庳博), *chaegyo* (梓校), and *syupyŏk* (슈벽) are all of similar origin, but possibly branched out later into different styles.

Compare the interpretations of Yi, *T'aekkyŏn*, p. 68; Chŏng, "A characteristic of taekgyeon as a traditional martial arts [sic]," pp. 101–2, Kim, and Hŏ, ["Past records on the etymology of *t'aekkyŏn*,"] pp. 195–203; for a detailed discussion see Cho, Moenig, and Nam, "The available evidence regarding *t'aekkyŏn* and its portrayal as a 'traditional Korean martial art,'" pp. 341–68.

44 The *Namwŏn'gosa* is in the collection of the library of the National Institute of Oriental Language and Civilization, Paris. The text was reprinted in Hong, [*The etymology of Yŏbo*].

45 Capener, "Problems in the identity and philosophy of *t'aegwondo* and their historical causes," p. 84.

46 Culin, *Korean games with notes on the corresponding games of China and Japan*, p. 39.

47 An Hwak, *Chosŏn musa yŏngungchŏn* (朝鮮武士英雄傳 *Chosŏn military heroes*), p. 76. However, I had no direct access to the book and do not know the publishing details.

48 Yi (in *T'aekkyŏn*), as cited and translated in Capener, "Problems in the identity and philosophy of *t'aegwondo* and their historical causes," p. 83. The characters 海東 in the book title mean literally 'East Sea,' but is another term for 'Korea.' I had no access to the original book.

49 As cited and retrieved from http://taekkyon.de/download/song_interview_translation_EN_DE.pdf. Original interview http://mov.taekkyonkorea.com/tkkorea/data/pds/2001/tk2001061713.asf; translation retrieved from www.youtube.com/watch?v=gWCLMmEH_88

50 Capener, "Problems in the identity and philosophy of *t'aegwondo* and their historical causes," p. 84.

51 The film, *Kŭki taekwondo*, was produced by the National Film Production Center (국립영화제작소) in 1971, the same year that taekwondo became the' national sport' of South Korea.

52 Only a few photographs and video clips of Song Tŏk-ki performing *t'aekkyŏn* exist prior to the first 1983 manual.

53 This is still true nowadays to some extent, although not all Korean children practice taekwondo anymore due to the wide availability of alternative activities, popular sports, and commercial entertainment.
54 As cited in Yook, "Kukkiwon Vice President Chong Woo Lee's shocking confession of Olympic competition result manipulation!", p. 307.
55 See Hobsbawm, "Introduction," pp. 1–14. Hobsbawm and Ranger collected articles that detail numerous cases of invention of tradition in many societies, cultures, and times.
56 See Kim, "Socio-cultural implications of the recent invention of tradition in Korea: An overview," pp. 7–28.
57 As cited in http://taekkyon.de/download/song_interview_translation_EN_DE.pdf. Original interview; http://mov.taekkyonkorea.com/tkkorea/data/pds/2001/tk2001061713.asf or @ www.youtube.com/watch?v=gWCLMmEH_88. During the interview, Song identifies "*kyŏllyŏn t'aekkyŏn*" as being a term for "self-defense *t'aekkyŏn*." However, '*Kyŏllyŏn*' is only a term for the combative activities during the *Tano Festival*, which included *t'aekkyŏn*, *ssirŭm*, and other games.
58 See Kim Ki-hoon, "The archery tradition of Korea," unpublished presentation paper, (2003). [Retrieved from http://ktarchery.com/sites/default/files/what%20is%20KTA/korean%20traditional%20archery%20presentation%20paper.pdf].
59 For example, Chinese martial arts are often associated with bandits and secret societies, which is not the case with *t'aekkyŏn*. *T'aekkyŏn* was only reportedly associated with ruffians.
60 Song, and Pak, *T'aekkyŏn*, p. 8.

Bibliography

Capener, Steven D. "Problems in the identity and philosophy of *t'aegwondo* and their historical causes." *Korea Journal*, 35, 4 (1995): 80–94. [Retrieved from www.eaglekd.com/images/STUDENT%20FORUM%20from%20Korea%20Journal.pdf].

Cho, Sihak Henry. *Korean karate – Free fighting technique*. Rutland and Tokyo: Charles E. Tuttle Company, 1968.

Cho, Sungkyun [Cho Sŏng-gyun] (조성균). 민속 지학적 관점에 의한 택견의 전수 형태 와 관점에 의 "Ethnographic approach to the initiation type of taekgyeon and its meaning [sic]." *The Korean Journal of History for Physical Education, Sport and Dance*, 1 (2006) 51–67. [In Korean only].

Cho, Sungkyun, Udo Moenig, and Dohee Nam. "The available evidence regarding t'aekkyŏn and its portrayal as a 'traditional Korean martial art.'" *Acta Koreana*. 15, 2 (2012): pp. 341–68.

[Ch'oe Song-nam] (최송남). 拳法敎本 [*Kwŏnbŏp textbook*]. Seoul: Donga Munhwasa, 1955. [In Korean only].

Choi, Hong Hi [Ch'oe Hong-hi] (최홍히). *Taekwondo – The art of self-defence*. Seoul: Daeha Publication Company, 1965.

[Chŏng Chae-sŏng] (정재성). 전통무예로서 택견의 특성 "A characteristic of taekgyeon as a traditional martial arts [sic]." Unpublished doctoral dissertation. Kookmin University, 2005. [In Korean only].

Culin, Stewart. *Korean games with notes on the corresponding games of China and Japan*. Philadelphia: University of Pennsylvania, 1895. [Retrieved from http://openlibrary.org/works/OL4288127W/Korean_games_with_notes_on_the_corresponding_games_of_China_and_Japan].

Funakoshi, Gichin. *Karate-dō kyōhan – The master text*. Trans. T. Ohshima. Tokyo:

Kondansha International Ltd, 1973. [Translation of revised edition of 1957; first edition published 1935].

Gu, Hyosong. "Aggression, Nationalismus und Kampfsport in Ostasien" ("Aggression, nationalism and combat sport in East Asia"). Unpublished master's thesis, University of Hamburg, 1994. [In German only].

Henning, Stanley E. "Traditional Korean martial arts." *Journal of Asian Martial Arts*, 9, 1 (2000): 8–15.

Hobsbawm, Eric. "Introduction." In *The Invention of tradition*. Eds. Eric Hobsbawm and Terence Ranger, 1–14. Cambridge: Cambridge University Press, 1983.

[Hong Yun-p'yo] (홍윤표). 여보의 어원 [*The etymology of Yŏbo*]. National Korean Institute e-book, Shimpyo Mach'impyo, 2007.

Hwang, Kee [Hwang Ki] (황기). 花手道教本 [*Hwasudo textbook*]. Seoul: Chosŏn Munhwa Ch'ulp'ansa, 1949. [In Korean only].

_____. 唐手道教本 [*Tangsudo textbook*]. Seoul: Kyerang Munhwasa, 1958. [In Korean only].

[Kim Ch'ŏn-t'aek] (김천택) 青丘永言 *Ch'ŏnggu yŏngŏn* (*Collection of ancient Sijo*). National Central Library of Korea, 1728. [In Korean only].

Kim, Kwangŏk. "Socio-cultural implications of the recent invention of tradition in Korea: An overview." *The Papers of the British Association for Korean Studies (BAKS)*, 1 (1991): 7–28. Leiden: Brill.

[Kim San, and Hŏ In-uk] (김산, 허인욱) 택견의 어원에 대한 소고 ["Past records on the etymology of *t'aekkyŏn*."] *Physical Education Bulletin*, 9 (2002): 195–203. [In Korean only].

Kim, Sang H. *Muye dobo tongji – The comprehensive illustrated manual of martial arts of ancient Korea*. Santa Fe: Turtle Press, 2000.

Lorge, Peter A. *Chinese martial arts*. Cambridge: Cambridge University Press, 2012.

Namwŏn'gosa [*History of Namwŏn*]. (Vol. 4). French Oriental Language School, [ca. nineteenth century]. [In Korean only].

[Pak Ch'ŏng-chŏng] (박청정). 武藝圖譜通志註解 [*Recorded documents of martial arts illustrations with commentary*]. Seoul: Dongmunsŏn, 2007. [In Korean only].

Pieter, Willy. "Notes on the historical development of Korean martial sports: An addendum to Young's history and development of tae kyon." *Journal of Asian Martial Arts*. 3, 1 (1994): 82–9.

Poliakoff, Michael B. *Combat sports in the ancient world*. New Haven and London: Yale University Press, 1987.

Pratt, Andrew. "Change and continuity in Chosŏn military techniques during the later Chosŏn period." *Papers of the British Association for Korean Studies*, 7 (2000): 31–48.

Rutt, Richard. "The flower boys of Silla (hwarang), notes on the sources." In *Transactions of the Korea branch of the Royal Asiatic Society*, 38 (October 1961):1–66.

[Sin Il-hŭi] (신일희). 武藝諸譜飜譯續集 [*Collection of martial arts documentations including interpretation*]. Taegu: Keimyung University Press, 1999. [In Korean only].

Son, Duk Sung [Son Tŏk-sŏng], and Robert J. Clark. *Korean karate – The art of Tae Kwon Do*. New York: Prentice-Hall, Inc. Englewood Cliffs, 1968.

Song, Hyeongseok [Song Hyŏng-sŏk] (송형석). 태권도사 강의 [*Taekwondo history lecture*]. Seoul: Yimun Publishing co., 2005. [In Korean only].

_____. 태권도 신론 [*New history discussion of taekwondo*]. Taegu: Yimun Ch'ulp'ansa, 2008. [In Korean only].

[Song Tŏk-ki, and Pak Chong-gwan] (송덕기, 박종관). 택견 *T'aekkyŏn*. Seoul: Sŏrim Munhwasa, 1983. [In Korean only].

Tikhonov, Vladimir. "Hwarang organization: Its functions and ethics." *Korea Journal*. 38, 2 (1998): 318–38.

World Taekwondo Federation. "History." (Last modified 2013). [Retrieved from www.worldtaekwondofederation.net/taekwondo-history].

[Yi Man-yŏng] (이만영). 才物譜 *Chaemulpo* (*Book of expertise*). (Vol. 6). Kyujanggak, 1798. [In Korean only].

[Yi Yong-bok] (이용복). 택견 *T'aekkyŏn*. Seoul: Taewŏn, 1995. [In Korean].

Yook, Sung-chul [Yuk Sŏng-ch'ŏl] (육성철). 이종우 국기원 부원장의 '태권도 과거'충격적 고백! "Kukkiwon Vice President Chong Woo Lee's shocking confession of Olympic competition result manipulation!". Trans. Lee Soo Han. *Shin Dong-A*, (2002, April). 290–311. [Retrieved from http://tkdreform.com/yook_article.pdf].

2 The relationship of taekwondo to karate

"I am one of those who wrote that [taekwondo history] in a book. To be frank, we did not have much to come out with... but now it's time to disclose the facts," acknowledged taekwondo pioneer Lee Chong Woo, former secretary general and vice president of the World Taekwondo Federation, and former vice president of the Kukkiwon, in an interview.[1]

Over the years, taekwondo has significantly contributed to advancing Korea's image around the world, by serving as a symbol of Korean culture and pride. As a consequence, a considerable amount of research in Korea is dedicated to finding some correlation between early Korean martial arts and taekwondo. However, the lines between fiction and reality often blur. Moreover, in the case of taekwondo, nationalism[2] plays a significant role in its historical portrayal, as well. General taekwondo literature and presentation will not reflect any relationship to karate whatsoever, insisting instead on an indigenous Korean origin.[3] Despite this popular portrayal, a variety of indisputable records and testimonies exist with regard to taekwondo's relationship to karate.

This chapter aims *not* to explain the relationship, or the lack thereof, between early Korean martial arts and modern taekwondo as discussed in the previous chapter, but focuses mostly on the latter's relationship with karate. This chapter will study the connection between taekwondo and karate by examining the existing records and testimonies. Following a brief, initial discussion of the origins of karate, the emphasis turns to the original *kwan*,[4] or schools, and their founders' relationship to karate. Then, this chapter describes the period when taekwondo leaders increasingly tried to distance themselves from taekwondo's karate roots. In particular, the influence of nationalism on this process will be examined. Finally, this study focuses briefly on the different taekwondo organizations that emerged from the power struggles among the early pioneers.

Karate in Okinawa and theories regarding its origin

In general, the Okinawan martial culture was significantly shaped by Japanese martial arts traditions.[5] In contrast, karate was strongly influenced or possibly transferred to Okinawa from China. Chinese boxing methods were introduced by soldiers, merchants, dignitaries, monks, Okinawans who ventured to the mainland to further their martial arts training, or simply settlers who immigrated to the island.[6] The first reference to a 'weaponless martial art' in Okinawa was in 1683 by the "Ryukyuan statesman, Junsoku."[7] Instructions were transmitted orally and the first few illustrations and descriptions of karate were only made during the mid-to-late nineteenth century.[8] However, prior to the twentieth century, there existed no "credible... documents" regarding the technical content, development, and history of karate.[9]

In the past, there have been several names for what is now called 'karate,' because the secretive schools preferred different names to distinguish their styles and lineages. According to Funakoshi Gichin, who is considered by many to be the 'father' of Japanese *karate-dō*, "we called the art merely *te* or *bushi no te*, 'warrior's hand(s)'."[10] '*Te*' was often combined with the area of origin, as *Naha-te*, *Shuri-te*, or simply *Okinawa-te*. In addition, '*kenpō*' ('fist method'), was another popular name and widely used term to describe China-based martial arts in East Asia referring to Chinese-style boxing (see Table 2.1).[11]

Table 2.1 Terminology used for Chinese *quanfa*

	Chinese	Japanese	Korean
拳 法	quan-fa	ken-pō	kwŏn-bŏp

Only over time, has 'karate' become the foremost name used to describe the art. At the beginning of the twentieth century, however, the Okinawan art was, by and large, known as '*tōdi-jutsu*' or '*karate–jutsu*.'[12] The original word '*kara-te*' is a combination of two Chinese characters, 唐 and 手, and was pronounced by the Okinawans with the alternative reading of '*tō-di*.' Like the Japanese language, the Korean language also borrows heavily from Chinese, and '*tang-su*' represents the respective Korean transliteration of the characters (see Table 2.2). The first character (*kara*, *tō*, or *tang*) refers to the Chinese Tang Dynasty (618–907 CE) and indicates an origin from China, and the second logogram (*te*, *di*, or *su*) means 'hand,' which is a reference to striking. Therefore, the original meaning of karate has been roughly translated as 'Chinese hand.'

Table 2.2 Terminology used for karate (I)

	Used in Okinawa	Japanese	Korean
唐 手	tō-di	kara-te	tang-su

A popular, fanciful hypothesis presented by some Korean scholars is that karate was actually transferred to Okinawa from Korea during the time of the long-vanished kingdom of Kaya (加倻 43–532 CE).[13] According to a K.B.S. documentary,[14] the ancient pronunciation of 'Kaya' had supposedly been 'Kara.' Therefore, some Korean scholars made the leap and claimed that '*kara*'-*te* was brought from the ancient kingdom of Kara (or Kaya) to Okinawa. The claim is based on the similarity of the pronunciations, and on the assertion that the name 'Tang' or 'Kara' (唐) had a broader meaning for the Okinawans, referring to both Korea and China. Furthermore, since Okinawan culture does bear some vague similarities to Korean culture, such as the *ondol* floor heating system and a *ssirŭm*-like wrestling game (which had possibly been transferred during earlier periods), these scholars speculated that the same might also have been the case with karate.[15] But this claim is easily disproved. First, even though the exact history of Okinawan karate is unclear, most evidence points to its formation during the period between the sixteenth to eighteenth centuries, originating from China as discussed before. However, the Kaya kingdom perished in the sixth century – leaving a thousand-year gap. Moreover, the Tang Dynasty (618–907 CE) was only established during the seventh century after the Kaya Kingdom had already vanished. In addition, there is no concrete evidence of any karate-like martial arts during the Kaya period in Korea or Okinawa. The earliest credible reference to the presence of any bare-handed martial arts in Korea occurred during the early twelfth century, in the *Koryŏsa* (*History of Koryŏ*), which refers to a China-based martial art called *subak* (see the discussion in Chapter 1, pp. 14–15). Second, the Okinawans used a variety of names for karate (as explained above) and the Chinese characters for 唐手 were not even pronounced 'karate' but '*tōdi*' by the Okinawans. Moreover, *tōdi-jutsu* only became popular at the beginning of the twentieth century as the general term used to describe the art.

Some other Korean scholars speculated that Korean martial arts were transferred to Okinawa with the advance of the *sambyŏlch'o* (elite military troops during the Koryŏ Dynasty) to the islands in the thirteenth century.[16] Even if this theory were true, it would only mean that Koreans introduced Chinese martial arts to Okinawa, because the known bare-handed Korean martial arts of that time were most likely of Chinese origin. There is no documented evidence for the above assertion and the first reference to a weaponless martial art in Okinawa was only made during the seventeenth century.[17] Empty-handed martial arts became important for the Okinawans only after 1477, as a result of a general weapons ban for commoners by the king, out of a fear of rebellion.[18] There are numerous references which suggest some martial arts transfer from China to Okinawa during this period, but no specific references to Korea. Moreover, even if there were some connection between long-ago Korean and Okinawan martial arts, this would still not address the fact that traditional martial arts in Korea ceased to exist at the beginning of the twentieth century. The only weaponless fighting contest still performed was wrestling-like *ssirŭm*, which represented a game-like activity unconnected to stand-up striking martial arts. Notably, another game-like fighting activity that survived, although on the verge of disappearance, was *t'aekkyŏn*. Although *t'aekkyŏn* cannot be classified as a martial art; in its original form, *t'aekkyŏn* resembled a folk game as discussed in the previous chapter.

The introduction of karate to Japan (1922)

At the beginning of the twentieth century, karate leaders from Okinawa decided to alter the implications of using the '*tang*' (唐) character. They replaced it with the 'empty' (空) character. In connection with the 'hand' (手) character, this refers to combat without using any weapons.[19] Both characters 唐 and 空 when used in connection with the 'hand' (手) logogram are pronounced the same way in Japanese, namely '*kara-te.*' However, the two respective combinations of Chinese characters are pronounced differently in Korean, hence the two Korean names '*tang-su*' and '*kong-su*' (see Table 2.3).

Table 2.3 Terminology used for karate (II)

	Japanese	Korean
唐 手 道	karate-dō	tangsu-do
空 手 道	karate-dō	kongsu-do

The suffix '-*dō*' (道 'way' or 'method'; Chinese: '*dao*'; Korean: '*do*'), which is sometimes used in connection with karate, was only adapted after the introduction of karate to Japan. It classifies the modern Japanese *bu-dō* sports, like *ken-dō* (kendo), *jū-dō* (judo), or *aiki-dō*, and symbolizes the transformation of the practically oriented classical '*jutsu*' (術 'skill') arts to the modern spiritually oriented '*dō*' arts with a moral dimension.[20] In Japanese culture, the martial arts changed its fundamental character as a 'craft for war' to a method for self-improvement and self-perfection, termed in popular literature as 'way of life.' This concept had never been used in Chinese martial arts, but was later adapted by the Koreans, as in '*taek-won-do*' (跆拳道) and '*hapki-do*' (合氣道 pronounced '*aiki-dō*' in Japanese where its origin is found).[21] For the Chinese, as well as the Koreans, '*dao*' or '*do*' originally had a supernatural or metaphysical connotation. Hence, many Chinese martial artists associated their training with mythical concepts of Daoist teachings, and their general ambitions were to, somehow, attain supernatural powers, longevity, or eternal life. In contrast, for the Japanese, the *dō* had a purely secular meaning of a 'way to follow in life.' This is a reflection of Japanese culture and life in general which is, on the whole, more utilitarian and pragmatic than otherworldly and metaphysical.[22] However, the concept of *dō* was not merely reserved for the Japanese martial arts, but also found expression in all kinds of aesthetic, artistic, and everyday activities, such as the tea ceremony (茶道 'way of tea'; Japanese: '*chadō*'; Korean: '*dado*'). Many of these spiritual activities and rituals were transferred into Korean culture during the colonial era.[23] In the case of Japanese martial arts, the *dō* became the symbolic expression for all the collective spiritual aspects attached to the *budō* arts. In this way, the *do* is understood in a symbolic manner in *taekwon-do* as well. The first to articulate and promote this concept in a methodical fashion was the modern judo founder Kanō Jigorō, during the late nineteenth century.[24]

Subsequently, the martial arts concept of '*do*' was first introduced along with kendo and judo to the colonial education system of Korea.[25]

Most sources attribute the official name change of karate to Funakoshi Gichin.[26] After moving to Japan from Okinawa in 1922, he was given most of the credit for the proliferation of the art in Japan. However, there were many other Okinawans, some more skilful than Funakoshi, who started teaching karate in Japan during those days. In fact Motobu Chōki (1870–1944), a well-known street fighter and pioneer in *kumite* (free fighting), already "ventured" to Osaka in 1921.[27] Motobu, who had some of the same teachers as Funakoshi, was opposed to Funakoshi, who saw the essence of karate in the training of *kata* (forms) and the development of spiritual and educational aspects.[28] The split between martial artists, who concentrate on sparring and fighting versus the ones who concentrate on forms training and self-cultivation, was already visible in those two, early pioneers.

Being Okinawan, this first generation of karate instructors in Japan faced a degree of discrimination in the ultranationalist atmosphere of the imperial era. In addition, during the 1930s, it would certainly have been difficult to propagate a martial art with a Chinese name, considering that Japan invaded Manchuria in 1931, and before long, started to wage war with China (Second Sino-Japanese War, 1937–1945). According to Funakoshi's own words, he wanted to avoid confusion with Chinese boxing. Therefore, he officially changed the name in 1933, a move that many other Okinawan masters at first strongly resented. In spite of this, the new name was soon universally accepted, and since that time, karate has carried the meaning of 'empty hand.'[29]

Funakoshi was also responsible for the incorporation of certain features of the "classical warrior spirit ethos" into the philosophical concepts and teachings of Japanese *karate-dō*, which did not exist in the original Okinawan karate teachings.[30] Since the warrior caste represented traditionally the upper class and elite in Japan, some philosophical refinement was necessary to appeal to this group.[31] The Japanese military was quick to recognize karate's value for its own purposes. Karate, along with kendo and judo, was exploited for military education by the Japanese imperial government. By incorporating some philosophical samurai concepts, the Okinawans tailored karate to the taste of Japanese audiences, and karate gained official recognition as a 'Japanese martial art.' However, the Japanese, with a rich martial arts' history, had no need to construct a narrative of ancient karate history rooted in Japan. It is well documented and common knowledge today that karate originated only about a hundred years ago from Okinawa. In spite of the introduction to Japan and the name change to go with it, the *tang* character has also been kept in use, at least among the Koreans.

Karate-dō was introduced to Korea under the Korean transliterations of *tangsudo* and *kongsudo*, or the Chinese term *kwŏnbŏp*. Karate was propagated under these names and, as will be discussed in the next section, the Korean *kwan* or school founders had no connection to *t'aekkyŏn* or any indigenous Korean martial art. Moreover, shortly after Korea's liberation from Japanese colonial rule in 1945, except for judo and kendo, no other martial art existed on the peninsula. *Ssirŭm* was considered a game-like sports activity and *t'aekkyŏn*, which was a folk game, had not been practised for some time.

The introduction of karate to Korea (1944)

Funakoshi Gichin (1868–1957), the most influential karate leader of the twentieth century, learned karate in Okinawa from two different *Shurite* instructors, Asato (Yasutsune) Ankō (1827–1906) and Itosu (Yasutsune) Ankō (1831–1915). Funakoshi studied the styles of *Shōrei-ryū* and *Shōrin-ryū*, respectively. After Funakoshi introduced karate to Japan in 1922, he purposely established karate clubs at Japanese universities to attract the educated and elite, which greatly contributed to its proliferation. His own headquarters gymnasium, called '*Shōtōkan*' (松濤館 'house of *Shōtō*' or 'house of pine-waves'),[32] was built in 1936,[33] and the name '*Shōtōkan*' was subsequently associated with Funakoshi's karate style. However, Funakoshi never considered his teachings as a distinctive karate method and opposed the classification of karate into different styles. The association of his teachings with the name *Shōtōkan* karate as a distinct discipline occurred only later, initiated by his students;[34] although, there developed not a single, unified style, but a myriad of *Shōtōkan* karate organizations. Students of Funakoshi sought to differentiate themselves from other schools because of Funakoshi's fame and popularity. In addition, association with Funakoshi and the name *Shōtōkan* promised better marketability.

In 1924, Funakoshi founded the first karate club at Keiō University,[35] the oldest university in Japan. By the mid-1930s, Funakoshi established over thirty karate clubs at various institutions of higher learning. These university clubs were also the places where Koreans, who were students at these respective universities, came into contact with karate.[36] Three of the founders of the original five 'taekwondo' *kwan* or schools,[37] Lee Won Kuk (the founder of *Ch'ŏngdo Kwan*), No Pyŏng-jik (*Songmu Kwan*) and probably Chŏn Sang-sŏp (*Chosŏn Yŏnmu Kwan Kwŏnbŏp Pu*)[38] studied karate directly under Funakoshi and his third son, Funakoshi (Yoshitaka) Gigō, in one of the various university clubs that they supervised (see Figure 2.1). In fact, Funakoshi was too old at this point, and the practical teaching was mostly left to his son. Several other Koreans learned karate in Funakoshi's clubs as well, and a few attended classes with instructors of different karate styles.

In Korea, karate was first exhibited by several karate masters from Japan during the late 1930s, who were invited to give some demonstrations. Funakoshi himself reportedly demonstrated karate with an eleven-member strong team during such an occasion at a judo school in Chongno, Seoul, in 1937.[39] It seems that the training of judo and kendo inspired alternative martial arts activities, and some of the judo schools were among the first to introduce karate classes to their *dojang* (gymnasium or school) a few years later.

*Lee Won Kuk (*Ch'ŏngdo Kwan*)*

Lee Won kuk (1907–2002), son of an affluent family, settled in 1926 in Tokyo to attend high school and later Chūō University, where he studied law. He likely started to learn karate during the early 1930s, and was perhaps the first Korean who received karate instruction in Japan. However, it seems unclear in which of Funakoshi's clubs Lee had begun to train karate.[40] Moreover, following his graduation from university, Lee never stated his exact activities until his return to Korea in 1944; although, he mentioned having visited Okinawa and different locations in China,[41] which makes him highly likely to have served the Japanese war effort or military establishment.

After returning home, Lee founded the first *tangsudo* or karate school in Korea, in 1944, due to his good connections with the Japanese authorities. As the most senior and highest ranking instructor, he was the leading figure during the early years of karate's proliferation in Korea. During the late 1940s, *Ch'ŏngdo Kwan* (*Chung Do Kwan*) had already a large membership base of about five thousand students, which attracted the attention of the governing party of the late president Rhee Syngman. However, Lee declined to get involved in the messy politics of those days. As a consequence, he was prosecuted and accused of having been a Japanese collaborator and continuing agitator because of his former close relationship with the Japanese authorities. Lee was arrested and spent some time in prison until his release in 1950. Subsequently, he fled to Japan in 1951, out of fear for continuing persecution. After Lee's departure, Son Duk Sung assumed the leadership of *Ch'ŏngdo Kwan* in 1951. Lee's disappearance opened the door for increasing fragmentation of the *kwan*. In the absence of firm leadership and seniority, a variety of students split from *Ch'ŏngdo Kwan* and established their own schools. In addition, the onset of the Korean War, in 1950, threw the martial arts world into further disarray.[42]

*No Pyŏng-jik (*Songmu Kwan*)*

In 1936, No Pyŏng-jik (born 1919) moved to Tokyo and, after some preparatory studies, entered also Chūō University. No must have started studying karate soon after his university admission, at approximately the same time that the karate club was established at Chūō University by Funakoshi Gikō in 1940.[43] Lee Won Kuk also recalled having once met No at the university club around that time.[44]

Following university graduation, No returned to Korea in 1944, where he began teaching karate in an archery school. However, soon after, due to difficult times, he had to close the school again because of a lack of students. Subsequently, No re-established *Songmu Kwan* (*Song Moo Kwan*) in a different location in 1946.[45] By naming his school '*Songmu Kwan*' (松武館 'pine tree martial arts school'), No fully associated with, and honoured, Funakoshi, whose pen name was 'Shōtō' (松 'pine tree'), which is transliterated into Korean to 'Song.' Moreover, through the choice of his school's name, No considered it an offspring of *Shōtōkan*.

*Chŏn Sang-sŏp (*Chosŏn Yŏnmu Kwan Kwŏnbŏp Pu*)*

Chŏn Sang-sŏp (dates unknown) was an offspring of an "elite" Korean family,[46] but details are not known about when he ventured to Japan. In his case the claims conflict as to exactly where he learned karate. Although, it seems likely that Chŏn studied at some point in one of Funakoshi's karate clubs since Takushoku University, which he presumably attended, had such a club. The karate club at Takushoku University, a place where many famous karate instructors began their careers, was founded in 1930;[47] therefore, it was a well-established training place during the late 1930s, when Chŏn likely took up his university life. Some also maintained that Chŏn was a student of Mabuni Kenwa, whose style of karate is called *Shitō-ryū*. It is also unclear exactly when Chŏn returned to Korea, but in 1943, he reportedly already taught judo and karate as a hired instructor at *Yŏnmu Kwan* in Seoul, which was a judo school at that time. After the disorder following the immediate surrender by the Japanese was settled, Chŏn reopened the school as its new leader in 1946. Few exact details about his life are known because he vanished during the onset of the Korean War, and his school was closed. However, details about his successors are well documented.[48]

His foremost successor, Yun K'wae-pyŏng (1922–2000), studied karate first under Mabuni Kenwa and later under Tōyama Kanken at Nihon University. Afterwards, Yun founded a sister school in Tokyo in 1940, called *Kanbukan* (韓武館 'Korean martial arts institute' or school). Once he returned to Korea in 1948, sometime later he joined the *Chosŏn Yŏnmu Kwan* as chief instructor. Consequently, Yun and Chŏn Sang-sŏp had likely some earlier relationship, perhaps practicing together at some point in Mabuni's school. After Chŏn Sang-sŏp disappeared during the beginning of the Korean War, Yun, together with Lee Chong Woo, reopened the school in 1951. They took over the leadership roles and renamed the school, *Jido Kwan* (see Figure 2.1).[49] Subsequently, Yun played an essential role in the introduction of full-contact sparring with protective equipment (see a detailed discussion in Chapter 4, p. 90).

Yun Pyŏng-in (YMCA Kwŏnbŏp Pu)

The karate school called *Shūdōkan* (修道館 'school for the reform of the way [of karate]') was founded by Tōyama Kanken (1888–1966). Together with Funakoshi, Tōyama was a student of Itosu Ankō. In 1924, Tōyama moved to Taiwan, where he worked in an elementary school and studied some Chinese *quanfa*. In 1930, he returned to Japan and opened his own *dōjō* or gymnasium,[50] naming it *Shūdōkan*. He taught Itosu's karate (and some *quanfa*), but did not consider it to be a distinctive style and continued calling it *Shurite* (首里手 'hand of Shuri') after the indigenous Okinawan name, which refers to the area of origin. Several Koreans attended Tōyama's karate classes at that time (see Figure 2.1). Among them were Yun Pyŏng-in (1919–1983), the founder of the *YMCA Kwŏnbŏp Pu* (1946), and Yun K'wae-pyŏng (the successor at *Chosŏn Yŏnmu Kwan/ Jido Kwan*), who are both officially listed as high-ranking *Shūdōkan* students under Tōyama's guidance.[51]

Yun Pyŏng-in was the descendant of a *yangban* (noble class) family. His father was an entrepreneur in Manchuria, where Yun was born. During his childhood in Manchuria, Yun studied *quanfa* from a Mongolian instructor, and became an accomplished student. In 1938, Yun went to Tokyo to study at Nihon University.

At the university, he attended *Shurite* karate classes under Tōyama Kanken. Since Yun and Tōyama both had some *quanfa* background, there are recorded exchanges between them. Most Korean authors portray Yun Pyŏng-in in a somewhat romantic fashion. They usually highlight anecdotes about Yun in which he supposedly defended Koreans and their pride with his superior *quanfa* skills against Japanese aggressors. However, the fact is that Yun became one of the most high-ranking members among the Koreans who studied karate in Japan, and he probably focused more on karate training than *quanfa*. Moreover, after returning to Korea, Yun reportedly taught mostly karate and only sometimes some *quanfa* to selected students. Unfortunately, Yun, too, disappeared in 1951 during the Korean War and the school was closed.[52] He was reportedly taken to North Korea. After briefly teaching *kuksul* (*kuk sool*) in Pyongyang from 1966 to 1967, the program was cancelled, and Yun was sent to work in a cement factory, where he died of lung cancer in 1983.[53] The style that Yun taught in North Korea was likely *quanfa*, because '*kuksul*' (國術 'national art' or literally 'national skill'), pronounced '*guoshu*' in Chinese, represented a modern, generic term for Chinese martial arts, which was introduced by the Kuomintang of the Republic of China (1928–1948) to replace the name *quanfa*.[54] Yun Pyŏng-in seems to have the only credible non-karate background among all the founders of taekwondo.[55]

After the Korean War in 1953, the *YMCA Kwŏnbŏp Pu* was reopened, with the new name *Ch'angmu Kwan* (*Chang Moo Kwan*), under the leadership of Yi Nam-suk (the former, second president) and Kim Sun-bae.

*Hwang Kee (*Mudŏk Kwan*)*

Hwang Kee (1914–2002), the founder of the *Mudŏk Kwan* (*Moo Duk Kwan*), opened his school in 1945, but soon after closed it and reopened in another location in 1947. Among the original *kwan* founders, only Hwang had never been to Japan. He reported having learned a Chinese martial art for one year while he was in Manchuria working for the South Manchurian Railway from 1935 to 1937, a semi-privately-held Japanese company. However, many senior taekwondo instructors regarded this claim as fabricated.[56] Moreover, Hwang also claimed that he "self-studied" some *t'aekkyŏn* as a small child, but this seems very unlikely because *t'aekkyŏn* had already vanished during the time of his youth. It seems that Hwang received little, if any, formal martial arts training, but was instead mostly self-taught. According to his own writings, he began studying Okinawan karate from books, after he started working for the Chosŏn Railway in 1939, which had a library holding some karate manuals.[57] Furthermore, Lee Won Kuk claimed that Hwang studied some *tangsudo* at his *Ch'ŏngdo Kwan*.[58] There seem to be many discrepancies in Hwang's personal historical accounts, and the portrayals by his followers, who often worship him in a cult-like fashion, are not too reliable, either. Hwang continuously had troubled relationships with many of the other martial arts leaders, and kept being a source of conflict and agitation.

All the founders of the original *kwan* (except Hwang Kee) went to Japan for educational reasons, with the goal earning a higher degree. At the universities that

The relationship of taekwondo to karate 43

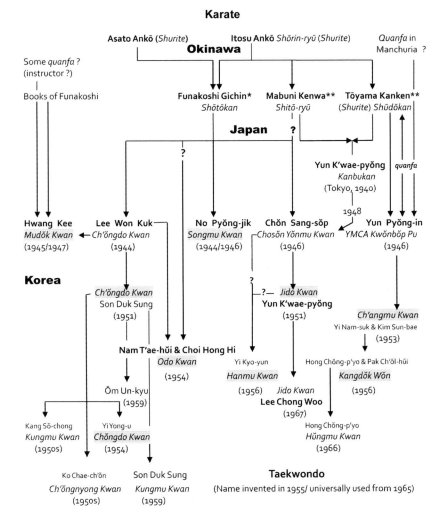

Figure 2.1 Connections of *kwan* or school founders to karate

Notes:
* From the mid-1930s on, due to Funakoshi's advanced age, most of the practical teaching in the *Shōtōkan* clubs was delivered by his third son, Funakoshi Gigō.
** Mabuni and Tōyama had a variety of other instructors. Both learned some *quanfa* from a Chinese instructor, as well.
• These nine *kwan* (highlighted in grey) are by most sources referred to as the main *kwan* that developed sometime later. Many more *kwan* developed over time.

they attended, they also started learning karate. Additional evidence demonstrating the Japanese origins of taekwondo can be seen in the lineages of those Koreans who also studied karate in Japan and came to dominate the Korean martial arts scene shortly thereafter, during the 1950s (see the discussion in

Chapter 2, pp. 46–7). Other notable Koreans who learned karate in Japan, such as Ōyama Masutatsu (with the Korean birth name Ch'oe Yŏng-ŭi), stayed in Japan and became respected personalities there. Ōyama moved to Japan in 1938 to enter Yamanashi Aviation School of the Imperial Japanese Army.[59] Consequently, he trained under a variety of famous karate instructors, among them also Funakoshi. After experimenting with many styles, he eventually created his *Kyokushin Kaikan karate* in 1957.

Early attempts to renounce the Japanese karate tradition

The early *kwan* or schools promoted their arts either under the names *tangsudo* or *kongsudo*. It is not clear why Lee Won Kuk, an assumingly devoted student of Funakoshi, would choose the name *tangsudo* over *kongsudo*. Lee likely started training karate during the early 1930s, when the old karate name with the '*tang*' character was still in use; however, Funakoshi had already started to advocate the new name with the 'empty' character. Therefore, either Lee did not agree with Funakoshi's name change, or he wanted to distance himself from his Japanese karate past. In contrast, his junior, No Pyŏng-jik, kept calling his art by Funakoshi's styled name, *kongsudo*.

From the beginning, Hwang Kee sought a Korean name for his art, and crafted the term '*hwasudo*' (花手道 'way of the flower hands'). According to Hwang, the logogram '*hwa*' (花 'flowers') was chosen to represent the post-war "blossoming" of liberated Korea.[60] In addition, the character '*hwa*' refers to the '*hwa-rang*' (花郞 'flower youth' or 'flower boys'), who were originally a social youth group of elites during the Silla Dynasty. In fact, only after Korea's independence were the formerly, little-known *hwarang*, all of a sudden, groundlessly elevated and associated with past Korean military glories.[61] Obviously, Hwang felt drawn to this kind of propagandistic rhetoric and crafted the name of his martial art in honour of the *hwarang*. He explained that *hwasudo* is derived from the terms *hwa-rang-do* and *tang-su-do*, but also admitted that he really does not know much about the long-ago existing martial art of *hwarangdo*.[62] Subsequently, in 1947, he adopted the term '*Tang Soo Do*' (*tangsudo*) because he could not attract any students with the self-styled name; in contrast, with the name *tangsudo* or karate, Hwang soon would draw an increasing number of followers. More than a decade later, the *Mudŏk Kwan* grew increasingly into one of the largest *kwan*. During the late 1950s, Hwang renamed his art, '*Soo Bahk Do*' (*subakdo*), again, with patriotic motives in mind. In his belief, '*subak*' represented the name of a long lost but 'real' Korean martial art; he did not know that it was merely the Korean transliteration of the traditional Chinese term for unarmed boxing, '*shoubo*' (手搏 see the discussion in Chapter 1, pp. 14–15). Even nowadays, the schools that affiliate themselves with Hwang's name are known, along with *Soo Bahk Do*, by the karate term '*Tang Soo Do*.'

In contrast to the karate names *tangsudo* and *kongsudo*, the *YMCA Kwŏnbŏp Pu* and the *Chosŏn Yŏnmu Kwan Kwŏnbŏp Pu* referred to their style as '*kwŏnbŏp*' (拳法), which is the Korean pronunciation of the Chinese term for '*quanfa*' (see Table 2.1).[63] However, according to Lee Chong Woo, who was one of the early members of the *Chosŏn Yŏnmu Kwan*, "I learned Karate in the Kwon Bup Division. Kwon Bup is the same as Japanese Karate. Since the national pride was concerned, we called it Kwon Bup instead of calling it Japanese karate."[64] National pride played a role from the beginning in the presentation of Korean martial arts. This was the reason the early founders often preferred to use the *tang* character instead of the *kong* character; its use obscured their art's origin from Japanese *karate* and suggested instead some ancient Chinese roots. For the same reason, some decided to call their art *kwŏnbŏp* (see Table 2.4).

Table 2.4 Founders and founding *kwan* of taekwondo

Original 5 schools	Founder	Called his art	Style(s) studied by founder
1. *Ch'ŏngdo Kwan** 青濤館 (1944)	Lee Won Kuk / **Successor**: Son Duk Sung (1951)	*tangsudo*	Yi: **Karate** under Funakoshi **in Japan**. Son: ***Tangsudo*** under Lee Won Kuk.
2. *Songmu Kwan* 松武館 (1944, closed, reopened 1946)	No Pyŏng-jik	*kongsudo*	**Karate** under Funakoshi **in Japan**.
3. *Mudŏk Kwan* 武德館 (1945, closed, reopened 1947)	Hwang Kee	*hwasudo* (1945) *tangsudo* (1947) *subakdo* (late 1950s)	**Karate** out of books; claimed to have studied *t'aekkyŏn* and a Chinese marital art.
4. *Chosŏn Yŏnmu Kwan Kwŏnbŏp Pu* (1946) 朝鮮研武館拳法部 later *Jido Kwan* 智道館 (1951)	Chŏn Sang-sŏp/ **Successor**: Yun K'wae-pyŏng (1951)	*kwŏnbŏp* and/or *kongsudo***	Chŏn: **Karate** under Funakoshi and judo **in Japan**. Yun: **Karate in Japan**.
5. *YMCA Kwŏnbŏp Pu* 拳法部 (1946), later *Ch'angmu Kwan* 彰武館 (1953)	Yun Pyŏng-in	*kwŏnbŏp*	*Quanfa* in Manchuria. **Karate in Japan**.
• *Odo Kwan* 吾道館 (1954)	Choi Hong Hi and Nam T'ae-hŭi	*tangsudo* taekwondo (1955)	Choi: **Karate in Japan**; claimed to have studied *t'aekkyŏn*. Nam: ***Tangsudo*** under Lee Won Kuk.

Notes:
* Eric Madis states that Lee Won Kuk called his school *Ch'ŏngdo Hwe* (會 '*hwe*,' 'assembly') in 1944, and Son Duk Sung changed the name in 1951 to *Ch'ŏngdo Kwan* (Madis, "The evolution of taekwondo from Japanese karate," p. 193.); however, this is not mentioned by other authors.
** There is some discrepancy among sources regarding the names used. Madis claims that the school was called *Yŏnmu Kwan Kongsudo Pu*. However, in an interview Lee Chong Woo referred to the art as *kwŏnbŏp* and the school as *Chosŏn Yŏnmu Kwŏnbŏp Pu*.
• There are also some minor divergences in the various reports regarding the closing and reopening of schools, and martial art names.

The emergence of new leaders in the post-Korean War period (1953)

In the aftermath of the Second World War, the Korean peninsula was divided into the American occupied South, and the Soviet dominated North, with two ideologically opposing governments emerging. The ultimate political goal of both Koreas was unification; but, each, under her own terms, and if necessary by force. The ensuing Korean War (1950–1953) brought extensive destruction and loss of life, and ended essentially where it started, with the 38th parallel as a dividing line between the South and North.[65]

When South Korea emerged from the ashes of the Korean War, with a continuing threat of annihilation from the North, nation building was necessary for physical survival. Moreover, in the struggle for legitimacy with North Korea, South Korean leaders could not appear to show appeasement with their former colonial ruler, especially since many of the South Korean elite formerly prospered under the Japanese.[66] The establishment needed to create a cultural identity that was 'pure' and untainted by connections with the Japanese colonial past. In contrast, the North Korean Communist leaders had a compelling anti-Japanese record.[67] The growing fervor of nationalism in South Korea, in tandem with an increasing anti-Japanese sentiment, meant that any connection with its former colonial ruler had to be denied. Therefore, karate, which was introduced to Korea by Koreans with a record and past history of embracing Japanese culture, had to be 'Koreanized' and its Japanese origins increasingly obscured.

The Korean War forced many martial arts schools to close, and their leaders and students often vanished or were killed. As a result, during and after the war, most of the *kwan* began to regroup. Out of the original five founding schools of taekwondo, many more sub-schools or branches developed, sometimes due to missing leaders, and at times, because of disagreements among key members that resulted in schisms and the opening of new gymnasia.[68] During these turbulent years, and as long as these various schools were not organized under an umbrella organization, some of the masters did not care too much about their art's name and Japanese origins. This soon became a greater issue after the disorder of the Korean War was settled, when the various *kwan* were gradually unified into a national organization.[69]

After the Korean War, Choi Hong Hi (1918–2002) progressively rose to become the most powerful among the new, emerging martial arts leaders. While studying in Japan, Choi also came in contact with karate. From 1938 to 1942, he attended first a Japanese high school in Kyoto, and then Chūō University in Tokyo. Following his return to Korea, willing or forced, he joined the Japanese military in 1943. Choi claimed of having trained *Shōtōkan* karate in Kyoto, and later at the Chūō University club under Funakoshi, where he supposedly earned a second degree black belt. However, his claims were highly inconsistent and could not be verified; more likely, Choi only gained some rudimentary knowledge of karate and available evidence does not support his having received a second degree black belt under Funakoshi.[70] After Korea's liberation, Choi joined the

South Korean military, and once in a position of power as a major general in 1952, he seems to have exaggerated his former martial arts accomplishments. Naturally, Choi sought association with Funakoshi, which promised recognition and prestige. During that time, Funakoshi was still highly regarded among the Korean martial arts elites, who would proudly boast of having studied under him.

Choi was largely responsible for the formation of the different schools under the name 'taekwondo.' He established his *Odo Kwan* (*Oh Do Kwan*) together with Nam T'ae-hŭi in 1954 in the military (see Figure 2.1). Nam and many other *Odo Kwan* members were originally affiliates of *Ch'ŏngdo Kwan* and learned *tangsudo* from Lee Won Kuk. Subsequently, Nam taught *tangsudo* in the military since 1947.[71] Moreover, the *Odo Kwan* style closely resembled *Shōtōkan* karate, due to its close connection to *Ch'ŏngdo Kwan*. Regarding Choi's personal martial arts experiences, "very few of Choi's men saw Choi do much martial arts during the fifty years in which they worked with him."[72] Instead, he gave instructions, and subordinates like Nam did the work.[73]

In his 1965 publication, Choi claimed to have studied *t'aekkyŏn* from his calligraphy teacher while he was in North Korea, and then later karate in Japan, afterward combining both.[74] Although it seems highly unlikely that a calligraphy teacher, who represented a sort of Confucian scholar, would also engage in teaching a folk game-like activity, often associated with lower classes and ruffians. In regards to Choi's martial arts skills, other martial arts leaders regarded him as inexperienced in karate, but paid him respect due to his powerful position as a military general.[75] Concerning the *tangsudo* or karate that his soldiers practiced, Choi was aiming from very early on to construct a narrative that connected his teachings to ancient Korean martial arts.[76] Moreover, Choi realized the ideological potential of martial arts education as well as the possibilities of sending instructors overseas for showcasing Korean culture.

Consequently, during the mid-1950s, Choi introduced taekwondo as a mandatory practice for soldiers. Some believe that from this time on, taekwondo was used as a tool for educating young Koreans in nationalism and militarism,[77] similar to the earlier abuse of karate in Japan. But this seems to be an oversimplification of the situation. During that time, South Korea was still in a state of near total destruction and one of the poorest countries on earth. Koreans were without hope and direction; the underlying motivation of teaching taekwondo was not just to instruct young soldiers how to fight and obey, but to turn them into proud Koreans.

With greater numbers of practitioners, especially those coming from the military, as well as the subsequent opening of new private gymnasiums and the establishment of various new schools or styles, a second generation of leaders emerged. The second generation had not studied in Japan, and was separated in both time and space from the original teachings. Naturally, some changes and modification in training styles appeared, as was seen when Japanese karate was handed to the next generation. In addition, the second generation leaders of Korean martial arts did not carry the burden of a pro-Japanese past. For them, it was easier to disconnect from taekwondo's karate origins.

Considering South Korea's desperate political and economic situation after the Korean War, nationalism was a necessary element of the nation building process. In this context, taekwondo's karate history became a liability. Taekwondo needed a 'useful' and legitimate cultural past; one that was accepted among fellow Koreans and one that could be marketed to the rest of the world. During this time of consolidation and expansion, the need for a unified umbrella organization became more urgent, and the process started with a name change.

A new name for the art: the dawn of taekwondo (1955)

The World Taekwondo Federation formerly stated on its homepage that when Rhee Syngman (1875–1965), the first president of South Korea, watched a "Taekkyon demonstration" by the Korean military in 1954, he was capable of "clearly distinguishing Taekwondo from the Japanese Karate which had been introduced by the Japanese ruler."[78] But the '*t'aekkyŏn* demonstration' was really a *tangsudo*, or karate, demonstration, which was practised under Choi Hong Hi in the Korean military at that time. The mention of the word '*t'aekkyŏn*' was probably a rather unconscious and innocent remark by the late president, who knew nothing about martial arts. But Choi apparently got the idea of renaming the Japanese art at a later time.[79]

Kang Won Shik (taekwondo pioneer and president of the Kukkiwon until 2013) and Lee Kyong Myong stated: "It was General Choi's determination that we should no longer use any Japanese or Chinese martial art names, but rather, use [names] derived from Korean tradition."[80] Most sources suggest that Choi Hong Hi proposed the name 'taekwondo' because of its close pronunciation to the native '*t'aekkyŏn*.' Choi himself claimed, "At the [1955] session for naming, the term worded in 'Tae' and 'Kwon' which I submitted was chosen unanimously among the many other ballots."[81] Son Duk Sung, another influential instructor of that era, who took over the *Ch'ŏngdo Kwan* leadership from Lee Won Kuk, also claimed later that he was in charge of crafting the term 'taekwondo' at that meeting.[82] Son and Kang Won Shik (member of *Songmu Kwan*) promoted Choi Hong Hi, who was relatively inexperienced in martial arts, to an honorary fourth degree black belt in 1955, due to his powerful position in the military. But some time later, they had disagreements over Choi's actions and further demands.[83] This dispute probably led to their later contradictory claims. Another popular name suggestion, also favored by Rhee Syngman, had been '*t'aekkyŏn-do*.' However, Choi instinctively knew that he could not promote his art, which was basically karate, with the name '*t'aekkyŏn*.'[84] The significance of this event is that it presents the beginning of the creation of a national, historical narrative for taekwondo. This episode was not so different from the earlier quest by karate leaders to ensure that karate became 'Japanese.'

Regarding the choice of the name '*taekwondo*,' a few points require clarification. Whereas '*t'aekkyŏn*' (택견) is a purely Korean name and cannot be written in Chinese characters (see also Chapter 1, p. 18), the name '*tae-kwon-do*' (跆拳道) is derived from three Chinese characters. The second character, '*kwon*' (拳), bears the meaning of 'fist' as in *quan-fa* or *kwŏn-bŏp*, and the last, '*do*' (道), is an indicator for the modern Japanese *bu-dō* sports, as mentioned earlier. However, the first character, '*tae*' (跆), is described by Choi Hong Hi in the following manner: "*Tae* literally means to jump or kick or smash with the foot."[85] This definition, or a definition very close to this one, has been adhered to in all later taekwondo literature. However, in fact, the character '*tae*' has the meaning of 'to step on,' 'to trample (or stamp) on or down,' and bears no connotation in meaning with kicking or jumping. The closeness in pronunciation of the words '*t'aekkyŏn*' and '*taekwondo*' was more important than its actual meaning for the founders. Currently, Sino-Korean (Chinese character) dictionaries also list to 'kick' and 'jump,' but only in association with taekwondo, as representing 'special Korean characteristics' of this Chinese character.[86] Over the years, this attractive fallacy has even been accepted by the administrators of the Korean language.

Regardless of the origin of the name, the main reason for the formation of the different schools under one national umbrella organization and name was the desire for expansion, with the ultimate goal of internationalization. While the name taekwondo was used at first only by Choi's *Odo Kwan* in the military, and the closely connected *Ch'ŏngdo Kwan*, in 1959, under pressure by Choi, the different schools unified for the first time under the name, the 'Korea Taekwondo Association' (KTA), with Choi as president. However, disagreements over the art's name persisted since most of the masters wanted to retain the name '*tangsudo*.' Soon thereafter, Hwang Kee was the first to split from the group as the result of a variety of internal issues.[87]

Following the 1961 military coup by Park Chung Hee (1917–1979), there was great turmoil in South Korean society and the martial arts world was affected as well. As a result, the organization was renamed the 'Korea Taesudo Association' ('*Taehan T'aesudo Hyŏphwe*'). However, factional strife and further disagreements between leaders kept undermining the establishment of a strong organization.[88] Finally, the term 'taekwondo,' hard-pressed and promoted by Choi Hong Hi, was officially recognized in 1965, when the Korea Taesudo Association changed its name back to 'Korea Taekwondo Association.' With the formation of the Korea Taekwondo Association, in concert with the drive for taekwondo's internationalization, any Japanese historical association had to be increasingly denied.

During the 1960s, the Japanese terminology was gradually changed. In early taekwondo many of the technical terms were often pronounced in Japanese. For example, several early Korean martial art manuals still sometimes used the Japanese pronunciation for names of forms, even though they were written in *han'gŭl* (the Korean alphabet). This was resolved by increasing the use of the Korean pronunciation of Chinese characters and by the introduction of new and sometimes purely Korean terms. Finally, the old karate forms and most of its terminology were replaced with newly developed taekwondo patterns during the late 1960s and early 1970s (see Chapter 3, pp. 67–71, for a detailed discussion).

However, in spite of several modifications, the traditional karate uniform (着 *gi* or 道着 *dōgi*) was still worn by Choi Hong Hi and other authors in the photographs of their books. Kanō Jigorō, the founder of judo, invented the uniform in 1907, using the traditional *kimono* garment (着物 literally 'thing to wear'), as model. The first uniforms consisted of simple, unbleached, heavy cotton, later models were bleached white. In Okinawa, karate students used to wear their everyday clothes during practice. However, Funakoshi, influenced by Kanō, at first introduced the standard judo uniform to karate training in 1924, which was modified over time, using lighter material and a design with a looser fitting. Judo training requires a strong garment for grappling and throwing, in contrast to karate, which needs a looser and lighter training uniform for kicking and punching. In taekwondo training, the traditional karate uniform was slightly modified only during the 1980s, with the introduction of a new style taekwondo '*dobok*' (道服 'uniform'), which featured a closed jacked with a v-shaped collar, instead of the traditional overlapping, open cover.[89]

In addition to the uniform, the belt ranking system was also invented by Kanō to structure judo training and its syllabus according to corresponding grades and ability levels of students. He divided the ranks into *kyū* (級 student ranks) and *dan* (段 master ranks). The *kyū* ranks are indicated by different color belts, and the *dan* grades are structured according to different black belt levels. Funakoshi adopted the same system, because it was a superior training method. Moreover, the '*Dai Nippon Butoku Kai*,' the official umbrella organization governing the Japanese martial arts, aimed for uniform standards across the whole spectrum of existing martial arts (see also Chapter 7, pp. 153–4), and Funakoshi aspired for karate to become a 'Japanese martial art.'[90] Naturally, the system was assimilated into taekwondo, although it has been slightly modified over the years, by any instructor choosing to do so. Nonetheless, taekwondo's *kŭp/dan* (級/段 the Korean transliteration of the Japanese *kyū/dan* terminology) system used by the World Taekwondo Federation nowadays was inherited from karate and is, in principle, judo-based.

Moreover, the main formalities and training curricula of early taekwondo were directly derived from Japanese karate and remain largely the same today. Yabu Kentsū (1866–1937), a military man, who also studied karate (just as Funakoshi) under Itosu Ankō, turned out to be another influential Okinawan karate master at the beginning of the twentieth century. Influenced by his military background, and likely by kendo and judo routines, Yabu pioneered and introduced the following training rituals and methods to karate training, when karate was first introduced to the public school system in Okinawa in 1901: "Bowing upon entering the training hall – Lining up students in order of rank [and in rows] – Seated meditation... – Sequenced training (warm-up exercises, basics, forms, sparring) – Answering the instructor with loud acknowledgment – Closing class with formalities similar to opening classes."[91] These are essentially military-style methods, which allow instructing and controlling a large number of students at the same time. None of these rituals or training methods existed in earlier Okinawan karate, Chinese martial arts, or Korean *t'aekkyŏn*, and had previously been used only in kendo and judo.[92] All of them still exist in present day taekwondo, along with the common appearance of the Korean flag on the *dojang* (gym) wall, which also represents an imperial Japanese martial arts tradition.

The formation of modern taekwondo

During the late 1950s, probably as a result of the post-war diaspora, immigrating Koreans started to introduce 'taekwondo' (called '*tangsudo*' or 'Korean karate' at that time) to the outside world, and opened the first Korean martial arts studios in the United States.[93] Until the early 1960s, however, taekwondo was largely proliferated by a variety of private groups and organizations, and the South Korean government had not yet begun to interfere directly in their activities. Direct state involvement occurred mostly in the ROK Army under the direction of Choi Hong Hi. While martial arts training was popular with police forces from the late 1940s, other military branches also introduced some martial arts classes during the late 1950s, sponsored by individual units and groups. In addition, presidential body guards were all trained in taekwondo, and later also sometimes *hapkido*, a self-defense and *aikidō-based* style. Moreover, many instructors started to teach at American military bases, which later helped to spread taekwondo when returning servicemen and invited Korean instructors started teaching in the United States.

During the mid-1960s, the government became increasingly involved in regulating martial arts activities. The Vietnam War provided another opportunity for the expansion and general recognition of taekwondo. Taekwondo trainers were among the first Korean troops sent to Vietnam to provide martial arts training to Vietnamese soldiers. Taekwondo was introduced during that time mostly as a means of training troops, conditioning, and as a lethal form of self-defense. Additionally, according to reports, the Korean CIA sent operatives disguised as martial arts trainers abroad to control and spy on the political activities of Koreans who lived or studied overseas.[94]

However, the fate and general direction of taekwondo during the 1960s depended on a power struggle between traditional and modernist leaders. The traditional oriented faction saw taekwondo foremost as a 'martial art' for practical self-defense and much less as a sport. They were not only politically opposed to the newly rising group, but also philosophically objected to the full-contact sparring and competition-based taekwondo style these new leaders promoted. Among the Korean leaders of that time, Lee Chong Woo (*Jido Kwan*) and Ŏm Un-kyu (*Ch'ŏngdo Kwan*) supported the development of a full-contact sport, while Choi Hong Hi (*Odo Kwan*) and Hwang Kee (*Mudŏk Kwan*) were among the most prominent individuals opposed.[95] Initially, Choi had the means to promote his vision of taekwondo due to his powerful position in the military. However, he was increasingly sidelined because of his animosity towards Park Chung Hee, who seized power in South Korea, through a military coup d'état, in 1961. At first, Choi was appointed ambassador to Malaysia with the aim of diminishing his influence and tactfully removing him from Korea. He remained in Malaysia from 1962 to 1964. After his return to Korea, Choi became the first president of the newly established Korea Taekwondo Association in 1965, but was soon labeled a constant agitator by other taekwondo leaders and eventually had to resign. Subsequently, in 1966, Choi established a competing umbrella organization, named the 'International Taekwondo Federation' (ITF), to promote taekwondo internationally.[96]

The Park Chung Hee regime introduced a policy of cultural revival under the catch-phrase "'Cultural Korea' (*Munhwa Han'guk*)." The movement, ironically, was based on former Japanese models, but used at times strong nationalistic, anti-Japanese rhetoric; although it was ultimately directed against the North, as a defense against Communist ideology. In this drive for spiritual, moral, and cultural restoration, the regime promoted sports in a systematic fashion as a form of cultural movement in order to energize and mobilize the masses,[97] but also as a means of advancing Korea's image in the world through achievements in competitive sports. Taekwondo increasingly served Park's "vision of diligence" and "self-discipline." The late dictator and president endorsed taekwondo under his slogan "Physical strength is national power."[98] As a result, taekwondo's status as a largely private undertaking changed in 1971, when it was upgraded to the 'national sport' of Korea. The same year, construction of the Kukkiwon, the so called 'World Taekwondo Headquarters,' began. The name 'Kukkiwon' (國技院 '*Kukkiwŏn*,' loosely translated 'hall or gymnasium of the national sport') was unimaginatively borrowed from the Japanese national sport *sumō* (Japanese wrestling) and its headquarters, the '*Ryōgoku Kokugikan*' (両国 国技館 '*Ryōgoku* gymnasium of the national sport'), built in 1909.[99] Furthermore, public schools introduced taekwondo officially into their physical education programs that year.[100] So, in a sense, these political decisions, helped launch the commercial taekwondo industry because, almost overnight, thousands of Korean children and young adults, began training taekwondo, leading to the development of a wide variety of related cottage industries, not the least of which was the overseas taekwondo expansion juggernaut.

From this time on, taekwondo has been exported throughout the world through a state-sponsored promotion campaign. It was then that, in order to find legitimacy as 'the Korean national sport,' taekwondo's history had to be 'officially' rewritten and its connection to Japan completely denied. The Park regime realized the potential power of creating a 'shared national past' that would transform 'mythological narratives' into 'national heritage.'[101] In regards to taekwondo, ironically, many of those who started this process, such as Choi Hong Hi, Hwang Kee, and other leaders of the first generation, were gradually marginalized due to political disagreements. A steady increase in the institutionalization of taekwondo also helped to erode their power base.

With the political support of the Park regime, Kim Un Yong was appointed as the president of the Korea Taekwondo Association (KTA), in 1971. According to Lee Chong Woo, as a teenager, Kim learned some "karate" at the *YMCA Kwŏnbŏp Pu*,[102] and after serving in the army, he joined the Korean CIA. As an ex-KCIA man, he would not accept any rivals or defiant views. Once and for all, Kim wanted to get rid of the old divisional politics and power struggles at work between the different schools and their leaders. Under Kim's leadership, the Ministry of Education subjected private taekwondo gymnasiums to a variety of government regulations in order to gain firm control over disobedient instructors.[103] Most emphatically, he would break the power base of the individual *kwan* leaders by depriving them of their ability to promote and issue independent *dan* (black belt) certificates for their students.[104] Finally, the *kwan* were officially dissolved in 1974 and brought under the direct control of the Korea Taekwondo Association and Kukkiwon. As a result of this monopolization of power by the new KTA leaders, many of the older generation leaders emigrated overseas during the 1970s and established or founded their own independent martial arts organizations outside Korea.[105] Choi Hong Hi fled to Canada in 1972, because of his fear of political prosecution by the Park regime. Simultaneously, he moved the headquarters of the International Taekwondo Federation to Toronto.[106] Hwang Kee relocated his son, Hwang Hyun Chul, from Greece to the United States in 1974, where he established his 'United States Tang Soo Do Moo Duk Kwan Federation.' However, taekwondo organizations established overseas tended to follow the long-standing pattern of splintering and fragmentation into different organizations brought on by disputes among leaders and students.

Hand-in-hand with the South Korean government, the newly founded 'World Taekwondo Federation' (WTF), in 1973, was intended to propagate and manage the sport-based style of taekwondo internationally. During the 1970s, in line with South Korea's increasing economic development, a growing number of international taekwondo organizations and schools associated with Choi's International Taekwondo Federation began to switch sides and joined the World Taekwondo Federation. This migration resulted in a situation of financial and political distress for Choi. Therefore, in 1980, after persuasion by North Korean agents and Kim Il Sung (the first leader of North Korea, 1912–1994) himself,[107] Choi introduced taekwondo to North Korea in order to gain sufficient funding to oppose the growingly powerful and heavily financed World Taekwondo Federation.[108] Prior to this event, karate, or taekwondo, had not existed in North Korea since all of the founders of the original taekwondo schools had settled in the South.[109] Only Yun Pyŏng-in, after his abduction to the North during the Korean War, reportedly taught a *kuksul* program for a brief period during the 1960s; this was, however, soon cancelled (see Chapter 2, p. 53). Moreover, Communist regimes, in general, viewed the traditional Asian martial arts with suspicion. For instance, the Chinese Communists suppressed traditional Chinese martial arts and labeled them part of a superstitious, bygone feudalistic era.[110] North Koreans, in particular, regarded taekwondo instructors and their activities as 'anti-communist' because of their involvement in the Vietnam War, where they had trained thousands of South Vietnamese soldiers in hand-to-hand combat.

In order to please the North Korean regime, Choi adjusted his anti-communist political ideology and expressed his change of heart through the introduction of some modifications regarding taekwondo's philosophy and presentation. For example, he eliminated a form named after a South Korean hero and patriot, called *Kodang*, and instead replaced it with a new form named after North Korea's official state ideology, '*Chuch'ae*' (literally 'self-reliance'). Moreover, he proclaimed that "North Koreans were practising 'pure Tae Kwon Do,'" and in turn, the North Koreans embraced his ideas and authority in martial arts matters.[111]

As a result, Choi's style of taekwondo was integrated as a physical training activity and a system of hand-to-hand combat in the North Korean military. On the international stage, however, even with the support of the North Korean regime, Choi's International Taekwondo Federation and other alternative taekwondo organizations became marginalized over the years, especially after the full acceptance of WTF-style taekwondo as an official Olympic discipline in 2000.

Kim Un Yong seemed to recognize from very early on the value of a sports-based martial art as a tool to advance Korea's image. Lee Chong Woo, who later became the secretary general and vice president of the World Taekwondo Federation, turned out to be perhaps the most central figure for the practical promotion of sport taekwondo, whereas Kim was responsible for its political lobbying. They promoted taekwondo as a sport with the idea of emulating the success of Japanese judo in becoming an Olympic discipline, while at the same time denying taekwondo's historical origins in Japanese karate. Moreover, in order to promote taekwondo in the Olympics, the presentation of taekwondo as a single unified organization was essential.

The South Korean government was exclusively committed to the support of the Korea Taekwondo Association. At the same time, the suppression of other taekwondo organizations, as well as state-sponsored political and financial support to the World Taekwondo Federation, made taekwondo's Olympic bid eventually possible. It would also prevail over a similar bid by karate which lacked a commensurate degree of strong support from the Japanese government. Moreover, by the 1990s, Kim Un Yong had become one of the IOC vice presidents, arguably, the most powerful Asian personality in the Olympic movement. In retrospect, an abundance of bribery allegations and irregularities during the long bidding process for taekwondo to join the Olympics surfaced.[112]

Choi Hong Hi died in 2002. As a result, due to political disagreements regarding its new leadership, the International Taekwondo Federation split into three organizations, each claiming to be the legitimate heir. While the early leaders eventually lost their leadership roles, the fictional history of taekwondo they invented is still formally recognized as 'taekwondo's history.' In addition, Choi's name was largely omitted from the taekwondo history presented by the World Taekwondo Federation due to the relationship he developed with North Korea and the rivalry that he created through his International Taekwondo Federation. The struggle for legitimacy between the World Taekwondo Federation, which was (and is) subsidized by the South Korean government, and the International Taekwondo Federation led by Choi and sponsored by North Korea, can be viewed as an extension of the general politics and attitudes of the two Korean nations towards one other.

Finally, Kim Un Yong fell in disgrace as well, accused of massive irregularities, briberies and vote rigging during the 2010 Winter Olympic bid by the Korean city of Pyeongchang. In addition, he was charged with running the KTA like a Godfather, surrounded by criminals and thugs. He had to resign from all his posts, was convicted of embezzlement by a Korean court, and sentenced to two years in prison in 2004.[113]

Summary

Contrary to the popular portrayal of Korean martial artists training underground as a sort of resistance against the Japanese suppressers, many Korean martial arts pioneers came from well-to-do families who prospered under the Japanese occupation. These families could afford to send their children for higher education to Japan, where they also came into contact with karate. All of the founders of the original five taekwondo schools studied *karate*, and all but Hwang Kee did so in Japan.

Immediately after liberation in 1945, Lee Won Kuk was the most important figure for the proliferation of the art. Lee, No Pyŏng-jik, and Chŏn Sang-sŏp learned *Shōtōkan* karate directly from Funakoshi Gichin. It is likely that the others had also had some contact with the *Shōtōkan* style, since it was the most popular and best organized. Only Hwang Kee was mostly self-taught from books, and possibly studied with some of Lee Won Kuk's students. Two of the founders probably had connections to Chinese martial arts. Yun Pyŏng-in learned *quanfa* (*kwŏnbŏp*) as a child in Manchuria, but in Hwang's case, the claim is more likely an exaggeration. Most obviously, there is no apparent connection between these individuals, their martial arts background, and *t'aekkyŏn*.

Nationalistic tendencies were visible from very early on in the presentation of Korean martial arts. Most Korean instructors preferred to call their arts *tangsudo* or *kwŏnbŏp* instead of *kongsudo* to obscure their Japanese roots. Through the choices of their names, Koreans tried to project some Chinese origins for their martial arts. In contrast, the lesser used term *kongsudo*, which was standard at this time in Japan, clearly indicated Japanese ancestry.

In reality, the early Korean schools merely represented new, 'off-shore' branches of the original Japanese karate schools. Korean martial art students simply continued the tradition of many Japanese karate students, and when they came of age, they founded their own schools and styles. The original founders of taekwondo all learned and basically taught karate.

Many Koreans like to refer to the martial arts practised in Korea in the 1950s and before as 'taekwondo.' The expression is often loosely used as a collective term for all early Korean weaponless martial arts, and the distinction between them and modern taekwondo is often purposely blurred. As a matter of fact, the term did not even exist until 1955, and had only been used by a few groups until 1965. The first Korean martial arts instructors who went overseas promoted their art mostly with the name 'Korean karate,' as in some of the book titles used for this study. Most people at that time were not able to distinguish taekwondo from karate and only,[114] over time, did the use of the term 'taekwondo' become the foremost name for the art.

During the formation process of the different *kwan* or schools under the term 'taekwondo,' Choi Hong Hi and many other respectable masters of that time and following generations purposely misrepresented taekwondo's history. At first, this process occurred in order to legitimize the Japanese art in the eyes of fellow Koreans, and later, to spread it internationally as an 'ancient' Korean national art form. Nationalism was the driving motivational force for this historical misrepresentation. During the 1950s and beyond, the South Korean nation was struggling for its survival, and nationalism was an essential tool for nation building.

The denial of taekwondo's karate past was a gradual process, accompanied by an institutionalization of taekwondo. First, various attempts were made to merge the schools, and then a unifying name was given. Subsequently, it was used in the military as a training tool, thus providing a source of authority and legitimacy. Finally, the different schools were united and taekwondo was proclaimed the 'national sport' of Korea. Consequently, taekwondo was also formally integrated into the public school physical education program; much like kendo and judo was in Japan. This was also the era of the total break from its Japanese past. Successively, taekwondo was promoted to the world by an organization and establishment supported financially and ideologically by the South Korean government. Moreover, taekwondo's historical narrative, which was largely framed by the taekwondo establishment of the 1960s, has been supported and propagated semi-officially by the South Korean state ever since.

Even today, many Koreans are unwilling to admit or accept taekwondo's historical roots in Japanese karate because of a fear that doing so would undermine taekwondo's legitimacy as a Korean national treasure and cultural icon. But historical inaccuracy seems to be the case with regard to the presentation of Asian martial arts in general, where history and mythology are often confused and blended. As a result, historical disciplines are not enhanced by the academic research undertaken by many scholars in the field of taekwondo, which, in general, is strongly biased and driven by nationalistic sentiments with the common goal of producing a unique, ancient indigenous Korean martial arts tradition.

The original reason for presenting taekwondo in such a fashion has to be seen in the broader context of South Korea's devastation and division after the Korean War, which required an internationally underwritten effort of nation building and cultural reconstruction. Such a policy conceivably may have had a place in the context of 1960s South Korea; however, this type of historical fiction should be discouraged in contemporary times because of the absence of scientific evidence and the inability to provide valid historical documentation. What is, perhaps, even more puzzling is that academicians continue to twist the logic of research in order to maintain the denial of taekwondo's roots in karate. The reluctance of the Korean taekwondo and academic establishment to update taekwondo's historical narrative seems clearly related to national pride, and even broader political and, perhaps, historical disputes among East Asian nations. However, regardless of the larger political environment, it is long overdue that the World Taekwondo Federation and the taekwondo community should present taekwondo's history in a more accurate and honest fashion, so that the martial art and sport may be better understood and grow in more meaningful directions.

This chapter has analyzed the historical roots of taekwondo and shown how these origins have been largely denied by scholars and the Korean taekwondo establishment. The next chapter will provide further evidence of taekwondo's evolutionary development from karate.

Notes

1 As cited in an interview with Yook, "Kukkiwon Vice President Chong Woo Lee's shocking confession of Olympic competition result manipulation!", pp. 306–7.
2 The term 'nationalism' is understood in this study in the sense that a shared history – along with common ethnicity, political heritage, and religion – is one of the factors that draw people together in nationalist movements. The presentation of the history of a group or nation is an important part of the group's or nation's sense of identity and serves to reinforce cohesion. However, histories and traditions are often partly, and sometimes altogether, 'inventions,' to one degree or another. See Hobsbawn, and Ranger, *The invention of tradition*; Smith, *Nationalism: Theory, ideology, history*.
3 See, for example, World Taekwondo Federation, "History."
4 '*Kwan*' (館) means literally 'hall,' but refers to a martial arts gymnasium, and in this context, to a school or style. See also Note 37.
5 The Ryūkyū Kingdom, consisting of a chain of volcanic islands located South of Japan in the East China Sea, started a tributary relationship with the Chinese empire in the fifteenth century, which developed into a profitable trading arrangement. However, in 1609, the kingdom was forced to enter into a similar relationship with a group of Japanese warlords. Despite the subordinated status, the Ryūkyū Kingdom maintained a considerable degree of independence. This changed after the Meiji Restoration in 1868, a political and social event which ended the traditional feudal society in Japan. Influenced by Western ideas, it ushered Japan into a seemingly modern era. Subsequently, Japan annexed the Ryūkyū Kingdom by military force and made it an official territory, the Okinawa Prefecture, named after the main island, in 1879.
6 See, for example, Draeger, *Modern bujutsu and budo*, p. 125; McCarthy, *Bubishi – The classic manual of combat*, pp. 78–85; Bittmann, *Karatedô – Der Weg der leeren Hand*, pp. 151–5.
7 McCarthy, *Bubishi – The classic manual of combat*, p. 14.
8 Bittmann, *Karated – Der Weg der leeren Hand*, pp. 43; 92.
9 McCarthy, *Bubishi – The classic manual of combat*, 14; see also Bittmann, *Karatedô – Der Weg der leeren Hand*, p. 92.
10 Funakoshi, *Karate-dō – My way of life*, p. 33.
11 Green, *Martial arts of the world – An encyclopedia*, p. 255.
12 Draeger, *Modern bujutsu and budo*, 125.
13 However, there are a variety of names with different Chinese characters for the kingdom.
14 K.B.S. Korean Broadcasting System.
15 Yi, and Samsŏng Yŏngsang Saŏbdan, [*Taekwondo searches for the Korean Wave – 1. Part*].
16 See, for example, Kim, and Kim, "Rediscussion on views about the Chinese origins of dangsu [sic]," pp. 21–39.
17 Bittmann, *Karatedô – Der Weg der leeren Hand*; Patrick McCarthy, *Bubishi – The classic manual of combat*, p. 14.
18 Hassell, *Shotokan karate – Its history and evolution*, p. 3.
19 The 'empty' (空) character is borrowed from Zen-Buddhism. According to Funakoshi, the new meaning of *karate* at a philosophical level refers to a "clear mind" and the "emptiness of the universe." See Funakoshi, *Karate-dō kyōhan – The master text*, p. 4.
20 See Draeger, *Modern bujutsu and budo*; Kanō, *Mind over muscle*, p. 19.
21 The founder of *hapikido,* Choi Yong Sool, learned *aikidō*, which was based on *Daitō-ryū aiki-jūjutsu*, in Japan, and introduced it during the 1950s to Korea. However, over time, *hapkido* likely incorporated many *tangsudo* or karate techniques, and techniques from other martial arts, including modern taekwondo.

Hapkido occasionally displays similar misrepresentation as taekwondo regarding its general history and philosophy.

22   Friday, and Seki, *Legacies of the sword – The Kashima-Shinryū and samurai martial culture*, p. 61; Draeger, *Classical budo – The martial arts and ways of Japan*, p. 24.
23   In the case of the tea ceremony, Koreans use the term '*tarye*' (茶禮) for tea ceremony as well. However, the Japan-based term *dado* shows clearly the Japanese influence.
24   See Kanō, *Mind over muscle*; Bittmann, *Karatedô – Der Weg der leeren Hand,* pp. 34–37.
25   Compare Capener and Gwang. Capener (in "The modern significance of taekwondo as sport and martial art: Overcoming cultural and historical limitations in traditional thinking," p. 337) states that kendo and judo were introduced to the education curriculum in 1914. According to Gwang (in *The Transformation of Modern Korean Sport*, pp. 169, 275), judo was first introduced to Korea in 1906, and kendo was introduced in 1938 to the physical education curriculum of colonial schools. Although in regards to the general portrayal of Korean martial arts, Gwang's book is full of factual mistakes and misinformation.
26   Funakoshi was not the first to introduce the new character. Hanashiro Chōmo used the 'empty' character already in his 1905 publication entitled, "Karate kumite."
27   McCarthy, "On Choki Motobu – Part 1."
28   Noble, "Master Funakoshi's karate – The history and development of the empty hand art Part II," p. 4.
29   Funakoshi, *Karate-dō – My way of life*, p. 4; Hassell, *Shotokan karate – Its history and evolution*, pp. 49–50.
30   Clayton, *Shotokan's secret – The hidden truth behind karate's fighting origin*, pp. 129–30.
31   However, Madis credits Itosu Ankō, who was the teacher of Funakoshi, with already "embra[cing] the promotion of karate as a means of developing Japanese spirit (*yamato dmashi*)." See Madis, "The evolution of taekwondo from Japanese karate," p. 188.
32   '*Shōtō*' was Funakoshi's pen name.
33   Funakoshi, *Karate-dō – My way of life*, p. 83. The *Shōtōkan* was destroyed during the Second World War, and later rebuilt.
34   Bittmann, *Karatedô – Der Weg der leeren Hand*, p. 102.
35   Keio Univ. Karate Team Official Website, ["Overview of the karate division"], (2014). [Retrieved from www.keiokarate.com/#!karatebu/c66t].
36   Regarding the exact history of the early *kwan* compare Kang, and Lee, *A modern history of taekwondo*, pp. 2–13; Madis, "The evolution of taekwondo from Japanese karate," pp. 191–200; "Storming the fortress: A history of taekwondo – Part two: The first Korean schools: The Shotokan schools"; "Storming the fortress: A history of taekwondo – Part three: The first Korean schools: The Shudokan schools"; "Storming the fortress: A history of taekwondo – Part four: The first Korean schools: The maverick schools"; and Hŏ, [*Taekwondo's formation history*], pp. 15–108. Madis provides the best account of the early *kwan*.
37   The term '*kwan*' (館 see also Note 4), in Japanese '*kan*,' was already used in *karate*, such as in *Shōtō-kan*. The classical Japanese martial arts used the term '*ryū*' (流) for style or school. *Karate* styles sometimes also use a combination of both, such as *Shōtōkan-ryū*.
38   '*Pu*' (部) refers to 'division' or 'section' since the school also taught judo.
39   Hŏ, [*Taekwondo's formation history*], pp. 15–6.
40   Madis ("Storming the fortress: A history of taekwondo – Part two: The first Korean schools: The Shotokan schools") stated: "The Chuo University karate club was established sometime between 1928 and 1935 (Cook, 2001: 76). Considering when Lee would have entered Chuo University, the earliest that he could have studied karate would have been 1929 or 1930"; This contradicts the club's history description, which states that the club was founded in 1940. Moreover, Funakoshi's

son Gikō was the first instructor during that time. See [Chūō University Karate Division], ["The history of the karate division"], (n.d.). [Retrieved from http://chuo-karate.jp/about/history].
41 Madis, "Storming the fortress: A history of taekwondo – Part two: The first Korean schools: The Shotokan schools."
42 Compare Kang, and Lee, *A modern history of taekwondo*, pp. 2–4; Madis, "The evolution of taekwondo from Japanese karate," pp. 191–4.
43 See Note 40.
44 Madis, "Storming the fortress: A history of taekwondo – Part two: The first Korean schools: The Shotokan schools."
45 SongMoo [sic] Kwan, "A short history of Song MooKwan [sic], " (2013). [Retrieved from www.songmookwan.com/index.php/hist-of-smk/short-history-smk-menu]; and Madis, "Storming the fortress: A history of taekwondo – Part two: The first Korean schools: The Shotokan schools."
46 Kang, and Lee, *A modern history of taekwondo*, p. 4.
47 See Takushoku University Karate Club, ["About Takushoku University Karate Club"], (n.d). [Retrieved from www.karate.ne.jp/takushoku/index.html]; for example, Nakayama Masatoshi entered Takushoku University in 1932, and started training karate at the club.
48 Hŏ, [*Taekwondo's formation history*], p. 15; Kang, and Lee, *A modern history of taekwondo*, pp. 4–6; Madis, "The evolution of taekwondo from Japanese karate," pp. 195–6.
49 Kang, and Lee, *A modern history of taekwondo*, pp. 5–6; Madis, "Storming the fortress: A history of taekwondo – Part three: The first Korean schools: The Shudokan schools;" "The evolution of taekwondo from Japanese karate," pp. 197–8.
50 '*Dōjō'* (道場), 'place of *dō*', refers to a karate school or training hall, and is pronounced '*dojang*' in Korean.
51 Madis, "Storming the fortress: A history of taekwondo – Part three: The first Korean schools: The Shudokan schools."
52 Kang, and Lee, *A modern history of taekwondo*, pp. 2–13; Madis, "The evolution of taekwondo from Japanese karate," pp. 191–200; "Storming the fortress: A history of taekwondo – Part three: The first Korean schools: The Shudokan schools."
53 McLain, "Master Yoon Byung-in's legacy: the Changmoo-Kwan and Kangduk-Won."
54 Modern '*kuksul*' in South Korea is very similar to *hapkido*. *Kuksul* (*Kuk Sool*) was founded by Suh In-hyuk in 1958. He claimed to have studied all kinds of martial arts and then combined them to form *kuksul*. However, more likely, he and other early *kuksul* members slightly modified *hapkido* and renamed it, '*kuksul*' (see also Note 21).

The Chinese term '*guoshu*' (transliterated '*kuksul*' in Korean) or 'national art' was originally introduced by the Chinese Nationalists to replace the term *quanfa* as a generic term for martial arts. It was thought to foster pride in the Chinese martial arts. However, when Chiang Kai-shek and the Nationalist forces were defeated by the Communists on the mainland in 1949, and had to retreat to Taiwan, the Communists suppressed the traditional martial arts. Suh In-hyuk borrowed the term '*kuksul*' from the Chinese to rename his *hapkido*-based style.
55 Kang, and Lee, *A modern history of taekwondo*, 9–11; Madis, "The evolution of taekwondo from Japanese karate," pp. 196–7.
56 Kang, and Lee, *A modern history of taekwondo*, pp. 7–8; Hwang, *The history of Moo Duk Kwan*, p. 12.
57 Hwang, *The history of Moo Duk Kwan* , pp. 9–18.
58 Kang, and Lee, *A modern history of taekwondo*, pp. 7–8; "Moo Duk Kwan," (last modified May 3, 2012). [Retrieved from www.tangsoodoworld.com/reference/reference_history_of_MDK.htm]; Madis, "The evolution of taekwondo from Japanese karate," pp. 198–200.

60 *The relationship of taekwondo to karate*

59 See Kyokushin World Union, (2011). [Retrieved from www.kwunion.com/official/]; Ōyama stayed in Japan and changed his nationality. He experimented during the 1950s with full-contact sparring, but without the use of body protectors, which eventually led to full-contact *Kyokushin* karate competitions in 1969. Ironically, many Koreans like to point out the fact that Ōyama was Korean. On the other hand, many also resent him for the fact that he became a Japanese citizen.

60 Hwang, *The history of Moo Duk Kwan*, p. 24.

61 According to Pieter, "Until the word *hwarang* was specifically used in relation to Korean martial arts and sports in the twentieth century, it had rather negative connotations." It had also some connections to shamanism and Buddhism. See Pieter, "Notes on the historical development of Korean martial sports: An addendum to Young's History and development of tae kyon," p. 86; see also Tikhonov, "Hwarang organization: Its functions and ethics"; Rutt, "The flower boys of Silla (hwarang), notes on the sources."

62 Hwang, [*Hwasudo textbook*], 1949, pp. 17–8; 37–40; see also Chapter 7, pp. 158–9.

63 Kang, and Lee, *A modern history of taekwondo*, pp. 2–13; Madis, "The evolution of taekwondo from Japanese karate," pp. 191–200; Hŏ, [*Taekwondo's formation history*], pp. 39–108.

64 As cited in Yook, "Kukkiwon Vice President Chong Woo Lee's shocking confession of Olympic competition result manipulation!", p. 298.

65 For more on the causes behind the division of Korea, the emergences of separate regimes, and the Korean War, see Cumings, *Korea's place in the sun: A modern history,* pp. 185–298; Eckert *et al.*, *Korea old and new: A history*, pp. 327–46.

66 Many former leading figures in politics and society from early South Korea had a pro-Japanese past. For example, the long-term military dictator and later president Park Chung Hee had volunteered and served as an officer in Japan's elite *Kantōgun* Army. In general, the ruling elite, such as landowners and industrialists, largely kept their positions and wealth in South Korea after the Second World War and liberation from Japanese colonial rule. Moreover, the American occupation forces did not dissolve the Japanese-built police force and bureaucratic structure (see, for example, Cumings, *The origins of the Korean War*, pp. 135–209). The witch-hunting of Japanese collaborators remained as a reoccurring event, and the handling of the colonial past seems, in general, to have been an unresolved problem in South Korea.

67 Armed Korean resistance against the Japanese was largely carried out only in Manchuria by groups associated or allied with the Communists. Among these guerrilla forces, Kim Il Sung (Kim Il-sŏng) emerged eventually as a leader with the help of the Russians and the Chinese. See for example, Cumings, *The origins of the Korean War*, pp. 31–38.

68 See Kang, and Lee, *A modern history of taekwondo*, pp. 2–50.

69 Capener, "Problems in the identity and philosophy of *t'aegwondo* and their historical causes," p. 85.

70 Madis, "Storming the fortress: A history of taekwondo – Part four: The first Korean schools: The maverick schools."

71 Kang, and Lee, *A modern history of taekwondo*, p. 13; Madis, "The evolution of taekwondo from Japanese karate," p. 201.

72 Gillis, *A killing art – The untold history of Tae Kwon Do*, p. 40.

73 Ibid.

74 Choi, *Taekwondo – The art of self-defence*, pp. 295–6.

75 Kang, and Lee, *A modern history of taekwondo*, pp. 26–8.

76 See Choi, [*T'aekwŏndo textbook*], p. 29; *Taekwon-do – The art of self-defence*, p. 22. Moreover, through the choice of the name 'taekwondo' (see next section), Choi tried to connect his art to 'ancient' Korean martial arts.

77 Gu, "Aggression, nationalism and combat sport in East Asia."

78 See World Taekwondo Federation, "History." Go to "Present day taekwondo," 2009. In 2013, the content of the history homepage of the WTF was slightly changed and the Rhee Syngman quote taken out.
79 Hyosong Gu, "Wer hat Angst vor der Wahrheit?" ["Who is afraid of the truth?"], (1992), pp. 20–1. [In German only]. [Retrieved from www.hessentkd.de/Geschichte/wer%20hat%20angst%20vor%20der%20wahrheit.pdf].
80 The English translation available on the internet was used for direct quotations. Kang, and Lee, *A modern history of taekwondo*, ch. 2, sect. 4.
81 Choi, *Taekwondo – The art of self-defence*, p. 22.
82 Burdick, "People and events of taekwondo's formative years," p. 40.
83 Kang, and Lee, *A modern history of taekwondo*, pp. 26–8.
84 Madis, "The evolution of taekwondo from Japanese karate," p. 202; Gillis, *A killing art – The untold history of tae kwon do*, p. 49.
85 Choi, *Taekwondo – The art of self-defence*, p. 14.
86 See, for example, 跆 and 跆拳, defined at Naver, 한자 사전 [*Chinese character dictionary*], (n.d.). [Retrieved from http://hanja.naver.com/search?query=%E8%B7%86]; see also Kim, *Principles governing the construction of the philosophy of taekwondo*, pp. 76–77.
87 Kang, and Lee, *A modern history of taekwondo*, pp. 29–31.
88 Ibid, pp. 33–43.
89 Compare the KTA's fanciful, historical description of the origin of the *dobok*, which seems to disregard any historical evidence. See Korea Taekwondo Federation, "Philosophical character of tobok," (2007). [Retrieved from www.koreataekwondo.org/KTA_ENG/html/ency/philo_index.asp].
90 See for similar discussions, Madis, "The evolution of taekwondo from Japanese karate," p. 190; Bittmann, *Karatedô – Der Weg der Leeren Hand*, p. 100; Clayton, *Shotokan's secret – The hidden truth behind karate's fighting origin*, pp. 102–3.
91 Madis, "The evolution of taekwondo from Japanese karate," pp. 188–9. Kanō Jigorō structured judo training in terms of the formalities first. Kendo training was influenced by Kanō as well (see Kanō, *Mind over muscle*, pp. 25–26). The karate instructors copied it.
92 Madis, "The evolution of taekwondo from Japanese karate," p. 189.
93 Nowadays, many taekwondo instructors claim that early Korean instructors in the U.S. used the term 'Korean karate' because the term 'karate' was already well-known and promised more membership. In reality, many early Korean instructors in the U.S. thought of their art as being karate. They adopted the term 'taekwondo' only much later, and the first to promote the name 'taekwondo' were those instructors dispatched by the ITF, Choi Hong Hi's organization. Some even call their art 'Korean karate' up to this day.
94 Gillis, *A killing art – The untold history of tae kwon do*, pp. 88–102.
95 Capener, "Problems in the identity and philosophy of *t'aegwondo* and their historical causes," pp. 84–5.
96 Ibid, p. 78.
97 See Park, "The paradox of postcolonial Korean nationalism: State-sponsored cultural policy in South Korea, 1965–Present," pp. 74–8. This was only one example of South Korea's wide-ranging mimicking of Japanese institutions, cultural movements, and modernization programs, despite an ongoing denial of any association with Japan. Most cultural movements or organizations and economic development projects in post-Korean War under the regime of Park Chung Hee were copies of Japanese pre- or post-Second World War models. For instance, the 'New Village Movement' ('*Saemaŭl Undong*') was modeled largely after the Japanese post-Second World War 'New Life Movement' ('*Shin Seikatsu Undō*').
98 Ibid, pp. 79–80.
99 Steven Capener pointed this fact out in a recent conversation with me. The first char-

acters in the terms '*Kuk-kiwon*' and '*Koku-gikan*,' 國 and 国, are the same. The former represents traditional Chinese characters (used in Korea and Taiwan), and the latter is the simplified version (used in mainland China and Japan). The first two characters in '*Kuk-ki-won*' (國技院) are the Korean transliteration of the first two characters of the Japanese term '*Koku-gi-kan*' (国技館). The Koreans only replaced the last character 館 with 院; both characters are very similar in meaning, literally 'hall.' The Korean taekwondo leaders probably tried to avoid association with the term '*kwan*' (館), since they tried to repress the individual taekwondo *kwan* during that time.

'*Ryōgoku*' is the name of the neighborhood in Tokyo where the *Kokugikan* is located. The Kukkiwon opened in 1973.

100 Yang, "A study on the history of modern Korean taekwondo," p. 14. Many schools also introduced taekwondo teams. However, the first taekwondo department at a university was only established in 1982, at the former Judo College, now Yongin University.
101 Sintionean, "Heritage practices during the Park Chung Hee era"; see also Chapter 1, p. 25.
102 Kim's practical martial arts experience and ability were questioned by many. See for example, Yook, "Kukkiwon Vice President Chong Woo Lee's shocking confession of Olympic competition result manipulation!", p. 300.
103 Kang, and Lee, *A modern history of taekwondo*, pp. 73–4.
104 Yook, "Kukkiwon Vice President Chong Woo Lee's shocking confession of Olympic competition result manipulation!", p. 305.
105 Madis, "The evolution of taekwondo from Japanese karate," pp. 204–5.
106 Madis, "Storming the fortress: A history of taekwondo. Part four: The first Korean schools: The maverick schools"; Gillis, *A killing art – The untold history of tae kwon do*, pp. 111–13.
107 The Soviet Union installed Kim Il Sung, a former anti-Japanese guerrilla commander, as official leader in the Northern part of the peninsula. Kim remained the North Korean dictator and leader from the establishment of North Korea in 1948 until his death in 1994.
108 Gillis, *A killing art – The untold history of tae kwon do*, pp. 125–41.
109 Koreans, who studied *karate* in Japan, generally had a pro-Japanese past. They were likely not to be keen on siding with the Communists, who were strictly anti-Japanese.
110 Chinese martial arts were revived only during the 1980s, in concert with political and leadership changes in China. See Lorge, *Chinese martial arts*, pp. 225–36.
111 Gillis, *A killing art – The untold history of tae kwon do*, pp. 143–4. '*Kodang*' was the pet name of the Korean nationalist Cho Man-sik. '*Chuch'ae*' is North Korea's state ideology of self-reliance.
112 See for example Ibid, pp. 167–78.
113 Ibid, pp. 191–7.
114 Yang, "A study on the history of modern Korean taekwondo," p. 65.

Bibliography

Bittmann, Heiko. *Karatedô – Der Weg der leeren Hand* (*Karatedô – The way of the empty hand*). Ludwigsburg: Verlag Heiko Bittmann, 1999. [In German, but also available in English].

Burdick, Dankin. "People and events of taekwondo's formative years." *Journal of Asian Martial Arts*, 6, 1 (1997): 30–49.

Capener, Steven D. "Problems in the identity and philosophy of *t'aegwondo* and their historical causes." *Korea Journal*, 35, 4 (1995): 80–94. [Retrieved from www.eagletkd.com/images/STUDENT%20FORUM%20from%20Korea%0Journal.pdf].

_____. "The modern significance of taekwondo as sport and martial art: Overcoming cultural and historical limitations in traditional thinking." *Korean History and Culture*, 30 (2005): 321–54.

Choi, Hong Hi [Ch'oe Hong-hi] (최홍희). 跆拳道教本 [*Taekwondo textbook*]. Seoul: Sŏnghwa Munhwa-Sa, 1958. [In Korean only].

_____. *Taekwondo – The art of self-defence*. Seoul: Daeha Publication Company, 1965.

Clayton, Bruce D. *Shotokan's secret – The hidden truth behind karate's fighting origin*. USA: Ohara Publications, Inc, 2004.

Cumings, Bruce. *The origin of the Korean War*. Princeton: Princeton University Press, 1981.

_____. *Korea's place in the sun: A modern history*. New York: Norton, 1997.

Draeger, Don F *Classical budo – The martial arts and ways of Japan*. (Vol. 2). New York: Weatherhill, Inc, 1973.

_____. *Modern bujutsu and budo*. (Vol. 3). New York: Weatherhill, Inc., 1974.

Eckert, Carter J., Ki-baik Lee, Young Ick Lew, Michael Robinson, and Edward E. Wagner. *Korea old and new: A history*. Seoul: Korea Institute, 1990.

Friday, Karl F., and Seki Humitake. *Legacies of the sword – The Kashima-Shinryū and samurai martial culture*. Honolulu, Hawai'i: University of Hawai'i Press, 1997.

Funakoshi, Gichin. *Karate-dō kyōhan – The master text*. Trans. T. Ohshima. Tokyo: Kondansha International Ltd, 1973. [Translation of revised edition of 1957; first edition published 1935].

_____. *Karate-dō – My way of life*. Trans. Tokyo: Kodansha International, 1975. [Original work published 1956].

Gillis, Alex. *A killing art – The untold history of tae kwon do*. Toronto: ECW Press, 2008.

Green, Thomas A (ed.). *Martial arts of the world – An encyclopedia*. (Vol. 1). Santa Barbara: ABC-CLIO, Inc, 2001.

Gu, Hyosong. "Aggression, Nationalismus und Kampfsport in Ostasien" ("Aggression, nationalism and combat sport in East Asia"). Unpublished master's thesis, University of Hamburg, 1994. [In German only].

Gwang, Ok. *The Transformation of Modern Korean Sport: Imperialism, Nationalism, Globalization*. Seoul: Hollym International Corp., 2007.

Hassell, Randall G. *Shotokan karate – Its history and evolution*. Los Angeles: Empire Books, 2007.

[Hŏ In-uk] (허인욱). 태권도형성사 [*Taekwondo's formation history*]. Kyŏngki-Do: Hanguk Haksul Ch'ŏngbo, 2008. [In Korean only].

Hobsbawm, Eric, and Terence Ranger (eds.). *The invention of tradition*. Cambridge: Cambridge University Press, 1983.

Hwang, Kee [Hwang Ki] (황기). 花手道教本 [*Hwasudo textbook*]. Seoul: Chosŏn Munhwa Ch'ulp'ansa, 1949. [In Korean only].

_____. 1995. *The history of Moo Duk Kwan*. Springfield, NJ: Tang Soo Do Moo Duk Kwan Federation, 1995.

Kang, Won Shik, and Lee Kyong Myong [Kang Wŏn-sik, Yi kyŏng-myŏng] (강원식, 이경명). 태권도 現代 史 *A modern history of taekwondo* [English title from the internet]. Seoul: Pokyŏng Munhwasa, 1999. [Parts published in English at www.martialartsresource.com/anonftp/pub/the_dojang/digests/history.html].

_____. 우리 태권도의 역사 *The history of our taekwondo*. Seoul: Tosŏch'ulp'an Sangakihwek, 2002. [Second, revised edition of *A modern history of taekwondo*; in Korean only].

Kanō, Jigorō. *Mind over muscle*. Trans. Nancy H. Ross. Tokyo: Kodansha International, 2005. [Original work not published].

[Kim Yŏng-man, and Kim Yong-bŏm] (김영만, 김용범). "당수의 중국 기원설에 대한 재논의 "Rediscussion for a view about Chinese origin of dangsu [sic]." *Taekwondo Journal of Kukkiwon*, 2, 1 (2011): 21–39. [In Korean only].

[Kim Yong-ok] (김용옥). 태권도철학의구성원리 *Principles governing the construction of the philosophy of taekwondo*. Seoul: T'ongnamu, 1990. [In Korean only].

Lorge, Peter A. *Chinese martial arts*. Cambridge: Cambridge University Press, 2012.

McCarthy, Patrick. *Bubishi – The classic manual of combat*. Tokyo.: Tuttle Publishing, 2008.

_____. "On Choki Motobu – Part 1." *Fighting Arts.com* (2012). [Retrieved from www.fightingarts.com/reading/article.php?id=398].

McLain, Robert. "Master Yoon Byung-in's legacy: the Changmoo-Kwan and Kangduk-Won." *Martial Talk* (2007). [Retrieved from www.martialtalk.com/forum/144-martialtalk-magazine-articles/43718-changmoo-kwan-kang-duk-won-history-photos-available-upon-request.html].

Madis, Eric. "The evolution of taekwondo from Japanese karate." In *Martial Arts in the Modern World*. Eds. Thomas A. Green and Joseph R. Svinth, 185–209. Westport: Praeger Publishers, 2003.

_____. "Storming the fortress: A history of taekwondo – Part two: The first Korean schools: The Shotokan schools." *EC Martial Arts Blog* (2011). [Retrieved from http://ec-ma.blogspot.kr/2011/02/storming-fortress-history-of-taekwondo_08.html].

_____. "Storming the fortress: A history of taekwondo – Part three: The first Korean schools: The Shudokan schools." *Fighting Arts.com* (2011). [Retrieved from http://fightingarts.com/reading/article.php?id=665].

_____. "Storming the fortress: A history of taekwondo – Part four: The first Korean schools: The maverick schools." *Fighting Arts.com* (2011). [Retrieved from www.fightingarts.com/reading/article.php?id=686].

Noble, Graham. "Master Funakoshi's karate – The history and development of the empty hand art part II." *Dragon Times*, 4 (n.d.): 6–9. [Retrieved from http://museum.hikari.us/].

Park, Sang Mi. "The paradox of postcolonial Korean nationalism: State-sponsored cultural policy in South Korea, 1965–Present." *The Journal of Korean Studies*. 15, 1 (2010): 67–94.

Pieter, Willy. "Notes on the historical development of Korean martial sports: An addendum to Young's history and development of Tae Kyon." *Journal of Asian Martial Arts*. 3, 1 (1994): 82–9.

Rutt, Richard. "The flower boys of Silla (hwarang), notes on the sources." In *Transactions of the Korea Branch of the Royal Asiatic Society*, 38 (October 1961): 1–66.

Sîntionean, Codruta. "Heritage practices during the Park Chung Hee era." In *Key papers on Korea*. Ed. Andrew David Jackson, 253–74. Kent: Global Oriental, 2013.

Smith, Anthony D. *Nationalism: Theory, ideology, history*. Cambridge: Polity Press, 2001.

Tikhonov, Vladimir. "Hwarang organization: Its functions and ethics." *Korea Journal*. 38, 2 (1998): pp.318–38.

World Taekwondo Federation. "History." (Last modified 2013). [Retrieved from www.worldtaekwondofederation.net/taekwondo-history].

Yang, Jin Bang (양진방). 해방이후 한국 태권도의 발전과정과 그 역사적 의의 "A study on the history of the modern Korean taekwondo." Unpublished master's thesis. Seoul National University, 1986. [In Korean only].

[Yi Yŏng-hŭi] (Director) and [Samsŏng Yŏngsang Saŏbdan] (Producer) (이영희, 삼성 영상 사업단). 태권도가 한류를 찾아서 (1. 부) [*T'aekwŏndo searches for the Korean*

Wave – 1. Part] [Television broadcast]. Korea: K.B.S. Documentary, 1995. [In Korean only].

Yook, Sung-chul [Yuk Sŏng-ch'ŏl] (육성철). 이종우 국기원 부원장의 '태권도 과거'충격적 고백! "Kukkiwon Vice President Chong Woo Lee's shocking confession of Olympic competition result manipulation!". Trans. Lee Soo Han. *Shin Dong-A*, (2002, April). 290–311. [Retrieved from http://tkdreform.com/yook_article.pdf].

3 The significance of forms

The following chapters will discuss taekwondo's technical evolution, although, taekwondo's development cannot be treated as a single event. Therefore, this study distinguishes, in principal, between 'traditional taekwondo' and 'WTF-style sport (sparring/competition) taekwondo.' This chapter examines the technical roots and modifications made in traditional taekwondo over time. Since the main training activity in traditional taekwondo consists of forms training, some overview of the forms used in early taekwondo, in comparison to karate pattern practice is helpful to establish and verify taekwondo's lineage. Moreover, this discussion may provide further proof of taekwondo's roots in karate. At first, this chapter explores the origin of forms training. Later, it documents the use of forms in early taekwondo, with the help of early Korean martial arts manuals. In addition, these manuals are briefly analyzed for their special features. Lastly, I will discuss recent developments regarding forms training.

The origins of forms training in Asian martial arts

A possible origin of modern forms training lays in ancient pattern-like "martial dances," performed by Chinese soldiers in rituals as a means of serving their spiritual needs and reinforcing social hierarchy.[1] Moreover, the fundamental method of forms instruction in Asian martial arts might be connected to the general mood of China-based Confucian style pedagogy which emphasizes repetition, ritual, and formalities.[2] However, with these characteristics aside, the *kata* (forms) training of the classical Japanese *bugei* (martial arts) and their modern offspring, judo and kendo, are fundamentally different from the forms training of Chinese martial arts, the Okinawa-based Japanese karate, and the modern Japan-based Korean martial arts. *Kata* training in the former mostly represents a set of prearranged exercises performed with a partner, whereas it is usually understood as a "solo-performance" of a practitioner by the latter.[3] These two distinct training methods and related philosophies are expressed with the use of different Chinese characters, 形 and 型; both are pronounced the same way in Japanese, namely '*kata*,' or the Korean transliteration, '*hyŏng*.' The first character (形) is generally used by the traditional Japanese *bugei*, and modern judo and kendo; whereas in karate and taekwondo writings, mostly the alternative logogram (型) is in use. According to

Karl Friday, a historian and expert on *kata*, the former it "is argued, better represents the freedom to respond and change-albeit within a pattern-essential to success in combat." In contrast, the latter "implies a rigidity and constraint inappropriate to martial training [according to Japanese *bugei* philosophy]."[4] That said, ordinary martial arts practitioners are generally not aware of any distinction.

In Korea, the only surviving bare-handed fighting-like activities during the end of the nineteenth century were *sirrŭm*, and the nearly extinct *t'aekkyŏn*. At that time, both, being simple folk-games, lacked any formal characteristics in terms of organization, official rules, and standardized training content or methods. Moreover, general formalities such as dress code, ranks, and designated training places were absent, as well. Most importantly for this study, both activities lacked any kind of standardized forms training, the hallmark of traditional Chinese and Japanese martial arts. Forms training or continuously repeated, uniform training exercises were neither a part of *sirrŭm* nor of *t'aekkyŏn*. *Sirrŭm* started only in 1912, at the onset of the Japanese colonial era, to incorporate some modern sports characteristics.[5] During the same period, the traditional martial arts concept of *kata* training was first introduced to twentieth century Koreans because of the expansion of judo and kendo to the colonial education system of Korea. In contrast, only during the early 1980s did *t'aekkyŏn* start to incorporate formal training characteristics and forms modeled after the pre-existing martial art in Korea, which was (and is) predominantly taekwondo. Subsequently, *t'aekkyŏn* leaders also created 24 forms named '*ponttae poeki.*'

Before the introduction of judo and kendo, and karate (in 1944) to Korea, neither kind of systemized forms training used in these martial arts existed as part of an indigenous Korean method of unarmed combat at that time. Martial arts instructions and concepts of earlier Korean periods were long forgotten. Moreover, there is no evidence that the term '*hyŏng*' (the transliteration of the term '*kata*') was ever used earlier than this in connection with Korean martial arts. The only surviving martial arts manuals of earlier periods in Korea are the China-based *Muye chepo* (1598) and *Muye tobo t'ongji* (1759). In both books, the term '*po*' (譜 'record' or 'table') is used to describe a series of Chinese *quanfa* illustrations intended as a training guide for the Korean military (see Chapter 1, p. 15).[6] The *Muye tobo t'ongji* was only rediscovered during the late 1950s by a librarian at Korea National Library,[7] and the existence of the *Muye chepo* became known only later on.

The origins of taekwondo forms

The importance that the Korean instructors of the first generations placed on forms training can be seen by the fact that in almost all of their publications, forms illustrations and instructions take up more than half of the entire space and content. Most of the forms mentioned and/or illustrated by the Korean authors in the books analyzed for this study resemble Funakoshi's orthodox *Shōtōkan* karate *kata* or *hyŏng* in terms of photographs, descriptive content, and names. Several of these forms were originally "modernized" or "created" by one of Funakoshi's teachers, Itosu Ankō.[8] Subsequently, when Funakoshi introduced these forms during the 1920s from Okinawa to Japan, he also modified some, renamed most, and created a few on his own. According to Funakoshi:

> The names of the kata have come down to us by word of mouth... many of which had ambiguous meanings... Since karate is a Japanese martial art, there is no apparent reason for retaining these unfamiliar and in some cases unclear names of Chinese origin.[9]

Funakoshi wanted to distance himself from the Chinese and Okinawan roots of karate in order to gain acceptance as a 'Japanese martial art.' A similar process happened several decades later with the introduction of karate to Korea, when the Korean leaders increasingly tried to distance themselves from their Japanese karate roots.

Funakoshi grouped his forms into the *'Shōrin'* (少林) and *'Shōrei'* (昭靈) *ryū* (流 'school' or 'style') named after the two most well-known styles of karate in Okinawa.[10] Given their well-documented origin and history, it would be fanciful to suggest that Funakoshi's or any of the other karate *kata* already existed as part of some indigenous Korean martial arts tradition prior to their introduction to Korea from Japan.

Next to Funakoshi's *Shōtōkan*, the most important karate styles or *ryū* that developed in Japan have been *Gōjū-ryū*, *Shitō-ryū*, and *Wadō-ryū*.[11] However, it seems that forms of other karate styles played a minor role in early Korean martial arts teachings since the majority of early Korean leaders studied *Shōtōkan* karate. While assumed, this cannot be concluded with certainty since all of these Japanese schools practiced a number of the same forms as Funakoshi. Some influence of other *ryū* on several of the Korean instructors can be seen by their use of the names for *kata*. Only Funakoshi's students started to use his newly introduced names for the passed down Okinawan *kata*; other schools usually kept the original Okinawan names.

In the period between the liberation of Korea in 1945 and the 1960s, some small changes from the original forms naturally occurred as the art was taught to the next generation. In addition, Choi Hong Hi created his own forms, called the *'Ch'anghŏn ryu'* or *'Ch'anghŏn school,'* but these are still heavily influenced by the technique and style of karate *kata* and are basically a remnant of *Shōtōkan* karate. In Choi's 1958 book, only five are mentioned and partly illustrated; by 1965 he mentions 20 (see Appendix D, Table 3.3). However, Choi's forms were mostly only used in his *Odo Kwan*, which he established in the military. Other schools kept using the original *Shōtōkan kata* of Funakoshi as displayed in the manuals used for this study. Furthermore, some *kwan* developed over the years a few other forms as well, such as Son Duk Sung, who invented some that he called "*Kuk Mu*" (*'Kungmu'*) *hyŏng*.[12] But apart from Choi's *hyŏng*, the others had only marginal influence and application. For example, during the early 1960s, the Korea Taesudo Association still used mostly Funakoshi's karate *kata*, in addition to a few of Choi's *hyŏng*, in their belt promotion tests.[13]

After Choi Hong Hi's break with the Korean taekwondo world during the second half of the 1960s, from 1967 to 1971, the Korea Taekwondo Association (KTA) developed and used the *P'algwae p'umsae*, which specify the level or rank of color belts. During the same period, the KTA also developed new forms for *dan* (black belt) ranks. Finally, in 1971, the modern *Taegŭk p'umsae* (*Taeguk Poomsae*) were introduced and are still used today. In accordance, the term '*p'umsae*' (before 1987 품세, after 품새) for forms was introduced during the early 1970s, and the old karate term '*hyŏng*' was discarded; there was no earlier use of the term *p'umsae* in any martial art. The stances in these forms are usually shorter than in karate, but the general technical features, movements, and biomechanical principles represent basically modified karate. Lee Chong Woo claimed he played a "central role," in association with other "masters who taught Karate" in developing these forms.[14] Although in comparison to karate *kata*, the taekwondo *p'umsae* are very poorly designed. From a practical standpoint of combat, most do not make any sense at all.

Many schools kept using some of the forms parallel past this general time line (see Figure 3.1). The *T'aegŭk p'umsae* have been only used by schools affiliated with the World Taekwondo Federation and KTA. Other organizations, such as Choi Hong Hi's International Taekwondo Federation are still using the *Ch'anghŏn hyŏng*, and Hwang Kee's affiliated organizations are still teaching mostly Funakoshi's *kata*. To distance their style from karate, Choi's ITF replaced the karate-based term *hyŏng* with the new name, '*t'ŭl*' (機 literally 'frame'), for forms.

Figure 3.1 Timeline for the general use of forms in taekwondo schools

Existing forms and interesting features in early taekwondo manuals

Early Korean martial arts publications give some helpful insight into the use of forms by the various *kwan* or schools. Moreover, these manuals also showcase the development of new forms and the disposal of older ones. All of the *kwan* founders or some of their accomplished students, with the exception of *Songmu Kwan*, left various early martial arts publications (see Figure 3.2). These manuals provide vital evidence of taekwondo's early technique and activity, as well as its relationship to karate. Just as their Japanese predecessors had done earlier, the writers of the early Korean martial arts manuals focused the majority of their content on forms. However, these manuals display a variety of other exercises as well, such as basics and prearranged sparring. Most of these manuals conclude

70 The significance of forms

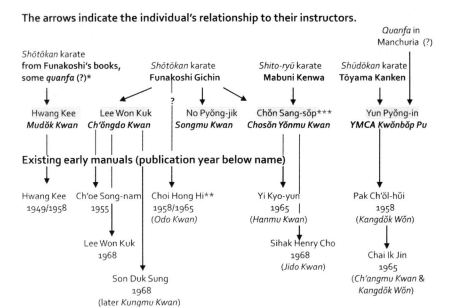

Figure 3.2 Existing publications of *kwan* founders, their students, and Choi Hong Hi
Note: The names of the original *kwan* founders are colored grey.

with a section on self-defense, which was the ultimate objective of all practical training activity at that time. In addition, most include a section on training with such typical karate tools as the *makiwara* (a padded striking post). Full-contact sparring is not described in any of the manuals, and the authors who mention it reject it vehemently. Non-contact sparring, which is mentioned in some of the literature, clearly plays a subordinated role. The following discussion of individual works focuses on the forms displayed in these manuals.

Until the late 1960s, primarily, all of the early Korean martial arts manuals display Funakoshi's conventional *kata*, which he renamed during the early 1930s. Table 3.1 lists the *kata* featured in Funakoshi's *Karate-dō Kyōhan* (1935), which was revised in 1957 and translated in 1973. In addition, Table 3.1 explains the original Okinawan names for these *kata*, the terms modified by Funakoshi and first introduced in his book of 1935, and the names used in Korean literature. In some cases, such as the *Taikyoku*, *Heian*, and *Tekki kata*, the Koreans changed from the Japanese pronunciation of the Chinese characters to the Korean transliteration. In other instances, such as the *Gankaku*, *Jitte*, and *Hangetsu kata*, they sometimes kept the Japanese pronunciation and spelled it in *han'-gŭl* (the Korean alphabet). And because of the relative proximity of the Japanese and Korean languages, the transliteration is sometimes almost identical, such as in the case of the *Jion*. Generally, there was a lack of any standardized language or curricula among the different Korean *kwan*. Tables 3.2, 3.3, and 3.4, in Appendix D, provide detailed lists of forms described in the early Korean manuals.

Table 3.1 Funakoshi's 13 *Shōrin-ryū* and 6 *Shōrei-ryū kata* in *Karate-dō Kyōhan**

Used in Okinawa	Used in Okinawa	Changed by Funakoshi	Japanese Pronunciation	Han'gŭl	Korean pronunciation
—	—	太極	Taikyoku 1–3 (introduced by Funakoshi)	태극/기조/ 기본	T'aegŭk/Kijo/ Kibon**
平安	Pinan	平安 unchanged	Heian 1–5	평안	P'yŏngan
バッサイ	Passai	披塞	Bassai	밧사이	Passai
クーサンクー or 公相君	Kūsankū or Kōsōkun	観空	Kwankū (Kankū)	공산군	Kongsanggun
ワンシウ	Wanshū	燕飛	Empi (Enpi)	엔피	Enp'i
チントウ	Chintō	岩鶴	Gankaku	간카쿠	Kank'ak'u
十手	Jutte or Jitte	十手 unchanged	Jutte or Jitte	짓데/십수	Jidde/Sipsu
半月	Seisan	半月 unchanged	Hangetsu	한겟츠/ 반월	Han'getch'ŭ Panwŏl
ナイハンチ, ナイファンチ or 騎馬	Naihanchi, Naifanchi or Kibadachi	鉄騎	Tekki 1–3	철기	Ch'ŏlgi
ジオン	Jion	慈恩	Jion	지온	Jion
—	—	天の方	Ten no kata*** (developed by Funakoshi)	—	—

Notes:
* See Funakoshi's *kata* in *Karate-dō kyōhan* (1935/2005), pp. 42–143; *Karate-dō kyōhan* (1957/1973), pp. 35–208. Compare table with Bittmann in *Karatedô – Der Weg der Leeren Hand*, p. 101. According to Bittmann, it is customary for the old Okinawan forms, for which multiple ways of writing with Chinese characters exist, to be written in *katakana*. There often exist several names for the old Okinawan *kata*, probably as a result of dialects and the different usage of Chinese characters. Likewise, there exist many different versions of Romanization in diverse literature.
** The forms were developed by Funakoshi. The term *T'aegŭk* (太極) is also used in Chinese martial arts, as in *Taiji,* but there is no direct relationship to karate *kata*. The modern taekwondo forms are also called *T'aegŭk p'umsae*, but they are also not related to Funakoshi's or Chinese forms. In addition, Koreans call Funakoshi's *T'aegŭk* forms also '*Kijo*' (basic) or '*Kibon*' (standard) forms. The *Taikyoku* 1–3 forms are not displayed in Funakoshi's original 1935 edition.
*** The *Ten no kata* is in addition to the 13 *Shōrin-ryū* and 6 *Shōrei-ryū kata*. It is a '*kumite* form.' Likely developed by Funakoshi's third son Gigō around 1941; therefore, it is not in Funakoshi's 1935 first edition, but in *Karate-dō nyūmon* (1943). The *Ten no kata* is not mentioned in any Korean literature.

72 *The significance of forms*

The following sections briefly discuss some of the interesting features of early Korean martial arts manuals. These manuals provide vital evidence of taekwondo's early techniques and activities, as well as its relationship to karate. If the claim that some instructors studied and incorporated martial art styles other than karate has merit, some differences should be evident when compared to karate.

Hwang Kee (founder of **Mudŏk Kwan***)*

Hwang Kee is the most eccentric figure among the early taekwondo leaders. He is the only author who features a non-karate form in his *Hwasudo textbook* (1949) next to Funakoshi's standard *kata* (see Appendix D, Table 3.2). It is not clear where Hwang learned the *quanfa* pattern. Reportedly, he studied *quanfa* in Manchuria from a Chinese instructor while working for the South Manchurian Railway,[15] but this claim remains disputed. The only existing school in Korea, where the instructor and a few students had knowledge of *quanfa*, was the *YMCA Kwŏnbŏp Pu*. Since Hwang allegedly trained on occasion with students from other schools,[16] he possibly learned it from one of them.

Hwang calls the Chinese form, '*Solim Changkwŏn*' (少林長拳 Chinese: '*Shaolin Changquan*' or '*Shaolin Long Fist*'). The term is frequently used in Chinese martial arts and broadly describes a northern Shaolin style. Hwang displays only three photographs while describing the form. The stances in the photographs that he poses for seem to convey a limited knowledge and lack of much formal training in Chinese martial arts.

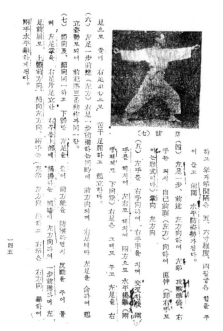

Figure 3.3 Solim Changkwŏn by Hwang Kee

Source: Hwasudo textbook (1949), p. 145.

Chinese forms are not described in Hwang's next publication, *Tangsudo textbook* (1958). He mentions only the *Solim Changkwŏn* again and a *T'aegŭkkwŏn* (太極拳 Chinese: '*Taijiquan*') form, among about forty karate *kata*, by name.[17] In addition, Hwang illustrates a few of Funakoshi's *Shōrim* school patterns and one form of the *Shōrei* school. However, when demonstrating basic techniques, Hwang displays a few technical dissimilarities to the *Shōtōkan* karate of that time for the likely reason that he lacked formal training and admitted to learning karate mostly from books.[18] The basic stances that he presents are mostly standard karate but, on a few occasions, he displays some stances that are not present in mature *Shōtōkan* karate; for example, a stance called "lowest position."

Some have suggested that Hwang incorporated movements from very early *Shōtōkan* karate that he learned out of Funakoshi's original manuals.[19] This theory seems plausible, because the exact same stance mentioned above is found in Funakoshi's 1925 publication (*Rentan goshin tōde-jutsu*),[20] but not in later *Shōtōkan* works. Although the stance is also very common in many *quanfa* styles, further support of the theory comes from the fact that Hwang often used the old Okinawan names for forms. Funakoshi used these terms in his 1920s publications, but subsequently replaced those with new names in his main, 1935 work (compare Tables 3.1 and the tables in the Appendix D, 3.2 and 3.3). Apart from this, the general range of technique presented by Hwang is, by and large, similar to standard karate at that time. However, he displays a modified kick, called '*bit*-kick,' and described it as being "between a front- and roundhouse-kick."[21] Also, in modern publications, he displays the 'inside-out-kick,'[22] which is a *t'aekkyŏn*-based kick, not shown in his early works. It is precisely this kicking technique that Hwang's organizations often showcase on their official homepages and advertisements, because they believe it proves that Hwang's style is different from karate.

Only in his 1970 book *Subakdo encyclopedia (tangsu)* (translated into English in 1977), does Hwang again illustrate and explain, next to Funakoshi's *kata*, two Chinese forms, namely the *T'aegŭkkwŏn* and the *Solim Changkwŏn* already mentioned earlier.[23] He possibly learned the *T'aegŭkkwŏn* later in life, since the form was not mentioned in his 1949 manual and only named in 1958. Hwang frequently uses the original Chinese characters of Okinawa for Funakoshi's forms, but also switches between the Okinawan, Korean, and Japanese pronunciations of the terms written in *han'gŭl* (the Korean alphabet) in his early books. This confusion could be the result of his lack of formal training and education in karate. Later, when he promoted his art in the United States and overseas, he often deliberately concealed the Japanese origin of many of the forms that he taught and claimed credit for its invention or introduction to Korea. For example, some *tangsudo* instructors and Hwang's son still claim "Hwang Kee brought the pyong ahn hyung [*P'yŏngan hyŏng*] back from China."[24]

Ch'oe Song-nam *(member of* **Ch'ŏngdo Kwan***)*

Ch'oe Song-nam, who learned *tangsudo* from Lee Won Kuk, describes a knife form that he calls '*Tando hyŏng*' in his *Kwŏnbŏp textbook* (1955). As there are no knife forms in karate, this form was probably created by him. Since Ch'oe was a soldier, it was possibly developed for use in the military. He calls his style *kwŏnbŏp*, but apart from this self-styled form, his book features exclusively standard karate technique and *Shōtōkan kata* (see Appendix D, Table 3.2).

Choi Hong Hi (founder of Odo Kwan)

The range and style of *Shōtōkan* karate and the taekwondo techniques displayed in Choi's publications, *Taekwondo textbook* (1958) and *Taekwondo – The Art of Self-Defence* (1965), are practically identical. The only exception is that karate literature of this time does not display a spinning-back-kick. However, the spinning-back-kick is also only displayed in Choi's 1965 English publication,[25] and not in his earlier 1958 Korean book, which would place its invention in the early 1960s.[26] Choi and some of the other Korean authors display a few more jump-kicks than Nishiyama in his manual *Karate the art of "empty hand" fighting* (co-author Brown, 1960). However, all are derived from regular kicking techniques and most are mentioned by Funakoshi in his earlier work.[27] Choi was accused of plagiarism when he released his book in 1965,[28] because of its resemblance to Nishiyama's work. Apart from re-naming some of the techniques, many of the pictures used in Choi's book are nearly identical to those of Nishiyama's. Choi admitted studying karate in Japan, but also claimed of having studied *t'aekkyŏn* and then combining them.[29] However, there is no content in Choi's early publications which shows he incorporated *t'aekkyŏn* or any martial art besides *Shōtōkan* karate. Both, Choi and Hwang Kee, included a few *t'aekkyŏn* techniques such as the frivolous inside-out-kick, but only in their much later publications. The earliest existing evidence of the use of the inside-out kick in taekwondo is from an instructional film produced by Choi, probably made in 1968. In this video, the kick is used as a blocking technique against a front-kick.[30] Its use was likely inspired by one of Song Tŏk-ki's public *t'aekkyŏn* performances. The claims that Choi or Hwang were exposed in their youth to *t'aekkyŏn* are likely more examples of wishful thinking.

Pak Ch'ŏl-hŭi (member of YMCA Kwŏnbŏp Pu)

Pak Ch'ŏl-hŭi and Hong Chŏng-p'yo split from *Ch'angmu Kwan* (the former *YMCA Kwŏnbŏp Pu*) in 1956 and founded *Kangdŏk Wŏn*. Prior to this, Pak's instructor, Yun Pyŏng-in, disappeared during the beginning of the Korean War, leaving no publications. Therefore, Pak's manual, *Kwŏnbŏp association – Kongsudo textbook* (1958), provides the only evidence of what the curriculum at the *YMCA Kwŏnbŏp Pu* possibly looked like. Pak's instructor, Yun, studied *quanfa* in his youth and later *Shūdōkan* (a *Shurite* style) karate in Japan, but the manual does not reveal the influence of any Chinese martial art. Pak displays exclusively karate technique and *kata*, although he does mention several Chinese forms by name (see Appendix D, Table 3.2). It is recorded that his teacher, Yun, taught some Chinese forms to selected students on occasion at the YMCA gymnasium, even though

Yun's main curriculum consisted of karate and Funakoshi's *kata* in particular.[31] The likely reason that Yun mostly taught Funakoshi's *kata* and not some *Shūdōkan* forms was that they were the most popular ones in Japan as well as in Korea, as a result of Funakoshi's status and fame. In addition, by using *Shōtōkan kata*, the evaluation in forms contests was streamlined and simplified.[32] In contrast, *quanfa* appears to have not been very popular among students, and after Yun's disappearance, his successors seem to have mostly given up practicing Chinese martial arts components in favor of karate in their general training activity, as presented in Pak's manual. Nevertheless, Pak acquired some basic skills in Chinese *quanfa*, which he is still known for in the Korean taekwondo community of today. Several of the original students of the *YMCA Kwŏnbŏp Pu* also had a little knowledge of *quanfa*. A few of them later founded or became members of *Ch'angmu Kwan* and *Kangdŏk Wŏn* where Chinese forms were also taught on occasion.[33] However, the comprehensive early taekwondo literature does not display any typical *quanfa* content, with the exception of Hwang Kee's 1949 book; therefore, it appears that *quanfa* had negligible influence on the general training activity of early taekwondo.

Yi Kyo-yun (member of Chosŏn Yŏnmu Kwan/Jido Kwan, *founder of* Hanmu Kwan*)*

Yi Kyo-yun had disagreements with Lee Chong Woo. As a consequence, he split from *Jido Kwan* and opened his own school in 1956. He named it *Hanmu Kwan* (*Han Moo Kwan*), after Yun K'wae-pyŏng's former school in Tokyo. *Hanmu Kwan* (韓武館) represents the Korean transliteration of *Kanbukan* (see Figure 2.1; see also the discussion in Chapter 4, pp. 87–8). Yi's manual, *T'aesudo textbook for the masses* (1965), seems to prove that the Korea Taesudo Association still used Funakoshi's *kata* until 1965, with no new forms yet developed (see Appendix D, Table 3.3).

Chai Ik Jin (member of Ch'angmu Kwan, *later* Kangdŏk Wŏn*)*

The purpose of Chai's book, *Taekwondo: A Way of Life in Korea* (1965, co-author Read), was to introduce and propagate taekwondo to an American audience. It described taekwondo's ethical values, martial arts history, and taekwondo's organizational structure, while blending fact with fiction. The authors claim that "following the liberation [from Japanese colonial rule]... Japanese *karate*, Chinese *chüan-fa*, and the earlier Korean *taekkyon* were combined to form what is today the art of *taekwondo*."[34] Chai stresses the *quanfa* roots in his book because he is a member of the *YMCA Kwŏnbŏp Pu* linage where its founder had a connection to *quanfa*.

Lee Won Kuk (founder of Ch'ŏngdo Kwan*)*

After Lee Won Kuk's eventual return to Korea from Japan, he belatedly published *Taekwondo manual* (1968), in which he introduced *Shōtōkan* karate technique

76 *The significance of forms*

and *kata* (see Appendix D, Table 3.4). However, by this time, he had long ceased to be a major player in Korean martial arts. Later on, Lee also claimed that he studied *t'aekkyŏn* in his youth, but there is no evidence of any *t'aekkyŏn* technique in his manual. He mentions in his book for the first time without any illustrations the *P'algwae hyŏng*, two of the *T'aegŭk hyŏng*, and most of the modern *dan* (black belt) forms. This was the period when the members of the Korea Taekwondo Association distanced themselves from Choi Hong Hi and developed new forms. It is interesting to note that the term '*p'umsae*' did not exist yet and Lee still used the karate term '*hyŏng*,' but in connection with the modern taekwondo forms.

Sihak Henry Cho (member of **Jido Kwan***)*

Henry Cho published four manuals in English between 1968 and 1970. He focuses mostly on self-defense and especially on free fighting, which is a reflection of his *Jido Kwan* background since *Jido Kwan* was the pioneering school in free, full-contact sparring. For instance, in his book titled *Korean Karate – Free Fighting Technique* (1968), Cho does not show any forms but only "free fighting techniques." The technical system that he shows is still karate and does not represent modern taekwondo. Moreover, he refers to his art mostly as "Korean karate." Cho's book is interesting for the fact that he clearly states, "Tae-kwon is the Korean word for karate… *Tae-kwon do*… is identical to Japanese karate… Some of the Korean public still uses the 'karate' pronunciation in conversation."[35]

Son Duk Sung (member and successive leader of **Ch'ŏngdo Kwan***)*

Son Duk Sung mentions in his book, *Korean Karate – The Art of Tae Kwon Do* (co-written Clark, 1968), that Funakoshi was the one who introduced *Okinawa-te* to Japan,[36] but fails to mention that his instructor, Lee Won Kuk, had learned karate directly from Funakoshi. Son's style is plainly *Shōtōkan* karate (see Appendix D, Table 3.4).

Lee Chong Woo (member and successive leader of **Jido Kwan***)*

As the Chairman of the Technical Committee of the Korea Taekwondo Association, Lee Chong Woo published a manual titled *Taekwondo textbook* (1972). Taekwondo was promoted the same year to the national sport of South Korea. The manual represents the first modern taekwondo textbook. It illustrates the *P'algwae* and modern *T'aegŭk p'umsae* and does only mention a few karate *kata* by name (see Appendix D, Table 3.4). Lee also comprehensively formulates, for the first time, the key points of taekwondo's modern, popular historical presentation: he presents the *hwarang* myth,[37] interprets early Koguryŏ paintings,[38] and uses the stone carvings of the Silla 'taekwondo warriors' in Kyŏngju[39] as proofs for the existence of 'ancient taekwondo.' In addition, he claims that taekwondo originated from *subak* and *t'aekkyŏn*.[40] Some elements of this presentation, such as the stone carvings of the Silla taekwondo warriors, are not included in the modern portrayal of taekwondo's history by the World Taekwondo Federation any longer because their connection with taekwondo has been thoroughly debunked. Instead of representing 'taekwondo warriors,' they symbolize fearsome Buddhist temple guardians commonly found at the entrances of East Asian Buddhist temples.[41] Despite the general rejection of the warriors as proof for taekwondo's ancient history, organizers in Kyŏngju city for the 2011 World Championships nevertheless decided to depict them as the main theme for advertising the games yet again. The popular myths created by Lee and others are prevailing and are often invoked when suited. In an interview in 2002, Lee confessed to his role in formulating taekwondo's history: "I am one of those who wrote that in a book. To be frank, we did not have much to come out with."[42]

Early Korean martial arts literature in comparison to karate publications

Early Korean martial arts literature is conveniently called 'taekwondo literature' by many instructors and academics. However, this is not an accurate title, because the name 'taekwondo' was not universally recognized at that time and most of the authors of early works thought of their martial art as something else. The evidence presented in these manuals provides solid proof for taekwondo's main origin in karate. None of the stances, hand striking techniques, striking points, blocking techniques, or kicking techniques displayed in these manuals, except for a few photographs in Hwang Kee's 1949 book, reflect any major differences with that of earlier karate publications. Photographs and descriptive content in these books are either identical or nearly so to earlier karate publications. In addition, an almost similar range of techniques is presented. If we would display, for instance, some *quanfa* stances, strikes, or kicking techniques adjacent to it, naturally, a host of similarities would occur, but also some differences in body posture and variety of techniques. Besides, none of the photographs presented by Choi Hong Hi or any other author resemble *t'aekkyŏn* techniques in posture or description. Taekwondo technique was identical to karate technique during the time when these photographs were taken.

Choi Hong Hi was the most important figure in taekwondo during the late 1950s and 1960s, and his leading publication of 1965 looks, in great part, like a copy of Nishiyama Hidetaka's earlier book of 1960 (*Karate: The art of "empty hand" fighting*). Hwang Kee is the only Korean author who shows some differences from contemporary karate in his 1949 and 1958 publications. It seems that Hwang incorporated some very early Okinawan *Shōtōkan* karate techniques into his style. Hwang admitted to having studied karate from books, and some of the stances that he displays resemble stances directly from Funakoshi's early 1925 publication (*Rentan goshin tōde-jutsu*). Hwang showed much interest in other martial arts, and incorporated a Chinese martial art form in his first publication in 1949, but this is not reflected in his later 1958 book. He might have had some contact with a Chinese martial art when he worked for the railway in Manchuria, or he might have learned the pattern from a student of the *YMCA*

Kwŏnbŏp Pu where a few had some knowledge of *quanfa*. However, Hwang ultimately relied on the Japanese karate style.

Even though several leaders of the early *kwan* did not publish anything tangible, some of their accomplished students authored manuals. These publications provide some physical evidence of the training activities of four of the original five schools. No significant difference from karate is reflected in any of the taekwondo literature presented by these individuals. Each of their books contains between two and three hundred pages, often with hundreds of illustrations, and this study concludes that only three photographs, which are part of a single *quanfa* form, are clearly recognizable as non-karate technique. The illustrational and descriptive content in these books greatly resembles karate. Furthermore, since the main training activity in early taekwondo schools was forms, an analysis of the early publications reveals that their main content consists of Funakoshi's *kata*. When considering the existing literature comprehensively, early taekwondo appears to be largely a product of Funakoshi's *Shōtōkan* karate.

The few *t'aekkyŏn* elements, such as the inside-out-kick, that exist in modern taekwondo are not displayed in any of the early manuals. They were only introduced to the technical body of taekwondo at much later times. Early taekwondo technique, forms, curriculum, most of its terminology, dress, and formalities were practically identical to that of karate.

Forms training in modern times

In principle, the forms and forms training have not changed since the formal introduction of the *T'aegŭk p'umsae* in 1971. The World Taekwondo Federation and its affiliated organizations, worldwide, are still using the same forms today. In South Korea, the Korea Taekwondo Association started to suppress the use of karate *kata* and Choi Hong Hi's forms with the introduction of the *T'aegŭk p'umsae*. However, in other countries, where alternative organizations flourished, Japanese *kata* and Choi's forms are still in use by various rival taekwondo associations.

The Korea Taekwondo Association and the World Taekwondo Federation neglected forms training to some extent during the 1970s and 1980s because of their drive to promote taekwondo sparring competitions as an Olympic sport. However, during the 1990s, general interest in *p'umsae* training was revived among practitioners. *P'umsae* championships had already become popular during the 1990s in the United States and Europe, but were somehow, belatedly, introduced to Korea. For instance, the European Taekwondo Federation already added *p'umsae* contests in 1985 as a promotional event at the European Championships.[43] This was probably the result of taekwondo's relatively diverse development in these countries. There existed alternative organizations, such as the ITF, and students often changed associations. Some of these students had more traditional ideas about taekwondo, and there was generally a greater diversification when contrasted to taekwondo's development in Korea, which was comparatively uniform because of the monopoly that the KTA held. *P'umsae* contests were first introduced to Korea in 1992, as part of the first *Hanmadang*, a taekwondo festival showcasing breaking, demonstrations, and forms contests. However, pure forms competitions did not become popular in Korea until sometime later. The first 'World Taekwondo Poomsae [*p'umsae*] Championships' was held in 2006, but has since been promoted to become an equal partner to sparring events (see Figure 3.4). The fundamental purpose of forms training has always been to copy the teacher as closely as possible. However, in breaking with this tradition, 'creative *p'umsae*,' in which students design their own forms, have been introduced as well.[44]

Ultimately, many would like to promote *p'umsae* competitions as a second taekwondo event in the Olympic Games. However, this seems to be a distant vision. Among several reasons, given the subjective nature of judging such competitions and the potential problems with disputes regarding decisions, taekwondo forms competitions will likely not become an Olympic discipline, at least in the foreseeable future.

Figure 3.4 World Taekwondo Poomsae Championships gold medalist, Noreen Thackery (USA)

Source: Courtesy of Noreen Thackery

Summary

The concept of forms training originated from China and appears to be related to military training which stresses drill and practice, as well as the general Confucian education system which favors repetition. Whereas the Chinese, Okinawan, and modern Korean martial arts usually conceive of forms training as a solo-practice by a practitioner, in the traditional Japanese martial arts and their modern offspring (judo and kendo), forms training typically characterizes prearranged partner exercises.

During the first decade after the introduction of karate to Korea, forms training was the main training activity in Korean martial arts schools, just like mainstream karate in Japan. At that time, the Korean schools exclusively used karate *kata* and more precisely, mostly Funakoshi's forms, which the existing literature confirms. However, increasingly over time, when a second generation of practitioners emerged, minor changes in the forms and their names began to appear. In addition, a few Korean pioneers created their own patterns. During the late 1950s, Choi Hong Hi was the first who tried to replace the karate *kata* with a new set of forms. During the late 1960s, because of Choi's break with the taekwondo establishment, the Korea Taekwondo Association decided to develop their own forms. Taekwondo forms and terminology changed because the establishment increasingly sought to conceal taekwondo's origin in karate, although the principle technical systems of these new forms, and the philosophical concept behind, were still based on the old karate system. With the baptism of taekwondo as South Korea's national sport in 1971, all rival organizations and their forms were suppressed by the Korea Taekwondo Association and subsequently the World Taekwondo Federation (founded in 1973).

However, simultaneously, another training system in taekwondo started to emerge during the 1950s and 1960s, unrelated to traditional mainstream karate and forms. This type of taekwondo, based on full-contact sparring, competitions, and sports training, will be described in the next three chapters.

Notes

1 See Lorge, *Chinese martial arts*, pp. 25–9.
2 Friday, and Seki, *Legacies of the sword – The Kashima-Shinryū and samurai martial culture*, p. 105.
3 Ibid, pp. 102–3.
4 Ibid, footnote, p. 107
5 UNSRC Korean Cultural Society, (March 4, 2011). [Retrieved from http://unkcs.org/wordpress/2011/03/04/ssireum-hopes-slimming-down-brings-back-fans/].
6 Reprinted in Pak, [*Recorded documents of martial arts illustrations and commentary*].
7 Hwang Kee claimed to have rediscovered the *Muye tobo t'ongji*; however, it was given to Hwang by a librarian. Subsequently, Hwang adopted the term '*subakdo*' for his marital art, named after the martial art described in the manual. See for example, Richard Chun, and Doug Cook, "History and philosophy of taekwondo – Part 2," (August 5, 2013). [Retrieved from http://ymaa.com/articles/2013/08/history-and-philosophy-of-taekwondo-part-2].
8 Madis, "The evolution of taekwondo from Japanese karate," p. 187.

9 Funakoshi, *Karate-dō kyōhan – The master text*, p. 35.
10 Hassell, *Shotokan karate – Its history and evolution*, p. 15; Bittmann, *Karatedô – Der Weg der Leeren Hand*, p. 101; see the forms in Funakoshi, *Karate-dō kyōhan – The master text*, pp. 35–208. Bittmann (*Karatedô – Der Weg der Leeren Hand*, p. 235) believes that the distinction between the two schools was possibly only a result of misspellings and dialects. The karate style of *Shōrin-ryū* is also referred to as *Shurite*, and *Shōrei-ryū* as *Nahate*, according to their places of origin.
11 Bittmann, *Karatedô – Der Weg der Leeren Hand*.
12 See Son, and Clark, *Korean karate – The art of tae kwon do*, pp. 64–88.
13 The forms are listed in Kang, and Lee, *A modern history of taekwondo*, pp. 45–6.
14 As cited in Yook, "Kukkiwon Vice President Chong Woo Lee's shocking confession of Olympic competition result manipulation!", p. 307.
15 Hwang, *The history of Moo Duk Kwan*, p. 12.
16 Madis, "The evolution of taekwondo from Japanese karate," pp. 198–201.
17 Hwang, *Tangsudo textbook,* p. 19.
18 Hwang, *The history of Moo Duk Kwan*, pp. 16; 18.
19 Madis, "The evolution of taekwondo from Japanese karate," p. 199.
20 An English version of Funakoshi's *Rentan goshin tōde-jutsu* was published under the title, *To-te jitsu*.
21 Hwang, [*Tangsudo textbook*], p. 64. The term '*bit*-kick' was later used for the under-kick (see Chapter 6, p. 126).
22 The 'inside-out-kick' is also referred to as the 'reverse roundhouse-kick.' It is called '*pitŭrŏ-ch'agi*' in modern taekwondo and '*tchae-ch'agi*' in *t'aekkyŏn*. It was only adapted later by some taekwondo instructors, mostly during the 1970s.
23 Hwang, [*Subakdo encyclopedia – tangsu*], pp. 604–22; 628.
24 Hancock, "Quest for the truth – the origin of Tang Soo Do's forms," (last modified 2009). [Retrieved from www.usadojo.com/articles/tang-soo-do-forms.htm].
25 See Choi, *Taekwondo – The art of self-defence*, p. 88. He calls the spinning-back-kick a "Reverse turning kick." The Korean version of Choi's book is titled, [*Taekwondo guide*].
26 See Gillis, *A killing art – The untold history of tae kwon do*, p. 62; see also Chapter 6, p. 133.
27 Funakoshi, *Karate-dō kyōhan – The master text*, p. 23.
28 Gillis, *A killing art – The untold history of tae kwon do*, p. 64.
29 Choi, *Taekwondo – The art of self-defence*, pp. 295–6.
30 Choi, and Yoo, *Historic taekwondo-do instructional film*. See the scene in the mid-section of the video.
31 Kang, and Lee, *A modern history of taekwondo*, pp. 10–1; Madis, "The evolution of taekwondo from Japanese karate," pp. 196–7; Hŏ, [*Taekwondo's formation history*], pp. 21–6.
32 Madis, "Storming the fortress: A history of taekwondo – Part three: The first Korean schools: The Shudokan schools."
33 McLain, "Master Yoon Byung-in's legacy: The Changmoo-Kwan and Kangduk-Won."
34 Read, and Chai, *Taekwondo: A way of life in Korea*, p. 48.
35 Cho, *Korean karate – Free fighting technique*, p. 19.
36 Son, and Clark, *Korean karate – The art of tae kwon do*, pp. 1–3.
37 Lee, [*Taekwondo textbook*], p. 18.
38 Ibid, pp. 17; 20.
39 Ibid, p. 19.
40 Ibid, pp. 20–3.
41 See for example Kim, *Principles governing the construction of the philosophy of taekwondo*, pp. 60–1.
42 As cited in Yook, "Kukkiwon Vice President Chong Woo Lee's shocking confession of Olympic competition result manipulation!", p. 306.

43 Lee, [*Taekwondo textbook*], p. 44.
44 See World Taekwondo Federation, "Poomasae competition rules – § 9 Creative poomsae," (May, 2003). [Retrieved from www.etutaekwondo.org/docs/WTFPRules.pdf].

Bibliography

Bittmann, Heiko. *Karatedô – Der Weg der leeren Hand* (*Karatedô – The way of the empty hand*). Ludwigsburg: Verlag Heiko Bittmann, 1999. [In German, but also available in English].
Cho, Sihak Henry. *Korean karate – Free fighting technique*. Rutland and Tokyo: Charles E. Tuttle Company, 1968.
[Ch'oe Song-nam] (최송남). 拳法教本 [*Kwŏnbŏp textbook*]. Seoul: Donga Munhwasa, 1955. [In Korean only].
Choi, Hong Hi [Ch'oe Hong-hi] (최홍희). 跆拳道教本 [*Taekwondo textbook*]. Seoul: Sŏnghwa Munhwasa, 1958. [In Korean only].
_____. *Taekwondo – The art of self-defence*. Seoul: Daeha Publication Company, 1965.
_____. 태권도지침 [*Taekwondo guide*]. Seoul: Chŏngyŏnsa, 1966. [Korean version of *Taekwondo – The art of self-defence*].
Choi, Hong Hi (Supervisor), and Yoo Hyun-mok (Director). *Historic Taekwondo-Do Instructional Film*. Seoul: The Dea Yeong Film Co [probably produced 1968].
Friday, Karl F., and Seki Humitake. *Legacies of the sword – The Kashima-Shinryū and samurai martial culture*. USA: University of Hawai'i Press, 1997.
Funakoshi, Gichin. 錬膽護身 唐手術 *Rentan goshin tōde-jutsu* (*Tōdi arts: Polish your courage for self defense*). Tokyo: Airyudo, 1996. [In Japanese; original work published in 1925].
_____. *To-te jitsu*. Trans. Shingo Ishida. Hamilton: Masters Publication, 1997. [Original work published 1925].
_____. *Karate-dō kyōhan – Master text for the way of the empty-hand*. Trans. Harum Suzuki-Johnston. San Diego: Neptune Publications, 2005. [Original work published 1935].
_____. *Karate-dō Kyōhan – The Master Text*. Trans. T. Ohshima. Tokyo: Kondansha International Ltd, 1973. [Translation of revised edition of 1957; first edition published 1935].
_____. *Karate-dō nyūmon*. Trans. John Teramoto. Tokyo: Kodansha International, 1988. [Original work published 1943].
Gillis, Alex. *A killing art – The untold history of tae kwon do*. Toronto: ECW Press, 2008.
Hassell, Randall G. *Shotokan karate – Its history and evolution*. Los Angeles: Empire Books, 2007.
[Hŏ In-uk] (허인욱). 태권도형성사 [*Taekwondo's formation history*]. Kyŏngki-Do: Hanguk Haksul Ch'ŏngbo, 2008. [In Korean only].
Hwang, Kee [Hwang Ki] (황기). 花手道教本 [*Hwasudo textbook*]. Seoul: Chosŏn Munhwa Ch'ulp'ansa, 1949. [In Korean only].
_____. 唐手道教本 [*Tangsudo textbook*]. Seoul: Kyerang Munhwasa, 1958. [In Korean only].
_____. 수박도 대감 (唐手) [*Subakdo encyclopedia – tangsu*]. Seoul: Samgwang Ch'ulp'ansa, 1970. [In Korean, but available in English under the title, *Soo Bahk Do Encyclopedia*].
_____. *The history of Moo Duk Kwan*. Springfield, NJ: Tang Soo Do Moo Duk Kwan Federation, 1995.

Kang, Won Shik, and Lee Kyong Myong [Kang Wŏn-sik, Yi kyŏng-myŏng] (강원식, 이경명). 태권도 現代 史 *A modern history of taekwondo* [English title from the internet]. Seoul: Pokyŏng Munhwasa, 1999. [Parts published in English at www.martialartsresource.com/anonftp/pub/the_dojang/digests/history.html].

[Kim Yong-ok] (김용옥). 태권도철학의구성원리 *Principles governing the construction of the philosophy of taekwondo*. Seoul: T'ongnamu, 1990. [In Korean only].

Lee, Chong Woo [Yi Chong-u] (이종우). 태권도교본 [*Taekwondo textbook*]. Seoul: Korean Taekwondo Association Publication, 1972. [In Korean only].

Lee Won Kuk [Yi Wŏn-guk] (이원국). 跆拳道教範 [*Taekwondo manual*]. Seoul: Jinsudang, 1968. [In Korean only; the first edition was probably published around 1965].

Lorge, Peter A. *Chinese martial arts*. Cambridge: Cambridge University Press, 2012.

McLain, Robert. "Master Yoon Byung-in's legacy: the Changmoo-Kwan and Kangduk-Won." *Martial Talk* (2007). [Retrieved from www.martialtalk.com/forum/144-martialtalk-magazine-articles/43718-changmoo-kwan-kang-duk-won-history-photos-available-upon-request.html].

Madis, Eric. "The evolution of taekwondo from Japanese karate." In *Martial Arts in the Modern World*. Eds. Thomas A. Green and Joseph R. Svinth, 185–209. Westport: Praeger Publishers, 2003.

———. "Storming the fortress: A history of taekwondo – Part three: The first Korean schools: The Shudokan schools." *Fighting Arts.com* (2011). [Retrieved from http://fightingarts.com/reading/article.php?id=665].

Nishiyama, Hidetaka, and Richard C. Brown. *Karate the art of "empty hand" fighting*. Vermont and Tokyo: Charles E. Tuttle Company, 1960.

[Pak Ch'ŏl-hŭi] (박철희). 破邪拳法 - 空手道教本 [*Kwŏnbŏp association – Kongsudo textbook*]. Seoul: Kudŏgwŏnsa, 1958. [In Korean only].

[Pak Ch'ŏng-chŏng] (박청정). 武藝圖譜通志註解 [*Recorded documents of martial arts illustrations with commentary*]. Seoul: Dongmunsŏn, 2007. [In Korean only].

Read, Stanton E., and Chai Ik Jin [Ch'oe Ik-chin]. *Taekwondo: A way of life in Korea*. Seoul: America-Korea Friendship Association, 1965.

Son, Duk Sung [Son Tŏk-sŏng], and Robert J. Clark. *Korean karate – The art of tae kwon do*. New York: Prentice-Hall, Inc. Englewood Cliffs, 1968.

[Yi Kyo-yun] (이교윤). 百萬人의 跆手道教本 [*T'aesudo textbook for the masses*]. Seoul: T'op'ik Ch'ulp'ansa, 1965. [In Korean only].

Yook, Sung-chul [Yuk Sŏng-ch'ŏl] (육성철). 이종우 국기원 부원장의 '태권도 과거'충격적 고백! "Kukkiwon Vice President Chong Woo Lee's shocking confession of Olympic competition result manipulation!". Trans. Lee Soo Han. *Shin Dong-A*, (2002, April). 290–311. [Retrieved from http://tkdreform.com/yook_article.pdf].

4 The origins of full-contact sparring

The most significant and largely unacknowledged event separating taekwondo from karate, not only in name, but also in substance, was the introduction of full-contact competition. This development shifted the nature of Korean karate from a martial art, with a central emphasis on self-defense, toward the formation of a competition-driven martial sport – taekwondo.[1] This process led to a gradual transformation of taekwondo's techniques, focus, and purpose.[2]

Generally, it is assumed that taekwondo sparring with a body protector is a Korean invention. However, this chapter will demonstrate that full-contact sparring with protective gear originated also from Japanese karate. Initially, this discussion focuses on the origins of free sparring in karate and the kinds of protective gear used in full-contact sparring. This chapter will then explain the circumstances and attitudes of Korean leaders when full-contact sparring was introduced to Korea. Lastly, it discusses the formation of the first full-contact sparring tournaments.

The introduction of free sparring to karate training

Originally, karate teachings in Okinawa were highly secretive with instructions individually transmitted from master to disciple. Moreover, karate was only a collection of a variety of different fighting techniques and *kata* varying in schools without any standard curriculum. Only during the late nineteenth century, was karate performed in the open. In 1901, it was first introduced to an Okinawan primary school. As a consequence of its introduction to the public education program, karate lessons received structure and a consistent methodology of instruction, largely modeled after the system already used in judo and kendo.[3]

Next to physical conditioning, forms or *kata* training (a solo-performance by a practitioner) had been the main focus in karate training in Okinawa. However, with karate's introduction to Japan, pre-arranged partner exercises, called '*yaksoku kumite*' (約束組手 'pre-arranged sparring,' also called '*kihon kumite*' 基本組手 or 'basic sparring'), copied from the training methods of the existing Japanese martial arts (predominately judo and kendo) were added to the training routine. Motobu Chōki, who moved around the same time as Funakoshi Gichin to Japan, pioneered these training routines or *kumite* drills, already during the

1920s; Funakoshi introduced these drills to his lessons only in the early 1930s.[4] During these drills, in its most basic form, the student attacks the opponent with a straight punch, and the opponent defends with a block, followed by a subsequent counterattack. The same kinds of exercises still exist in present-day taekwondo under the name '*yaksŏk daeryŏn*' (約束 對鍊 'prearranged contest'). These kinds of exercises represented the pre-stage for free sparring and are, in principle, similar to the concept of *kata* training in judo and kendo.

In judo and kendo, most training activities are geared toward free sparring. However, Funakoshi only reluctantly introduced free, non-contact sparring to the daily training routine of karate during the mid-1930s, because the Japanese students ultimately longed for some combative activity and spirit. Nakayama Masatoshi, who became one of Funakoshi's most famous students, remembered:

> My seniors...knew only *kata*; it was the only thing Master Funakoshi taught them. But in my generation, things began to change...all of us had studied judo and kendo...[which] were centered around combat. So, the idea of combat was deeply ingrained in us, and we really needed the combative aspect that karate lacked.[5]

Subsequently, university clubs regularly gathered for sparring contests. However, these supposedly 'non-contact' matches only too often frenzied into, essentially, bare-knuckle fights applying karate skills which resulted in many bloody injuries.[6] However, the majority of karate leaders, most prominently Funakoshi, strongly disapproved of full-contact sparring, advocating the use of non-contact engagements, only. While already an integral part of karate training at the late 1930s and 1940s, non-contact sparring played a subordinate role in karate's training activities and philosophical attitude.[7] Instead, Funakoshi and many other karate instructors kept emphasizing the forms aspect in training.[8]

Full-contact, popular exhibition fights already existed for centuries in many parts of Asia, especially in some regions of China and South East Asia. For example, during the 1920s, Thai-boxing pioneered modern rules and the use of a ring and boxing gloves as mandatory protective equipment for matches.[9] Around the same time, full-contact exhibition fights were also frequently held in Japan. Since the late nineteenth century, wrestling and boxing contests, with few rules, in which wrestlers, boxers, judo, and karate practitioners faced off against one other, were quite popular.[10] A legendary match happened in 1922, when Motobu Chōki crushed a Russian heavy weight boxing contestant in a "bare-handed bout" with karate skills, which gave him a reputation as a fearless fighter. Even though, Motobu was physically very strong, the fact that he defeated a larger Caucasian contributed to his fame. However, Funakoshi was later often erroneously credited for the victory, because the author of an article recounting the fight that was published in a Japanese magazine in 1925, wrongly featured Funakoshi's image instead of Motobu's. Motobu represented the principal rival and antagonist of Funakoshi, both mutually disliked each other on grounds of different personality and karate philosophy.[11]

86 *The origins of full-contact sparring*

During the 1930s, some Japanese karate students experimented with full-contact sparring using boxing gloves and baseball equipment as protectors; however, this kind of gear proved too cumbersome.[12] Others experimented with protective gear from kendo, called '*bōgu*' (防具 'protective equipment'). *Bōgu* (or '*kendōgu*,' 剣道具 'kendo equipment') in kendo refers to the combined protective gear used in sparring, which includes a mask, gloves, waist, groin, and a body protector (see Figure 4.1). Karate students came to use this gear selectively in full-contact sparring training. Naturally, over time, the various items of equipment used became modified and adapted, as well.

Figure 4.1 Kendo *bōgu* gear
Source: Courtesy of Michael Han

Motobu Chōki, famous for full-contact engagements, was possibly also the initiator of free full-contact sparring with protective equipment (see Figure 4.2).[13] Although Motobu's training methodologies never became mainstream because, unlike Funakoshi, he was not able to establish a large number of followers and schools in Japan. This was possibly the result of Motobu's allegedly poor Japanese language skills. Moreover, most crucially, Motobu lacked the support that Funakoshi had in the established Japanese martial arts community through backers, such as Kanō Jigorō. Patrick McCarthy, a karate expert and historian, speculated that Kanō might have even detested and opposed Motobu, equating Motobu with the old *jūjutsu* community that he despised.[14]

Among a number of full-contact sparring pioneers from *Shurite* karate was also a Korean immigrant, Yun K'wae-pyŏng, who moved to Japan during his high school years, and started learning karate first from Mabuni Kenwa. Subsequently, as a student at Nihon University, Yun attended *Shurite* karate classes under Tōyama Kanken. Once Yun became an accomplished student, he established a sister-school in Tokyo, in 1940, which he named '*Kanbukan*' (韓武館 'Korean martial arts institute' or school, see Figure 2.1). This school attracted students from diverse karate styles who wanted to compare and test their skills in full-contact sparring. The protective equipment also consisted of a modified kendo

Figure 4.2 *Bōgu* sparring at Tōyō University in Tokyo, in 1937, at Sensei Motobu Chōki's karate club, experimenting with a baseball pitcher's protective equipment

Source: Courtesy of Motobu Chōsei (third son of Motobu Chōki)[15]

bōgu. Yun was highly regarded for his proficiency and advancements in full-contact sparring with protective gear. After the Second World War and Korea's liberation, Yun decided to return to Korea in 1948, to contribute to the development of his native country. Consequently, in 1950, his '*Kanbukan*' school was renamed, under new leadership, as '*Renbukan*' (練武館 'Institute of martial arts training'). A few years later, in 1954, *Renbukan* introduced an annual, full-contact tournament using the *bōgu* as a protector in which mostly Japanese and Koreans participated, as well as a few American servicemen from the military occupation forces.[16] As an unconventional karate style, *Renbukan* karate has survived and expanded until present times.

During the late 1950s, conventional, mainstream karate also introduced sparring competitions. The general competition format of mainstream karate tournaments, such as the approximate court size, the number of judges and referees, and the flag system indicating points, greatly mimicked the already existing kendo and judo competition rules. In 1957, the Japan Karate Association (JKA),[17] which was a product of mostly senior *Shōtōkan* students, organized the first nationwide 'All Japan Karate Championship,' representing the dawn of modern sport karate.[18] However, the event was divided into '*kata*' ('forms') and '*kumite*' ('sparring') competitions. The sparring arrangement naturally applied non-contact rules without any protectors, since most traditional karate instructors rejected full-contact sparring. The second element, the forms competition, was an essential component of the event, since traditional instructors regarded it as fundamental to their philosophy. For example, Funakoshi stated, "it must be emphasized that sparring does not exist apart from kata but for the practice of kata...karate...should be practiced with kata as the principal method and sparring as a supporting method."[19] Traditional Japanese karate instructors could not conceive of conducting sparring tournaments, exclusively. At that time, traditional Japanese karate was advanced nearly to its present form, both technically as well as philosophically.[20] In contrast, Korean karate, which changed its name officially to taekwondo in 1965, was only in its infancy.

The attitudes of Korean leaders toward full-contact sparring

Until the 1950s, free sparring during practice in Japan had a clearly subordinate role in most karate styles, which continued to focus on forms training. Moreover, full-contact sparring was not at all widespread among the majority of karate schools at that time. Funakoshi, in particular, strongly opposed any full-contact engagements. As a result, when karate was introduced to Korea, the emphasis of the first Korean instructors was also on forms training and self-defense, since most of them had learned conventional *Shōtōkan* karate. Non-contact, free sparring was rarely performed during the 1940s in the five existing Korean taekwondo organizations at that time. However, this gradually changed with the proliferation of karate in Korea during the 1950s.[21] Accordingly, some schools shifted their training activities from drills perceived as preparation for self-defense and combat, toward sparring-related exercises geared for sporting competitions, eventually leading to the first taekwondo tournaments during the 1960s.

The only globally recognized full-contact sport at the time of the introduction of taekwondo competitions was Western boxing. The obvious choice for the leaders in Korea would have been to imitate boxing and use some kind of hand and foot protectors in full-contact sparring. However, a possible reason for the rejection of boxing gloves was the concern that realism in combat would suffer; a belief that was similar to Ōyama Masutatsu's regarding *Kyokushin* karate, a full-contact style that he developed during the late 1950s in Japan.[22] Besides, tradition-minded instructors opposed, in principal, the use of any padding equipment in sparring. For instance, Choi Hong Hi had great reservations about the use of gloves. He declared:

> Striking points are restricted; for example, if a glove is worn, the knife-hand, spear finger and other parts of the hand would not be able to be used ... [and] ... [s]ince one blow might finish the contest, it would be almost impossible to appreciate the whole power and skill of Taekwon-Do through actual hitting, as in other sports such as boxing [or] wrestling.[23]

However, Choi had similar concerns about the use of body protectors. He thought that because of its weight, the fighters would no longer be able to move freely; therefore, he rejected it, as well. In fact, Choi rejected all safety equipment and opposed full-contact competitions for the reason that "it would not be a proper test of skill and power any longer." He tried to maintain the myth that taekwondo is a lethal form of self-defense and stated, "One blow might cause the instantaneous death of a person."[24] Son Duk Sung declared, "A well-trained Taek Kwon Doist's attack with full force would put the opponent out of business if it would not actually kill him." And regarding the use of padding equipment, Son thought, "Wearing protection removes the whole point of Tae Kwon Do because ... the student is supposed to learn to protect himself, not how to buy protective devices at sporting goods stores."[25] Choi, Son, and many other instructors, retained the traditional karate philosophy of perceiving martial arts as foremost a practical means for lethal combat. On the other hand, a new group of leaders emerged, who sought to promote taekwondo as a competition sport.

Since the new leaders opted to advance taekwondo as a full-contact sport, the use of some kind of protective equipment for athletes became necessary. Like their Japanese predecessors, the first Koreans who practiced full-contact sparring basically utilized the available equipment which consisted of conventional kendo protectors. Japanese samurai had used body protectors stuffed with bamboo sticks as early as the eighteenth century in sparring with mock weapons (see Figure 4.3),[26] and since kendo had been introduced to the Korean public school system under Japanese colonial rule, this kind of gear was abundant and familiar to the Korean martial arts community.

Figure 4.3 Kendo fencing at an agricultural school in Japan during the early twentieth century
Source: Courtesy of Project Gutenberg[27]

The introduction of full-contact sparring to Korea

After Yun K'wae-pyŏng, a former karate student of Tōyama Kanken, returned to Korea from Japan in 1948, he was hired at the *Chosŏn Yŏnmu Kwan* as the chief instructor. However, during the confusion of the Korean War, Chŏn Sang-sŏp, the founder of the *Chosŏn Yŏnmu Kwan* disappeared and the school was closed. Subsequently, in 1951, Yun became the school's leader, when he, together with Lee Chong Woo, reopened it and renamed it *Jido Kwan* (see Chapter 2, pp. 40–1).[28] Since Yun had previously taught *bōgu* karate at the *Kanbukan* in Tokyo, it is apparent that once he became the person in charge, he introduced the idea of Japanese *bōgu* sparring to the general training curriculum of the *Jido Kwan*.

During the 1950s, Yun K'wae-pyŏng must have been aware of the annual full-contact *Renbukan* tournaments in Japan, since they were established by his former school that he founded in Tokyo. Moreover, Yun kept in contact with the Japanese martial arts community, which might have also influenced the training activity at *Jido Kwan*. While many other schools kept the focus during training on forms, the *Jido Kwan* pioneers completed the shift from non-contact to full-contact sparring during the second half of the 1950s. In addition to *Jido Kwan* athletes, some students from the *YMCA Kwŏnbŏp Pu* lineage seemed to have also started full-contact sparring during that time. This was possibly a result of the close relationship between Yun K'wae-pyŏng and Yun Pyŏng-in, who both trained together under Tōyama Kanken in Japan. For instance, students of *Ch'angmu Kwan*, the successor of the *YMCA Kwŏnbŏp Pu*, also already used kendo protectors during the late 1950s (see Figure 4.4, and Figure 2.1). Nevertheless, the *Jido Kwan* advocates turned out to be the dominating athletes in the first full-contact competitions of the early 1960s.[29]

Figure 4.4 1958 demo at presidential mansion square (Seoul, Korea). "1st Korean President Syn Mahn Rhee's [Syngman Rhee] birthday celebration demo. Free sparring demo between Ik-jin Chai [Ch'oe Ik-chin, member of *Ch'angmu Kwan*] and Kim Soo [Kim Pyŏng-su, member of *Ch'angmu Kwan*]."

Source: Courtesy of Grandmaster Kim Soo[30]

Note: Both athletes wear a kendo body protector and Kim Soo seems to wear, in addition, kendo headgear as well some sort of as shin protection (compare to Figure 4.1). The photograph possibly represents the earliest existing evidence of *bōgu* or *hogu* sparring in Korea.

Lee Chong Woo, who became *Jido Kwan*'s successive leader in 1967,[31] recalls that, at first, conventional kendo body protectors and helmets were used in sparring, but punching the solid headgear with bare knuckles resulted in many bloody fist injuries and head trauma (see Figure 4.1). Therefore, they started to construct some headgear made of softer materials, which, it seems, did not solve the problem of serious injuries.[32] Consequently, punches to the head of the opponent had to be excluded from sparring during the first nationwide tournaments.

In 1962, at the 43rd National Sports Festival in Taegu, the promoter included, for the first time, a full-contact sparring event as a demonstration sport, albeit without any protectors. This contest was sponsored by the Korea Taesudo Association, which was the representative martial arts body in Korea from 1961–1965. The following year, 1963, when the National Sports Festival was held in Chŏnju, Chŏnbuk province, a stronghold of the *Jido Kwan* gymnasiums, its leaders were able to lobby for the elevation of the full-contact sparring event to official sport status. As a sparring aid for this competition, Chŏn Il-sŏp, another member of *Jido Kwan*, designed a modified body protector, called '*hogu*' (護具 'protective gear,' see Figure 4.5),[33] by using the kendo body protector as a model.[34] Lee Chong Woo strongly promoted the *hogu*'s use at this contest, and was also responsible for the organization of the competition.[35] Even though athletes wore a *hogu* from this time on during tournaments, its use in sparring did

Figure 4.5 1960s-style modified body protector: *hogu* with bamboo stick inserts
Source: Courtesy of Gregory S. Kailian

not become officially mandatory according to the competition rules until 1968.[36] Lee, perhaps, had more than safety in mind when he pushed for the use of the *hogu* in competition: anecdotal evidence suggests Lee might have wished to help a friend who owned a clothing factory by contracting him to produce the body protector.[37] But, regardless of his motivations, Lee clearly acknowledged the effect of the *hogu* on taekwondo after its introduction: "the use of body armor and other innovations in the competition system in the early 1960s stimulated a process of technical development which resulted in many new techniques which had not existed before";[38] although, during the first taekwondo tournaments, matches still resembled karate-style sparring.[39]

During the 1960s, until the early 1970s there were continuing exchanges between Korean and Japanese karate schools. Yun K'wae-pyŏng kept good relationships with the All Japan Karate-do Federation (AJKF), which was officially founded by his teacher Tōyama Kanken in 1946. Thus, *Jido Kwan* and *Mudŏk Kwan* athletes, as part of the 'Korea Subakdo Association,' traveled to Japan several times during that period. They reportedly visited Japan in 1961, 1964, and 1970, to participate in karate goodwill tournaments and the World Karate Championships,[40] and a Japanese team came to Korea for a friendship match in 1963. The *Mudŏk Kwan* students' participation, under the umbrella of the Korea Subakdo Association, was the result of Yun K'wae-pyŏng's decision to join Hwang Kee's Korea Subakdo Association that Hwang formed in 1960, in opposition to the first Korea Taekwondo Association (1959–1961). Subsequently, Yun kept the succeeding Korea Taesudo Association (1961–1965) and second Korea Taekwondo Association (1965–present) at arm's length. On the other hand, Lee Chong Woo, in disagreement with Yun, favored joining the Korea Taekwondo Association. As a result, in 1967, *Jido Kwan* split into two organizations with two conflicting leaders, Yun and Lee. During the same period, Hwang and his *Mudŏk Kwan* organization also lost the bulk of its members over the same issue.[41] In the end, Lee Chong Woo gained the upper hand in these power struggles, when he rose to assume one of the leading positions in the Korea Taekwondo Association.

Summary

Motobu Chōki introduced karate to Japan from Okinawa around the same time, or even slightly earlier than Funakoshi Gichin. However, due to the connections that Funakoshi developed with the Japanese elites, and in particular with Kanō Jigorō, Funakoshi was able to establish his vision of karate and was later credited as being the 'father' of Japanese *karate-dō*. Funakoshi, a life-long school teacher, saw karate's value foremost from an educational point of view, as a tool for character building. He stated proudly, "I have never injured anyone in all the years of studying karate. In fact, winning without fighting is the greatest victory."[42] Consequently, Funakoshi advocated forms training only, and rejected free sparring, especially violent full-contact engagements. On the other hand, Motobu had a reputation as a practical street fighter who pioneered free, full-contact sparring and training methods; he ridiculed Funakoshi's training system as an unrealistic sham.[43] However, due to Motobu's lack of connections to the Japanese martial arts establishment, his style of karate did not become mainstream in Japan.[44] Although the split and antagonism between forms advocates and free sparring proponents crystallized already in these two early individuals. As a result of these dynamics, full-contact sparring became only a marginalized training method in Japan; in contrast, full-contact sparring became a conventional training routine in Korea later on.

The general assumption that full-contact sparring with a body protector was an invention of taekwondo leaders is not supported by historical evidence. In all likelihood, it was a continuation of the early Japanese full-contact *bōgu* sparring system. Originally, the idea of using a body protector in sparring was copied by karate instructors, such as Motobu, from kendo. Later, the training method was probably introduced by Yun K'wae-pyŏng from Japan to Korea when he became the leader of *Jido Kwan* in 1951. Therefore, he could be considered the actual initiator of modern full-contact taekwondo. Subsequently, *Jido Kwan*'s students pioneered full-contact sparring with a *hogu* in Korea, and second-generation leaders paved the way for the introduction of full-contact competitions. Lee Chong Woo seems to have been instrumental during this process.

In contrast to the All Japan Karate Championships, the Korean tournaments, focused only on free sparring matches and excluded forms competition. Moreover, the Koreans opted for full-contact sparring. Consequently, the actual introduction of large-scale, full-contact sporting competitions was a Korean contribution to the evolution of East Asian martial arts. Full-contact competitions existed in Japanese karate only at an experimental level with the annual *Renbukan* tournaments, which were not considered mainstream events.

The origin of full-contact sparring with body protectors seems to provide further evidence of taekwondo's roots in Japanese karate. Moreover, the original competition format of taekwondo was also modeled largely after a Japanese standard, which is discussed in the following chapter.

Notes

1 Capener, "Problems in the identity and philosophy of *t'aegwondo* and their historical causes," p. 87.
2 Yang Jin Bang coined the term 'competitionalization' (경기화 '*kyŏnggihwa*') for this process. The English translation was termed by Steven Capener.
3 Hassell, *Shotokan karate – Its history and evolution*, p. 19; Madis, "The evolution of taekwondo from Japanese karate," pp. 188–9; Tom Ross, "Examining Yasutsune Itosu," *Fighting Arts.com*, (n.d.). [Retrieved from www.fightingarts.com/reading/article.php?id=1].
4 Hassell, *Shotokan karate – Its history and evolution*, p. 44; Bittmann, *Karatedô – Der Weg der Leeren Hand*, p. 127.
5 As cited in Hassell, *Shotokan karate – Its history and evolution*, pp. 43–5.
6 Ibid, pp. 45; 74.
7 Bittmann, *Karatedô – Der Weg der Leeren Hand*, pp. 100–1; Funakoshi, *Karate-dō kyōhan- The master text*, p. 211.
8 Funakoshi, *Karate-dō kyōhan – The master text*, preface; *The essence of karate*, p. 102. According to Nishiyama, when he started training in Funakoshi's school in 1943, the training content was about 80% *kata* and only 20% basic technique (as cited in

"Hidetaka Nishiyama," [last modified October 9, 2012]. [Retrieved from http://en.wikipedia.org/wiki/Hidetaka_Nishiyama].
9   Kraitus, and Kraitus, *Muay Thai*, pp. 15; 23; Lorge, *Chinese martial arts*, p. 132.
10 Green, and Svinth, "Maeda's Judo and Gracie's jiu-jitsu," 61–70; Friday, and Seki, *Legacies of the sword – The Kashima-Shinryū and samurai martial culture*, p. 3.
11 McCarthy, "On Choki Motobu – Part 1."
12 Koharu, [*Research in early Ryukyu karate*], p. 234.
13 Email correspondence with Peter Kobos, January 13, 2014.
14 McCarthy, "On Choki Motobu – Part 1." Contrary to McCarthy, Christopher M. Clarke believes that Motobu, due to his noble background, was certainly not "illiterate" and possible also spoke Japanese, but refused to speak Japanese "out of disdain for Japan's destruction of his society." See Clarke, *Okinawan karate: A history of styles and masters – Volume 1: Shuri-te and Shorin-ryu*, pp. 151–2.
15 Courtesy of Motobu Chosei Soke, son of Motobu Chōki, a direct descendant of the Royal Family of Okinawa and founder of *Motobu Kenpō Karate*. According to Motobu Chosei Soke: "The art in this picture is *Motobu-Ryū (Motobu Kenpō Karate)*. Sensei Motobu Chōki was the first instructor to open a school of karate (named *Daidokan*) in Mainland Japan and one of the first pioneers to introduce karate there." See also www.motobu-ryu.org or www.fb.com/Motoburyu.Japan
16 Madis, "The evolution of taekwondo from Japanese karate," pp. 197–8; "Storming the fortress: A history of taekwondo – Part Three: The first Korean schools: The Shudokan schools"; see also "Kanbukan karate," (n.d.). [Retrieved from www.karateindia.co.in/renbukai_history.htm]; Urban dictionary, "Kanbukan," (n.d.). [Retrieved from www.urbandictionary.com/define.php?term=kanbukan].
17 The Japan Karate Association (JKA) was formed in 1949, by senior *Shōtōkan* students, among them also Nishiyama Hidetaka.
18 Hassel, *Shotokan karate – Its history and evolution*, p. 77. The 'All Japan Karate Championship' has been held annually since 1957.
19 Funakoshi, *Karate-dō kyōhan – The master text*, p. 211.
20 Karate's development was mostly accomplished during the 1920s and 1930s. See Bittmann, *Karatedô – Der Weg der Leeren Hand*, pp. 128; 254.
21 Kim, "A study on how the taekwondo games rules can [have] influence on the changes of game skills [sic]," pp. 18–19; Madis, "The evolution of taekwondo from Japanese karate," pp. 185–209; "Storming the fortress: A history of taekwondo – Part two: The first Korean schools: The Shotokan schools."
22 See "Kyokushin kaikan," (August, 2007). [Retrieved from http://encyclopedia.thefreedictionary.com/Kyokushin+kaikan].
23 Choi, *Taekwondo – The art of self-defence*, p. 292.
24 Ibid, p. 292.
25 Son, and Clark, *Korean karate – The art of tae kwon do*, pp. 268–9.
26 Draeger, *Modern bujutsu and budo*, p. 97.
27 Photo from *The foundations of Japan: Notes made during journeys of 6,000 miles: In The rural districts: As a basis for a sounder knowledge of the Japanese people* (1922), by J.W. Robertson Scott. This eBook is for the use of anyone anywhere at no cost and with almost no restrictions whatsoever. You may copy it, give it away or re-use it under the terms of the Project Gutenberg License included with this eBook or online at www.gutenberg.org. [Retrieved from http://en.wikipedia.org/wiki/File:FENCING_AT_AN_AGRICULTURAL_SCHOOL.jpg].
28 Kang, and Lee, *A modern history of taekwondo*, p. 6; Madis, "Storming the fortress: A history of taekwondo – Part three: The first Korean schools: The Shudokan schools."
29 Kim, "A study on how the Taekwondo games rules can [have] influence on the changes of game skills [sic]," pp. 19; 41–2.
30 Kimsookarate, (n.d.). [Retrieved from http://kimsookarate.com/].
31 See Kang, and Lee, *A modern history of taekwondo*, p. 6.

32 As cited in Yook, "Kukkiwon Vice President Chong Woo Lee's shocking confession of Olympic competition result manipulation!", p. 309. Even modern headgear does not prevent concussions sufficiently. See Fife, Pieter, O'Sullivan, Cook, and Kominski, "Effects of Olympic style taekwondo kicks on an instrumented head-form and resulted head injury measures," pp. 310–84.
33 *Hogu* (護具) is an alternative term for protective equipment and similar to the Japanese term, '*bōgu*' (防具), which is pronounced '*panggu*' in Korean.
34 Ko Eui Min, personal interview, January 13, 2010; Kang, and Lee, *A modern history of taekwondo*, p. 127.
35 Ko Eui Min, personal interview, January 13, 2010; Kang, and Lee, *A modern history of taekwondo*, p. 104.
36 Kang, and Lee, *A modern history of taekwondo*, p.120.
37 This information is from my conversations with Steven D. Capener, who worked for several years under Lee Chong Woo at the WTF (at that time located in the Kukkiwon), during the early 1990s. Lee told this story.
38 As cited in Capener, "Problems in the identity and philosophy of *t'aegwondo* and their historical causes," p. 94.
39 Kim Sei Hyeok, personal interview, March 23, 2010; see also Chapter 6, p. 118..
40 Ko Eui Min, personal interview, January 13, 2010; Madis, "Storming the fortress: A history of taekwondo – Part three: The first Korean schools: The Shudokan schools"; Sŏ, [*Modern taekwondo history – The course*], pp. 42–3; Kimsookarate, "Letter from Kanken Toyama student," (n.d.). [Retrieved from www.kimsookarate.com/intro/Kanken%20Toyama%20Ltr.pdf].
41 Kang, and Lee, *A modern history of taekwondo*, p. 6; Madis, "The evolution of taekwondo from Japanese karate," p. 200.
42 Funakoshi, "Speaking about karatedo," in *Funakoshi Gichin tanpenshu*.
43 McCarthy, "On Choki Motobu – Part 1."
44 Clarke, *Okinawan karate: A history of styles and masters – Volume 1: Shuri-te and Shorin-ryu*, p. 157.

Bibliography

Bittmann, Heiko. *Karatedô – Der Weg der leeren Hand* (*Karatedô – The way of the empty hand*). Ludwigsburg: Verlag Heiko Bittmann, 1999. [In German, but also available in English].

Capener, Steven D. "Problems in the identity and philosophy of *t'aegwondo* and their historical causes." *Korea Journal*, 35, 4 (1995): 80–94. [Retrieved from www.eagletkd.com/images/STUDENT%20FORUM%20from%20Korea%0Journal.pdf].

Choi, Hong Hi [Ch'oe Hong-hi] (최홍히). *Taekwondo – The art of self-defence*. Seoul: Daeha Publication Company, 1965.

Clarke, M. Christorpher. *Okinawan Karate: A history of styles and masters – Volume 1: Shuri-te and Shorin-ryu*. Huntingtown: Clarke's Canyon Press, 2012.

Draeger, Don F. *Modern bujutsu and budo*. (Vol. 3). New York: Weatherhill, Inc., 1974.

Fife, G., Pieter W., O'Sullivan D., Cook D., and T. Kominski. "Effects of Olympic style taekwondo kicks on an instrumented head-form and resulted head injury measures." *Br J Sports Med*, 45 (2011): 310–84.

Friday, Karl F., and Seki Humitake. *Legacies of the sword – The Kashima-Shinryū and samurai martial culture*. USA: University of Hawai'i Press, 1997.

Funakoshi, Gichin. *Karate-dō kyōhan – The master text*. Trans. T. Ohshima. Tokyo: Kondansha International Ltd, 1973. [Translation of revised edition of 1957; first edition published 1935].

_____. *Funakoshi Gichin tanpenshu*. Trans. Partick and Yuriko McCarthy. Aspley: International Ryukyu Karate Research Society, 2006.

_____. *The essence of karate*. Trans. Richard Berger. Tokyo: Kondansha Internationa, 2010. [Original work not published].

Green, Thomas A. and Joseph R. Svinth. "Maeda's judo and Gracie's jiu-jitsu." In *Martial Arts in the Modern World*. Eds. Thomas A. Green and Joseph R. Svinth, 61–70. Westport: Praeger Publishers, 2003.

Hassell, Randall G. *Shotokan karate – Its history and evolution*. Los Angeles: Empire Books, 2007.

Kang, Won Shik, and Lee Kyong Myong [Kang Wŏn-sik, Yi kyŏng-myŏng] (강원식, 이경명). 태권도 現代 史 *A modern history of taekwondo* [English title from the internet]. Seoul: Pokyŏng Munhwasa, 1999. [Parts published in English at www.martialartsresource.com/anonftp/pub/the_dojang/digests/history.html].

[Kim Chong-min] (김종민). 태권도 규칙이 경기기술의 변화에 미치는 영향에 대한 연구 "A study on how the taekwondo games rules can [have] influence on the changes of game skills [sic]." Unpublished master's thesis, Kyung Hee University, 2002. [In Korean only].

Koharu, Iwai. 本部朝基と琉球 カラテ [*Research in early Ryukyu karate*]. Tokyo: Airyudo, 2000. [In Japanese only].

Kraitus, Panya, and Pitisuk Kraitus. *Muay Thai*. Bangkok: Asia Books, 1988.

Lorge, Peter A. *Chinese Martial Arts*. Cambridge: Cambridge University Press, 2012.

McCarthy, Patrick. "On Choki Motobu – Part 1." *Fighting Arts.com* (2012). [Retrieved from www.fightingarts.com/reading/article.php?id=398].

Madis, Eric. "The evolution of taekwondo from Japanese karate." In *martial arts in the modern world*. Eds. Thomas A. Green and Joseph R. Svinth, 185–209. Westport: Praeger Publishers, 2003.

_____. "Storming the fortress: A history of taekwondo – Part two: The first Korean schools: The Shotokan schools." *EC Martial Arts Blog* (2011). [Retrieved from http://ec-ma.blogspot.kr/2011/02/storming-fortress-history-of-taekwondo_08.html].

_____. "Storming the fortress: A history of taekwondo – Part three: The first Korean schools: The Shudokan schools." *Fighting Arts.com* (2011). [Retrieved from http://fightingarts.com/reading/article.php?id=665].

[Sŏ Sŏng-wŏn] (서성원). 태권도 현대사 와 길동무하다 [*The course of modern taekwondo history*]. Seoul: Dosŏ Ch'ulp'ansa Sangakihoek, 2007. [In Korean only].

Son, Duk Sung [Son Tŏk-sŏng], and Robert J. Clark. *Korean karate – The art of tae kwon do*. New York: Prentice-Hall, Inc. Englewood Cliffs, 1968.

Yook, Sung-chul [Yuk Sŏng-ch'ŏl] (육성철). 이종우 국기원 부원장의 '태권도 과거' 충격적 고백! "Kukkiwon Vice President Chong Woo Lee's shocking confession of Olympic competition result manipulation!". Trans. Lee Soo Han. *Shin Dong-A*, (2002, April). 290–311. [Retrieved from http://tkdreform.com/yook_article.pdf].

5 The origins of taekwondo competition rules

In 1962, for the first time, the 43rd National Sports Festival in Taegu included a full-contact sparring event, and the following year, 'taekwondo' (at that time called '*t'aesudo*') became an official sport. Afterward, a variety of competitions were launched at the high school and university level. In 1973, the World Taekwondo Federation (WTF) was founded, and that same year the first World Championships were held in Seoul.

Supported by the South Korean government, Korean taekwondo leaders were aiming for taekwondo's inclusion as an Olympic discipline. Subsequently, taekwondo was aggressively promoted over the following decades as an internationally recognized sport, to be first included at the 1986 Asian Games, held in Seoul. Two years later, taekwondo earned its debut as a demonstration sport at the 1988 Seoul Olympics. It was included again as a demonstration sport at the 1992 Games in Barcelona and, at last, taekwondo gained the status of an official, medal event at the 2000 Sydney Olympics.

Chapter 6 examines the roots and causes for the evolutionary direction of taekwondo as a sport, over the past sixty years. The foremost characteristic of Olympic taekwondo is that it is a combat sport which, almost exclusively, uses kicking techniques in sparring. Moreover, the preferred sparring tactics keep changing along with revisions in the rules, as well as advancements in protective gear and innovations in scoring technology. However, the current competition system was not only the result of technical rule and equipment changes, but also of political decisions and struggles among Korean taekwondo leaders.

During sport taekwondo's infancy, there was much trial and error in the development of new rules and regulations. This chapter will seek to demonstrate how these rules were formulated, and examine how improved equipment and further rule modifications have affected the technical direction of sport taekwondo. Finally, this chapter will conclude by discussing the most recent developments regarding the issues mentioned, above.

The original competition rules

The original rules and format of taekwondo competition were strongly influenced by early non-contact karate competitions, possibly the *Renbukan* full-contact tournaments and, to some extent, by boxing, such as the rule of victory by legal knock-out.[1] In addition to the introduction of full-contact sparring with a body protector, the basic sparring rules profoundly shaped the technical direction of taekwondo. The legal striking techniques, the permitted striking areas, and other formal regulations determined the preferred use and evolution of sport taekwondo's techniques. Moreover, through procedural changes and the introduction of new rules and equipment, the taekwondo establishment tried to influence and improve the technical direction of taekwondo sparring, over time. Although minor adjustments of the regulations happened throughout the history of taekwondo competition on an almost yearly basis, there were several especially important periods for the introduction of new rules and sparring gear that had great influence on the technical direction of taekwondo sparring. Official amendments of the World Taekwondo Federation competition rules were enacted twenty two times between 1973 and 2015.[2]

Early taekwondo was essentially karate and many of the striking techniques were performed with the hands, elbows, and knees, and various kicking techniques were also executed. In addition, some grappling and throwing moves were practiced; however, ground fighting (such as taught in judo and wrestling) was largely excluded from the training routines. Consequently, the training routines of the early taekwondo athletes shaped the selection of the competition rules; the focus was on stand-up striking.

Since the organizers of the first tournaments opted for full-contact sparring, the danger of knock-outs and serious injuries needed to be minimized by limiting the legal striking techniques and target areas. During the first, full-contact competitions in Korea in 1962 (conducted without body protector or *hogu*), and in 1963 (conducted for the first time with *hogu*), the core rules resembled those used today, and victory through knock-out was possible. Kicking to the face scored two points, and body kicks and punches scored one point each; however, intentional strikes with the hands to the face of the opponent were prohibited and led to point deductions. Even though some individual *kwan* or schools would still allow striking techniques with the hands to the head of the opponent during their internal contests, the association in charge of the 1962 tournament had already barred these techniques in national competition. In addition, the competition rules would no longer permit low-kicks, elbow and knee strikes, and grappling. However, throwing techniques to incapacitate or humiliate the opponent were still practiced and popular, but no points were awarded for their use. As a consequence of the selected rules, the range in the athlete's choice of authorized techniques was considerably narrowed. Moreover, the scoring area was sharply reduced: only strikes to the front and side areas of the head and torso were allowed.[3]

Just as the duration of a match influences the tactics used, the structure, shape, and size of the competition area has a direct influence on the development of technique. The choice of an open court, as opposed to, for example, a closed ring with ropes, also had important implications for kicking techniques. A taekwondo court is larger than a boxing ring, with no ropes or any kinds of physical restraints; there is always room to escape. The court size for the first competition, in 1962, was 8 × 8 meters, which was also the size of the court used in the non-contact, All Japan Karate Championship. Other court regulations, such as the number of judges and referees, also followed karate rules.[4] In the choice of the competition format, it seems that early taekwondo leaders simply followed the Japanese, non-contact karate competition layout of the Japan Karate Association. The most obvious alternative format would have been the Western-style boxing regulations with a ring. However, early taekwondo was essentially karate, as was its competition format and many of its basic rules.

Important competition rule changes during the 1960s and 1970s

Subsequent improvements in equipment and modifications to the rules shaped the technical direction of taekwondo and ultimately made it different from karate. During the first few years of competition, a variety of minor rule modifications were introduced, but the more important rule changes happened during the late 1960s. A significant rule modification allowed uninterrupted fighting (despite points being scored) without intervention by the referee.[5] In non-contact karate competitions, the fight was stopped after each exchange of blows because of the philosophical concept of 'one blow – certain death' (一拳必殺 'ikken hissatsu'), which emphasized the belief in the lethality of a single strike. During "one blow matches," the victor was declared after inflicting a single "killing blow";[6] a reason why karate developed so few combination techniques. During the first years of sport taekwondo competition, as in karate, points were only awarded for single strikes and not after a wild exchange of blows. This policy changed only after a rule revision in 1967.[7]

Another important rule revision that same year was related to the body protector: the scoring of points with instep roundhouse-kicks to the body. In karate, the roundhouse-kick was only executed with the ball of the foot, a technique which is not very suitable for full-contact sparring (for a detailed discussion, see Chapter 6, pp. 119–21). However, the traditional *hogu* with bamboo stick inserts was still very hard and resulted in many bloody fist and foot injuries when struck with full force.[8] As a consequence, during the mid-1970s, protectors of a higher quality were introduced. These protectors had an ethafoam filling which gave them a distinctive sound, especially, when hit with the instep roundhouse-kick. Gradually, the 'bang' sound became a criterion for scoring a point, which rapidly increased the use of the instep roundhouse-kick.[9] In addition, Ko Eui Min introduced the groin protector, which was adopted soon after 1972, as a mandatory safety item in competition.[10]

A second period of substantial rule revisions was initiated between 1977 and 1980. In 1977, the size of the outer boundary of the fighting court was enlarged to 12 × 12 meters with the introduction of a two meter-wide safety area, which indirectly, but significantly, enlarged the competition area. This increase led to a tactical development wherein an athlete could easily leave the fighting area and effectively run away from the fight. Avoiding direct exchanges by athletes became a lingering problem with taekwondo matches.

According to Kang Won Shik and Lee Kyong Myong, another substantial rule change in 1977 was the introduction of two points for a "strong kick to the body," or three-points for a "strong kick to the face," both followed by an eight-count. Subsequently, however, multiple point scores were abandoned altogether in 1980 and replaced with single point scores only.[11] In 1979, at the fourth World Championships in Sindelfingen, Germany, multiple point scores were still used.[12] However, Kang and Lee's statement partly conflicts with WTF amendments, enacted in 1977; only much later, in 1982, was there a subsequent revision.[13] In any case, multiple point scores were abandoned around that time. The rule could have been changed based on suspected manipulation of scoring results.

The revision of evenly awarding single points for punches and kicking techniques to the body and face of the opponent contributed to the gradual disregard of high kicks because of the higher risk of counterattack as well as the difficulty involved. Since the distance from the foot to the head of the opponent is greater than that to the trunk, high kicks give the opponent more time to react. In addition, high kicks require much more flexibility and balance. Finally, high kicking greatly exposes the kicker, significantly increasing vulnerability. As a result, the instep roundhouse-kick to the body was, from then on, the most-used kicking technique in taekwondo sparring. At the same time, with a rising level of kicking skill, athletes increasingly chose to develop effective counterattack techniques (see Chapter 6, pp. 123–6), which are safer for scoring points since athletes open their guards during an attack, thus opening themselves to counterattack. As a consequence, a defensive game style became a persistent tactic in many taekwondo matches during the 1980s and beyond.

The quest to join the Olympics: competition rule changes during the 1980s and 1990s

In order to gain admission to the Olympics as a demonstration sport in 1988, a variety of equipment modifications had to be introduced to qualify for the safety standards of the IOC. During the mid-1980s, shin guards, forearm guards, and headgear were gradually adopted as mandatory safety equipment. In addition, a soft mat, which was first used in Taiwan in 1985, was added to protect against head injuries as a result of falling.[14] In the beginning, the introduction of headgear was less intended as protection from direct blows but, rather, to prevent critical injuries to the back of the head as a result of falls to the floor, especially at events without padded courts. The first headgear in Korea, specifically made for taekwondo, had merely some light padding at the back of the head.

Weight divisions were reduced from ten to eight during the mid-1980s. This act and the introduction of new protective equipment was all done in anticipation of membership in the Olympic Games. The advancement in gear development was also partly a result of the growing worldwide market for taekwondo equipment. During the late 1980s and 1990s, this demand led to an increased participation by a number of newly founded companies, and eventually involvement by some leading sports firms such as Adidas.[15]

A key issue during the 1980s was the relatively low scoring results of taekwondo matches. For example, an end result of three or four points after a three round contest was considered a high scoring match. Points were only awarded when a technique was executed with considerable power upon impact, which was a very subjective judgment. After the 1988 Seoul Olympics, the low scores were perceived as a specific problem for audiences, because Olympic level spectator sport matches came to require more visible action and effect, such as point totals. As a result, corner judges were instructed to award more points. From that time on, blows with lighter impact were often awarded with points as well.[16] This decision led to much higher scores, although as a consequence, during the 1990s, many techniques were executed with the front leg, which is less powerful but faster.[17] Additionally, double-kicks, which are also relatively weak but fast, became very popular during the 1990s. As a general result, most kicking techniques used by athletes during that time, turned out to be some type of roundhouse-kick, with an almost universal disregard for high kicks and other complex techniques. Furthermore, a defense-oriented game style persisted throughout that period (see the discussion in Chapter 6, pp. 126–8) often resulting in lackluster matches that failed to attract spectators.

Comprehensive changes of competition rules after 2000

Before admission to the 2000 Sydney Olympics as an official sport, taekwondo faced a variety of accumulated problems. The IOC would only allow a limited number of taekwondo athletes to participate in the games. Consequently, the weight divisions for the Olympic Games were reduced to four each for males and females, and pre-qualification tournaments were required to limit the number of athletes. Moreover, during the 1990s, Korea was still the undisputed leader in international championships and she won the majority of gold medals. Therefore, the maximum participation of a nation was limited to four athletes, two male and two female, in order that no single country would seize all the gold medals and grossly distort the overall ranking of the Olympics.[18]

Another major concern of the 1990s, and early 2000s, was that many spectators perceived taekwondo as too boring to watch because of the often passive game style of athletes, and the almost exclusive use of a few variations of the roundhouse-kick to the body during matches; others questioned its scoring transparency.[19] Moreover, after a variety of high-level corruption scandals surrounding the taekwondo leadership, the establishment feared for taekwondo's continuing membership at the Olympic Games.[20] As a result, the World Taekwondo Federation progressively initiated a variety of major rule modifications after the new millennium.

A display of more spectacular techniques for the audience was necessary to tackle the general perception that taekwondo games were boring to watch. Therefore, multiple point scores for kicking techniques were re-introduced in stages to stimulate more high kicks as well as a diversification of kicking techniques. According to the last rule revision concerning multiple points (2009), spinning and turning kicks to the head were awarded four points, conventional high kicks with three, and successful back-turning kicks to the trunk with two points.

A ten-second 'stall rule' was introduced to punish passivity, and the fighting time of matches was reduced from three to two minute rounds to stimulate more action. The Korea Taekwondo Association also experimented with an octagonal ring which reconfigured the competition area to discourage athletes from going out of bounds or avoiding the fight.

These changes substantially influenced strategy, fighting style, and technique. In a smaller fighting arena, athletes are more forced to confront each other. In addition to the reduction of the size of the fighting court, an immediate point deduction for crossing the boundary with both feet was introduced to discourage running away from the fight, as well as to encourage aggressive, attack-oriented behavior. Moreover, among the major changes, a 'sudden death' rule was established in case of a tie score at the end of a match, with the intention of introducing a dramatic element for the audience.[21]

More protective gear was introduced as well. Athletes were required to use light protective gloves and a mouthpiece. In addition, light instep padding was occasionally allowed in some competitions. Consequently, the added protective gear helped to prevent injuries and thus allow the competition to proceed without interruption for the full duration of the match. Lastly, to meet certain IOC demands for scoring accuracy and transparency, an electronic scoring body protector (probably inspired by fencing) was gradually introduced. After several years use in national and international competitions, the electronic body protector was finally also introduced to the Olympic venue in the 2012 London Summer Games.

Improvement of scoring transparency

Scoring transparency and a perceived lack of objectivity are controversial issues in all sports and, especially, in combat sports. Until the late 1980s, the scoring results of taekwondo matches were released at the end of each match, similar to boxing. However, on countless occasions, many of the results and decisions by judges were often disputed in heated verbal arguments and sometimes even physical scuffles among coaches and ring officials.[22] The first attempt to improve scoring transparency was the visual display of results after each round by the center referee extending fingers to denote the score, or using cards with scoring numbers. This was gradually improved with the introduction of electronic scoreboards, first used at the World Championships in Seoul in 1985.

However, there was a problem with the method of aggregating points using the 'paper and pencil' scoring system. Prior to 1985, the individual corner judge score sheets were simply totaled up at the end of the match, and a single judge could distort the entire scoring outcome by awarding a disproportionally high number of points to one athlete. The introduction of the 'majority score' system in 1985, represented an improvement by requiring the round score to be the point-total awarded by a *majority* of the judges. For example, if four corner judges awarded two points to the blue competitor, and a fifth (the center referee) awarded eight points, the score would be two points for blue, because a majority of the five score sheets awarded blue no more than two points. The introduction of the 'majority score' policy could also explain why round scores may have dropped. Before 1985, score cards were simply totaled, sometimes yielding higher match results. Use of the majority score method, lowered scores because the overall round total was a rough average of the number of scoring judges.

The majority score innovation was designed to make scoring fairer, but a new flaw, peculiar to the majority score method of tabulation, appeared because paper and pencil scoring could not accommodate the requirement for judges to score at the same time, or within one second of the first judge to identify a point. "Competitors could randomly *gain* or *lose* points," as a result of the new method of point computation which used "a majority of judges' scores" as the criteria for points to be awarded. Because scores were not immediately published, but only handed to the senior referee seated at the head table for tabulation after each round, it was possible to win or lose points (and matches), "by chance"[23] (see sample Table 5.1).

However, this arithmetical fault in the scoring computation was clearly never recognized by the taekwondo establishment at the time. The problem lay in the fact that there was no way of knowing if the marks on any judge's scoring sheet correlated (within the one second time frame) with the marks on any other judge's scoring sheet. Points are awarded when a majority of judges score, but with the paper and pencil method, there is no way of determining the *time* of a score. During the 1990s, this flawed process eventually developed into a better system in which the judges' scoring would be indicated instantaneously on the

Table 5.1 Paper and pencil scoring limitations – losing points

	Kick/ punch 1	Kick/ punch 2	Kick/ punch 3	Kick/ punch 4	Judges' Score card	Actual score
Corner Judge 1	/		/	/	/// (3)	
Corner Judge 2		/	/	/	/// (3)	
Corner Judge 3	/		/		// (2)	
Corner Judge 4		/			/ (1)	
Center Referee (Judge 5)	/	/		/	/// (3)	
Jury's summary score (based upon the judges' score card results from column 5)					3	
Actual score (computed vertically)	/	/	/	/		4

Source: Courtesy of Gregory S. Kailian, *Sport Taekwondo Referee Primer*[24]

scoreboard by pressing a button.[25] With the innovation of electronic scoring, the computer software could determine how many corner judges scored a strike, as well as if the confirming judge/s pressed the button within one second of the initiating corner judge. Although subjective decision-making by judges continued to be an issue, it was thought the problem would eventually be eliminated with the introduction of a purely electronic protector scoring system without any human input in the process. Therefore, an electronic body protector, similar to those used in fencing, was designed, using a small radio transmitter instead of a cable (see Figure 5.1). Lee Chong Woo was again one of the driving forces behind these developments. He thought that a "scoring machine" would finally bring "peace" to the constant disputes and clashes of athletes and coaches regarding scoring results.[26]

In addition, another well-intended contribution to the enhancement of scoring transparency was the introduction of instant video replay, modeled on American football and tennis, and first introduced at the World Championships in Copenhagen in 2009. Although, somewhat controversial at first, the system is popular with coaches and seems to significantly enhance taekwondo's fair-scoring processes.[27]

Another issue, which was never openly addressed in a satisfactory manner, was that the referee corps at international tournaments was almost exclusively

Figure 5.1 First officially recognized electronic body protector by the WTF. Made by the LaJust company, introduced in 2006

Source: Courtesy of Peter Bolz

dominated by Koreans, or ethnic Koreans holding non-Korean-passports. Non-Korean athletes did not begin regularly winning gold medals until the referee corps began to be integrated with non-Korean referees, another requirement urged by the IOC (see Figure 5.2). Athletes and coaches complained for years about possible corruption and incompetence regarding scoring decisions in taekwondo matches. Ultimately, the final resolve to tackle the problem came from the top down because of a concern that taekwondo might lose its Olympic status. Many of the recent reforms were introduced after the World Taekwondo Federation and its leadership under Kim Un Yong (president of the WTF 1973–2004, and former IOC vice president, see also Chapter 2, p. 54) faced charges of corruption amid significant irregularities. In an interview in 2002, Lee Chong Woo admitted to being part of extensive game fixing in taekwondo tournaments and also at the Olympic Games in Sydney in 2000.[28] Later, he partly retracted his revelations, but his statements left great controversy and confusion, and the problem of manipulated taekwondo scoring became one of the foremost issues of the time.

Figure 5.2 The center referee
Source: Courtesy of Gregory S. Kailian

Unanticipated outcomes of recent competition rule changes

Although publishing scores instantly was a good solution to resolving the former scoring discrepancies, doing so affected the game in a tactical as well as a psychological way. When competitors did not know the score until the end of the fight, they fought fiercely to dominate the match. However, when electronic scoring made it possible to know the score at all times, scoring leaders only needed to stay ahead by one point to win. As soon as they were one point ahead, many delayed fighting in favor of 'defending' their lead by stalling, falling, feigning injury, running out of bounds, fixing equipment, and creating and accepting penalties to consume match time. Even though referees punished such behavior with warnings and point deductions, the problem was never completely resolved and remains an issue to this day.

In relation to points, scores to the trunk and head (but not the exposed areas of the face) are now determined by the electronic body protector and helmet (currently referred to as the PSS, 'Protector Scoring System'). However, many coaches and athletes are not satisfied with the functioning of the PSS, regardless of the system used. Nevertheless, it is pointed out, with some degree of irony that even if the PSS does not function as hoped, it is equally inefficient or "equally unfair,"[29] which is reluctantly preferred to the endless arguments and disputes that frequently erupted among coaches, athletes, and ring officials over points awarded by corner judges. Up to 2015, however, the scoring of multiple points for high kicks to the head and face and also punches to the chest continued to rely on human judgment. Many matches were now decided by high kicks motivated by the multiple points awarded, in contrast to body strikes that may, or may not, receive only one uncertain point awarded by the electronic protector. Currently, because many strikes to the head (and face) go unrewarded, the necessity for an expensive and technically immature PSS becomes questionable. In addition, (until the introduction of the e-helmet in 2015) unexpectedly, many coaches and athletes still preferred the reliable, subjective-corner-judge awarded points, to the uncertain, objective points earned by kicking the PSS. Some coaches felt that in close situations, human judgment was sometimes more reliable than the difficult-to-score-upon electronic protector. A number of sport taekwondo equipment manufacturers are actively developing electronic head gear systems to compete for the WTF market, but given the less than satisfactory performance of the PSS after many years of development and use, the introduction of a reliable electronic head gear system and PSS suite seems many years away. Moreover, taekwondo federations, schools, and clubs may now be forced to change their expensive PSS for the third time in a decade, as the WTF leans to adopt yet another new system.

In the years immediately prior to 2015, many of sport taekwondo matches resembled the light-contact point matches of certain karate styles.[30] Tournament judges were instructed to award points, when *any* part of the foot touched the opponent's head.[31] This criterion provided more transparency and was also compatible with the newly introduced video replay innovation in which coaches could challenge decisions by judges and referees. However, front leg kicks, which are relatively weak but the easiest to execute, were generally favored. In addition, the PSS tended to easily give points for front leg side- or push-kicks to the body, a simple, peculiar flaw in the system. As a result, many athletes tend to over-rely on kicking techniques with the front leg to the body and face. And, it seems there are a considerable number of athletes and coaches whose primary concerns are to exploit the rules and shortcomings of the PSS, instead of engaging in proper fights to test the superiority of skills, tactics, and techniques. Some would call this 'strategy,' but it could also be considered an unsportsmanlike manipulation of the game to gain victory at all costs.

Although it is clear that high kicks in tournaments are more often used than in the past, a comparison in the frequency of injuries is difficult because of a lack of available, reliable data.[32] A further general problem of the new rules is that the complexity of the scoring system makes it very difficult for ordinary spectators to follow and comprehend the flow and results of a match.

As a result of these recent developments, the KTA, which always had slightly different rules than the WTF, was forced to adapt to WTF rules, because only a few Korean athletes were able to win any medals during international championships in the last decade. The KTA leaders perceived this as necessary, even though they had arguably a superior system in regards to rules, the PSS, and the octagon ring.

The competition system of the International Taekwondo Federation (ITF)

Choi Hong Hi founded his International Taekwondo Federation in 1966, after his break with the KTA. In contrast to the full-contact-based competition style of the KTA, which was later internationally promoted by the WTF, Choi's ITF tournaments closely resembled Japanese karate competitions. The ITF kept the principle format of the All Japan Karate Championship, introduced by the Japan Karate Association, and divided tournaments into two main events: patterns and sparring. Moreover, the sparring competitions continued the traditional karate format of non-contact engagements, which allowed fist strikes to the head. Nowadays, modern ITF tournaments feature patterns, sparring, self-defense routines, breaking, and acrobatic breaking contests, also called "Special Technique" events.

In modern tournaments, the sparring event applies the use of lightly padded hand and foot protectors, which are similar to Jhoon Rhee's 'Safe-T equipment' (first developed around 1969) to make sparring safer, since injuries often occur when athletes accidentally really strike the opponent. Moreover, light padding allows light-contact matches. However, full-contact strikes, defined as strikes with "excessive contact," can lead to point deductions, or even disqualification, if the opponent is unable to continue the fight as a result of an excessively strong blow. In ITF scoring rules, one to five points are awarded depending on the technique.[33] As a result, the rules are as complicated as modern WTF competition rules. Moreover, the use of non-contact, or light-contact rules, leads generally to even more disputes regarding scoring decisions than in full-contact matches. The challenge in full-contact matches is usually to determine if a strike was powerful enough to constitute a point. In non- and light-contact matches the opposite dilemma occurs; referees have to decide if strikes were executed with too much force, therefore constituting illegal blows. In addition, in light- and non-contact tournaments, judges have to conclude if a strike could in fact have been executed with enough force to characterize a technique worthy of rewarding a point.

In comparison to WTF full-contact competitions, ITF competitions still resemble traditional karate tournaments in terms of technique and spirit. ITF sparring technique could not evolve as much as WTF sparring, because of the continuing use of light-contact rules in addition to an equal emphasis on forms contents during these competitions. As a result, in ITF taekwondo and traditional karate, the biomechanical execution of techniques corresponds much more between forms and sparring than in WTF taekwondo.

Safety considerations in taekwondo sparring in comparison to other combat sports

In all fighting systems, the rules are a compromise between the safety of the athletes and realism in combat. In order to create a safe sparring environment for training and competition, all modern sparring systems forbid certain techniques, such as strikes to the groin, head butting, biting, or attacking an opponent's eyes and ears. However, intentional punches to the head and face of the opponent constitute a particular problem since they are relatively easily executed and able to inflict great damage. They tend to be the most frequently used and most effective of self-defense striking techniques. Naturally, stand-up kicking techniques to the head can do even greater harm, but they are much less frequent and, by far, more difficult to execute than punches.[34]

In order to create a safe sparring environment for training and competition in martial arts, there are essentially three options. The first choice is to restrict the use of full force when striking, as in traditional non-contact karate and also the later styles of light-contact karate and ITF taekwondo. A second option is to introduce boxing gloves in full-contact sparring, which reduces open cut wounds and, arguably, head trauma; a good example would be the introduction of lightly padded gloves in the mixed martial arts' Ultimate Fighting Championships (UFC). During the first tournaments in the 1990s, bare knuckle fighting resulted in excessively bloody injuries which forced the promoters to introduce some minimal safety measures in the form of light gloves. The third and final alternative is to exclude hand strikes to the head altogether, such as in WTF taekwondo and *Kyokushin* karate. Since full-contact sparring without the use of boxing gloves leads to too many injuries and is too dangerous, and also since early taekwondo leaders either rejected or did not consider the idea of using boxing gloves, they were necessarily led to the conclusion that punches to the head and face must be banned under taekwondo sparring rules.[35] To date, there is no viable head protector which could be used as an alternative to the use of boxing gloves, allowing full force bare knuckle strikes to the head. Table 5.2 illustrates, rough and simplified, the use of rules and protective equipment in the major martial arts striking systems.

Summary

The initial choice of the full-contact sparring arrangement with a sporting character was very controversial among early Korean taekwondo leaders, later leading to a split of taekwondo into different organizations. As discussed in

Table 5.2 The use of protective equipment in combat sports

Name of art	Introduced	Protector used	System	Permitted striking techniques
Modern Western Boxing	1743	**Boxing gloves.**	Full-contact	Only fists.
Thai-boxing (modern form)	1920s	**Boxing gloves.**	Full-contact	Fists, legs, knees, and elbows. Grappling and some throwing.
Karate (traditional)	1957 First All Japan Karate Championship	Originally none.	**Non-contact**	Fists, legs, knees, and elbows. Some throwing.
Taekwondo (WTF style)	1963	Originally only a body protector.	Full-contact	Legs and fists. **Exclusion of hand strikes to the head.**
Kyokushin Karate	1969 First Open *Kyokushin* Full-contact Karate Tournament	None.	Full-contact	Legs, fists, knees, and elbows. **Exclusion of hand strikes to the head.**
Ultimate Fighting Competition (UFC mixed martial arts)	1993	Originally none, but had to introduce **light gloves** due to frequent and serious injuries.	Full-contact	Fists, legs, knees, and elbows. Grappling, throwing, and ground fighting.
K-1 kick-boxing	1993	**Boxing gloves.**	Full-contact	Fists, legs, and knees.

Chapter 2, the rise of full-contact sport taekwondo was ultimately the result of political decisions. The traditional leaders, who saw taekwondo as first and foremost a martial art, most notably Choi Hong Hi, lost their influence in Korea due to political situations and a modern-minded, new order that wanted to promote taekwondo as a combat sport. Choi's downfall was tied to his animosity towards the Park Chung Hee regime and his numerous disagreements with other taekwondo leaders. On the other hand, as a sport, taekwondo fitted the general ideology of the regime, which used physical education as a form of national anti-Communism, and competitive sport to improve its international standing as a rising nation. Lee Chong Woo in particular was instrumental in the development and promotion of full-contact sport taekwondo. He was responsible for the practical implementation of technical issues, while Kim Un Yong was in charge of political lobbying and the promotion of taekwondo as an international sport and ultimately its admission into the Olympics.

Many of the early sparring rules and regulations during the first competitions were a replica of those already used in Japanese JKA, non-contact karate tournaments. For instance, the competition area and format were an imitation of the preceding karate format at the All Japan Karate Championships, which in turn were judo and kendo-based. The difference with traditional mainstream karate was that taekwondo leaders opted for full-contact sparring instead of continuing the traditional non-contact method. In choosing the original rules, most leaders, both old and new, seemed to agree that the use of boxing gloves was not an option, because of the fear that it would impair combat realism in sparring; in addition, there existed no viable headgear. Therefore, punches to the head in full-contact sparring had to be necessarily excluded from the arsenal of permitted strikes as a result of frequent injuries. This essential rule, in combination with the other selected regulations, shaped taekwondo into a combat sport that almost exclusively uses foot techniques in sparring.

Through changes in scoring rules and other regulations, the taekwondo establishment tried to influence the direction of the game throughout its history, with the goal of making sport taekwondo competition more interesting for spectators to watch and/or to correct perceived deficiencies. Minor revisions happened almost on a yearly basis, but there were several periods of especially far-reaching amendments which contributed significantly to changes in technique, although the anticipated outcome did not always materialize. The introduction of new and improved equipment occasionally altered the scoring behavior of corner judges. Furthermore, rule and regulation modifications were sometimes related to improvements in protective equipment and scoring tools. Because of a large-scale expansion of competitions and an increasing number of athletes, taekwondo was able to develop many new techniques and sparring methods over time that made it distinctive from karate. It eventually became a completely new martial sport, and today taekwondo probably greatly exceeds karate in terms of international membership and popularity.

Over the years, various new game modifications have been made, but the ongoing equipment modifications, as well as revisions to rules, scoring, and game settings are especially far-reaching and significant. They might influence the continuing popularity of taekwondo, its ongoing membership in the Olympics, and whether or not it can compete for increased membership and audience with the mixed martial arts.

The focus of this chapter was an examination and analysis of the origins and transformation of taekwondo's protective equipment, competition rules, and regulations. The next chapter will discuss some of the impact these changes have had on fighting techniques. The primary focus is on the evolution of kicking techniques, since kicking is the favored feature of taekwondo sparring.

Notes

1 Lee Chong Woo draws many comparisons to boxing, but does not mention the prior Japanese non-contact competition format, which had much more influence than boxing. See Yook, "Kukkiwon Vice President Chong Woo Lee's shocking confession of Olympic competition result manipulation!", p. 309.
2 See World Taekwondo Federation, *Competition rules and interpretation*.
3 Kang, and Lee, *A modern history of taekwondo*, pp. 116–7; email correspondence with Ch'oe Yŏng-nyŏl, October 28, 2011. Ch'oe, a member of *Jido Kwan*, was the leading heavy-weight fighter during the 1960s.
4 Compare with the karate game settings in Nishiyama, and Brown, *Karate – The art of "empty hand" fighting*, pp. 187–8.
5 Capener, "Problems in the identity and philosophy of *t'aegwondo* and their historical causes," p. 85.
6 Nishiyama, and Brown, *Karate – The art of "empty hand" fighting*, p. 188. In addition, there existed "three-blow matches" and "winner by points matches."
7 Kim, "A study on how the Taekwondo games rules can [have] influence on the changes of game skills [sic]," p. 24.
8 Kim Sei Hyeok, personal interview, March 23, 2010; Kang, and Lee, *A modern history of taekwondo*, p. 127.
9 The improved *hogu* was first used in 1975.
10 Ko Eui Min, personal interview, January 13, 2010; Kang, and Lee, *A modern history of taekwondo*, p. 120.
11 Kang, and Lee, *A modern history of taekwondo*, p. 125; Kim, "A study on how the taekwondo games rules can [have] influence on the changes of game skills [sic]," p. 29.
12 Eugen Nefedow, telephone interview, October 20, 2013. Nefedow placed second in the -84 kg division during this tournament.
13 See World Taekwondo Federation, "Competition rules and interpretation."
14 Kang, and Lee, *A modern history of taekwondo*, 129.
15 Ibid, p. 129.
16 Steven D. Capener, personal interview, January 13, 2011.
17 Kim, "The analysis of the frequency of attempts and the success ratio according to the attacking and bal-no-rim patterns of taekwondo patterns [sic]," p. 35; see also Chapter 6, pp. 134–6.
18 Steven D. Capener, personal interview, January 13, 2011.
19 See Yook, "Kukkiwon Vice President Chong Woo Lee's shocking confession of Olympic competition result manipulation!", pp. 296–8.
20 Gillis, *A killing art – The untold history of tae kwon do*, pp. 193–201.
21 Steven D. Capener, personal interview, January 13, 2011. Capener was actively involved in these rule revisions. See also World Taekwondo Federation, *Rules and interpretations* (last modified January 1, 2015).

22 See also Kailian, *Sport taekwondo referee primer*, pp. 97–109.
23 Ibid, Appendix A, pp. 429–33.
24 Reprint of table with the permission of Gregory S. Kailian. See, ibid, Appendix A, p. 433. For the analysis of "gaining points," see Appendix A (pp. 429–33) of Kailian's book, which discusses the problem in detail.
25 Kang, and Lee, *A modern history of taekwondo*, pp. 132–5.
26 As cited in Yook, "Kukkiwon Vice President Chong Woo Lee's shocking confession of Olympic competition result manipulation!", p. 298; see also "History of Jidokwan," (n.d.). [Retrieved from www.taekwondojidokwan.com/page6.html].
27 Kailian, *Sport taekwondo referee primer*, pp. 50–6.
28 As cited in Yook, "Kukkiwon Vice President Chong Woo Lee's shocking confession of Olympic competition result manipulation!", pp. 295–8.
29 Kailian, *Sport taekwondo referee primer*, pp. 44–8.
30 See for example the final game of the 2011 World Championships in the male 58 kg division on YouTube (Filimonov [Poster], 2011 WTF World Taekwondo Championships male 58kg final competition [Video], [May 3, 2011]. [Retrieved from www.youtube.com/watch?v=YjPkQ2OrGmg].
31 See World Taekwondo Federation, *Rules and interpretations* (modified July 14, 2013). However, a clear definition was taken out in the amendment of July 4, 2014.
32 Terry L. DeFreitas, and Jae-ok Koh, "Baseline concussion testing in youth taekwondo sparring participants at the 2013 Canada Open: A pilot project" (paper presented at The 4th International Symposium for Taekwondo Studies, Puebla, July 16–17, 2013), see abstract pp. 50–1; Jae-ok Koh, and Janice C. Dunn, "Effects of competition rule changes on incidence of head kicks and possible concussions at the 2011 World Taekwondo Championships" (paper presented at The 4th International Symposium for Taekwondo Studies, Puebla, July, 16–17, 2013), see abstract pp. 48–9.
33 International Taekwon-Do Federation, *ITF tournament rules*, pp. 22–4. After Choi Hong Hi's death in 2002, the ITF splintered into different organizations. These rules were issued by the North Korea supported ITF. Its president is Chang Ung, who is an IOC member from North Korea.
34 Only in taekwondo sparring are kicking techniques more frequently used than punches because of its particular rules.
35 The same reason is also cited in the case of *Kyokushin* karate. See 'Kyokushin kaikan,' (August, 2007). [Retrieved from http://encyclopedia.thefreedictionary.com/Kyokushin+kaikan].

Bibliography

Capener, Steven D. "Problems in the identity and philosophy of *t'aegwondo* and their historical causes." *Korea Journal*, 35, 4 (1995): 80–94. [Retrieved from www.eagletkd.com/images/STUDENT%20FORUM%20from%20Korea%0Journal.pdf].
Gillis, Alex. *A killing art – The untold history of Tae Kwon Do*. Toronto: ECW Press, 2008.
International Taekwon-Do Federation. *ITF tournament rules*. September, 2011. [Retrieved from www.itftkd.org/?Content=TournamentRules].
Kailian, Gregory S. *Sport taekwondo referee primer*. Pennsylvania: Word Association Publishers, 2010.
Kang, Won Shik, and Lee Kyong Myong [Kang Wŏn-sik, Yi kyŏng-myŏng] (강원식, 이경명). 태권도 現代 史 *A modern history of taekwondo* [English title from the internet]. Seoul: Pokyŏng Munhwasa, 1999. [Parts published in English at www.martialartsresource.com/anonftp/pub/the_dojang/digests/history.html].
[Kim Chong-min] (김종민). 태권도 규칙이 경기기술의 변화에 미치는 영향에 대한 연구 "A study on how the taekwondo games rules can [have] influence on the changes

of game skills [sic]." Unpublished master's thesis, Kyung Hee University, 2002. [In Korean only].

Kim, Sei Hyeok [Kim Se-hyŏk] (김세혁). 태권도 경기의 공격 및 발놀림 유형에 따른 시도횟수와 성공도 분석 "The analysis of the frequency of attempts and the success ratio according to the attacking and bal-no-rim patterns of taekwondo patterns [sic]." Unpublished master's thesis, Inha University, 1993. [In Korean only].

Nishiyama, Hidetaka, and Richard C. Brown. *Karate – The art of "empty hand" fighting*. Vermont and Tokyo: Charles E. Tuttle Company, 1960.

World Taekwondo Federation. *Competition rules and interpretation*. Seongnam: World Taekwondo Federation, last modified 2015, January 1.

Yook, Sung-chul [Yuk Sŏng-ch'ŏl] (육성철). 이종우 국기원 부원장의 '태권도 과거'충격적 고백! "Kukkiwon Vice President Chong Woo Lee's shocking confession of Olympic competition result manipulation!". Trans. Lee Soo Han. *Shin Dong-A*, (2002, April). 290–311. [Retrieved from http://tkdreform.com/yook_article.pdf].

6 The evolution of sparring technique

In spite of its status an official Olympic sport, taekwondo lacks any in-depth studies regarding its technical evolution as a combat sport. Moreover, any uniform vocabulary and definitions regarding kicking techniques in sparring are absent, as well. Since taekwondo sparring and tournaments originate from Korea, Korean athletes have enjoyed a historical, as well as numerical advantage. Korea simply outnumbered other countries in terms of active athletes, who also enjoyed greater experience. As a result, Korean athletes dominated international tournaments until recently, and the innovation of new skills happened primarily in Korea. As this study dismisses claims that taekwondo is an offspring of *t'aekkyŏn* or other early Korean martial arts, it treats the evolution of technique from early karate to present day taekwondo as a consecutive development. This chapter demonstrates how taekwondo technique transformed gradually from karate technique, and how taekwondo eventually progressed in becoming a distinctive martial art.

The selected rules and other specific regulations in taekwondo sparring promoted the development of kicking techniques more than in any other martial art. Therefore, this chapter also provides a 'history of kicking techniques,' since modern taekwondo sparring mostly consists of kicking.

Kicking techniques in early karate and taekwondo

Despite frequent depiction in popular martial arts movies, the use of high and flying kicks is a very recent development. Early Chinese martial arts manuals show exclusively a few types of low and front-kicks to the trunk. In Okinawan karate, which was an offshoot of early Chinese martial arts, the use of foot techniques was also very limited. In his first publications during the 1920s, Funakoshi Gichin showed only a front-kick to the mid-section of the body.[1] In subsequent karate manuals, Motobu Chōki demonstrated kicking techniques in a few photographs of low front- and side-kicks in 1926 and 1932.[2] Other notable karate instructors who ventured to Japan during that time, such as Mabuni Kenwa, also only displayed front-kicks in their publications.[3] As its name implies, original Okinawan karate focused on hand techniques.

However, with karate's introduction to Japan from Okinawa, young Japanese students started to incorporate new training ideas. The university clubs, which were often *Shōtōkan* clubs established by Funakoshi, played a significant role in karate's swift proliferation and transformation. However, Funakoshi was not pleased with the direction and development that karate took during that time, and he disagreed with many of the modernizations. He principally opposed the introduction of a sports character to karate training and did not value free sparring as an appropriate training activity. In contrast, the Japanese youth longed for some competitive characteristics that they were accustomed to from judo and kendo. Therefore, Funakoshi reluctantly approved the inclusion of '*jiyū kumite*' (自由組手 'free sparring')[4] to the training routine of karate by the mid-1930s.[5] Free sparring stimulated the development of new techniques, similar to taekwondo's evolution, which essentially began in the 1960s. High kicks in karate, however, did not become fashionable until sparring rules prohibited the use of low kicks to the groin.[6] Funakoshi stated: "No other martial art has developed foot techniques (*ashiwaza*) to the high degree of refinement that they found in karate. Indeed, foot techniques are a major strength of karate."[7] Funakoshi's third son, Funakoshi Gigō, managed mostly the daily training routines of the *Shōtōkan* clubs by the 1930s, because of Funakoshi's advanced age. Consequently, Funakoshi Gigō is credited with introducing many modernizations to karate. Some also claim that Funakoshi Gigō developed a few of the modern kicking techniques, such as the roundhouse-kick, and they credit him as being one of the first to use high kicks in sparring.

During the 1930s, karate in Japan transformed into a very distinctive art from the original Okinawan teachings. By that time, a number of Koreans attended classes in Japan, and subsequently introduced karate to Korea.

The existing karate and taekwondo literature of the 1950s and 1960s, generally displays a similar range of kicking techniques. Table 6.1 demonstrates some of the differences in range of technique:

Important features of these kicking techniques

- **Front-kick/side-kick/roundhouse-kick/back-kick**: They represent the original, basic striking techniques with the feet in Japanese karate. The roundhouse-kick and back-kick were likely invented during the 1930s, in Japan, and did not exist in the original Okinawan teachings. The roundhouse-kick is not mentioned by Funakoshi in 1935, yet.
- **Front-kick/push-kick**: The push-kick (described as *thrust*-kick) is basically a variation of the front-kick (described as *snap*-kick). Not all authors distinguish between them.
- **Crescent-kick**: Both variations (inside-out/outside-in) were considered blocking techniques and not striking techniques in traditional karate and early taekwondo.
- **Front-rising-kick/side-rising-kick**: The predecessor of the modern axe-kick, the front-rising-kick was most likely used only for stretching and warming-up at that time. The side-rising-kick was never regarded as a real kicking technique, but merely a means for stretching.

Table 6.1 Samples of kicking techniques in early karate and taekwondo manuals

Basic kicks (no jump- or low-kicks) as illustrated in these authors' respective manuals								
Kicking techniques:*	Funakoshi Gichin	Choi Hong Hi	Hwang Kee	Nishiyama Hidetaka	Choi Hong Hi	Yi Kyo-yun	Cho Henry	Son Duk Sung
	1935	1957	1958	1958	1960	1965	1965	1968	1968
Front-kick	O	O	O	O	O	O	O	O	O
Side-kick	O	O	O	O	O	O	O	O	O
Roundhouse-kick		O	O	O	O	O	O	O	O
Back-kick	O	O	O	O	O	O	O	O	
Push-kick (or *thrust*-kick)			O		O	O		O	
Crescent-kick	O	O	O	O	O	O		O	
Front-rising-kick			O	O	O	O		O	O
Side-rising-kick			O	O	O	O		O	O
Spinning-back-kick						O	O	O	
Hook-kick								O	

Note:
* The authors use a variety of different names for the respective kicking techniques. The above terms are commonly used, modern names.

- **Snap-kick/thrust-kick**: Some of the authors, especially Nishiyama and Cho, demonstrate several variations of the front-, side-, and roundhouse-kicks. A common differentiation is made between a '*snap*' and '*thrust*' kick.
- **Spinning-back-kick/hook-kick**: The spinning-back-kick is illustrated first in 1965.[8] Cho describes the hook-kick as a variation of the spinning-back-kick.[9]
- **Roundhouse-kick**: The roundhouse-kick was only executed with the ball of the foot, not with the instep, yet.
- Hwang also displays a self-styled kick that he calls '*bit*-kick' ('*bit*' implies 'change of direction,' or 'turn slightly'). He describes it as a between a front- and roundhouse-kick.
- All of the kicks were used only as attack kicks, or in the sequence 'block and then counter-attack.' No direct counterattack kicks existed yet.
- **Jump kicks**: Nishiyama and Funakoshi show only the front- and side-kicks as jump kicks. Some of the Koreans also display the roundhouse-kick as a jump kick.[10] Funakoshi already mentions several jump kicks in 1935. Choi also mentioned several additional jump kicks.
- **Low kicks**: Almost all authors illustrate a few low kicks, but Nishiyama shows the greatest variety. Generally, the Japanese seemed to have used more low kicks than the Koreans.
- Most of these kicking techniques had to be modified for application in full-contact sparring.

Modification and innovation of techniques in early taekwondo full-contact sparring

In traditional karate and taekwondo, force projection behind a strike is usually not a priority, since during most exercises, such as forms training, self-defense drills, and non-contact sparring, practitioners do not engage in contact with the target. The only time a strike actually hits a target, is when breaking boards, roofing tiles, or cement blocks. In addition, traditional *makiwara* drills (knuckle toughening by punching wooden boards and bricks wrapped in straw or rope) require some degree of force upon impact. Even though, power was very much emphasized during that time, and techniques were executed with strength, most traditional martial arts techniques lacked the efficient use of force projection behind a strike for application in full-contact sparring.

With the introduction of full-contact sparring in taekwondo, the biomechanical execution of punches and kicking techniques had to be modified since scoring rules in full-contact sparring require a strong impact on the target (the opponent). In full-contact sparring, the goal of the fighter is to project the maximum body weight behind a strike; combined with speed, to gain maximum force upon impact. The impact force is not the result of some magical *ki*-forces (氣), but of simple laws of physics.

Newton's Second Law of Motion states that force is the product of mass times acceleration (F = ma). Therefore, athletes can increase their impact force by either projecting more mass (their body weight) behind a strike, or by increasing the acceleration of a technique.[11] Heavier and faster athletes potentially deliver stronger blows than lighter, slower ones. Athletes can increase their muscle mass through weight training to gain more strength and weight, or they can improve their speed to develop a stronger strike. In addition, athletes can also achieve stronger strikes by improving their technique. Improved technique and timing translates into the ability to maximize the projection of one's body weight or mass behind a punch or kick. Projection of body weight toward the target is the key to efficient technique. Therefore, with the introduction of full-contact sparring, punches, kicking techniques, and the stances of early taekwondo athletes had to progressively adjust to the new system.

Early taekwondo sparring

Early taekwondo matches focused more on power and less on speed. Former heavy weight champion Ch'oe Yŏng-nyŏl recalled that during the first tournaments of the 1960s, "the front-kick was the most often used technique."[12] Ko Eui Min, the Korean national team head coach for the 1975 and 1977 World Championships, also stated that athletes mostly used front-kicks, blocks, and punches during sparring.[13] In addition, the main characteristics of the 1960's taekwondo tournaments were power and strength. Side- and roundhouse-kicks were lesser used techniques.[14] According to Kim Sei Hyeok, athletes did not use any flexible steps during the first tournaments of the 1960s. Moreover, their wide stances and strikes resembled karate technique, entirely.[15]

The development of short stances and a variety of agile steps

With an increasing number of athletes and tournaments came a growing necessity to develop new skills to outwit and beat rivals. After almost a decade of competition, the techniques and skill of athletes started transforming rapidly toward the end of the 1960s. During that time, shorter and flexible stances and various 'steps' were introduced to sparring. The weight concentration in these stances also became more forward directed similar to other full-contact sports. For instance, Ko Eui Min, who was one of the leading sparring instructors at that time, incorporated such stances and steps modeled after boxing. Ko illustrated the existing steps of the early and mid-1970s in his publication titled, *Taekwondo competition* (1980),[16] the first modern taekwondo sparring manual. According to Ko, the notes (not the photographs) for the steps displayed in this book, date back to the early 1970s; feinting motions were only developed sometime later.[17] The relatively large size of the fighting arena, and the efforts by athletes to keep away from strikes and blows executed with full force, played a decisive factor in this progression. As a consequence of these developments, sparring became much more dynamic. In accordance, the importance of speed during matches increased at the expense of power.

The adjustment of the roundhouse-kick to full-contact sparring

A newly introduced scoring rule in full-contact sparring triggered a major change in the customary, technical execution of the roundhouse-kick, which progressed over time to become the most frequently used kicking technique in taekwondo sparring. According to Kim Sei Hyeok,[18] during the early years of competition, no points were awarded for instep roundhouse-kicks to the trunk. This was reversed with a rule amendment in 1967. In traditional karate and early taekwondo, the contact point with the target was the ball of the foot, which is useful when breaking boards but highly impractical for full-contact sparring (see Figure 6.1).

There is a high possibility of injuring one's toes when executing a roundhouse-kick with the ball of the foot in full-contact sparring. This can happen, especially, when the opponent blocks the kick. Moreover, when kicking with the ball of the foot, the calf muscles are tightened up, which hinders a relaxed and swift execution of the kicking motion. Additionally, it also slows down a follow-up or combination kick. Roundhouse kicking with the ball of the foot creates a rotational configuration, which inhibits the reciprocal motion which is necessary for forward moving attacks.

In contrast, for effortless use in full-contact sparring, the instep as the contact area of the foot with the target is much more suitable (see Figure 6.2). The use of the instep allows for a faster and more natural execution of the roundhouse-kick, especially, when carried out with a strong 'snap' or 'whipping' motion. Following the introduction of a new and improved body protector during the mid-1970s, the use of the instep roundhouse-kick became widely popular. The old body protectors made with bamboo-stick inserts were not really suited for the use of the instep

120 *The evolution of sparring technique*

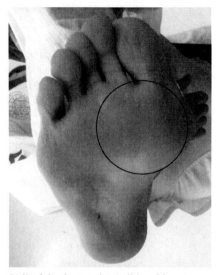 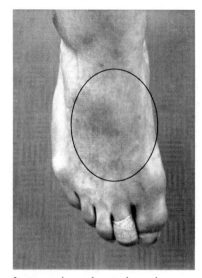

Ball of the foot, as in traditional karate and early taekwondo

Instep, as in modern taekwondo

Figure 6.1 The contact area of the roundhouse-kick
Source: Courtesy of Michael Han

Figure 6.2 The instep roundhouse-kick
Source: Courtesy of Peter Bolz

roundhouse-kick yet, because of the hard impact and potential for injury. The new protectors had an *ethafoam* filling, which is comparably soft and ideal for hitting with the instep. In addition, over time, the 'bang' sound when kicking the body protector with the instep became synonymous with the execution of a successful scoring technique; the 'snap' instep roundhouse-kick was particularly suited for this effect.[19] Moreover, using the instep allows multiple and repetitive attacks. The instep roundhouse-kick is biomechanically much more suited for full-contact sparring than the traditional roundhouse-kick, executed with the ball of the foot. In fact, all full-contact competition systems use the roundhouse-kick in a similar way.

The general effect of rules combined with the type of fighting arena on kicking techniques: power versus speed

During the first decade of competition in the 1960s, power was the main emphasis during sparring, and the roundhouse-kick was executed in the traditional manner of a wide, round circle, hence its name. This changed over time, as a variety of footwork techniques were developed, and speed in sparring gained greater importance. As a result, instead of kicking in a wide circle, the kick became straighter and more forward, or obliquely, directed (see Figure 6.3). A modified version of the roundhouse-kick, between a front- and roundhouse-kick, also became very popular in sparring during the late 1960s. This kicking technique is also straight, forward directed and relatively easy to execute.[20]

The necessary phenomenon of using straighter kicking techniques can be further explained: if we compare a basic roundhouse-kick (out of a basic stance and not in a changing fight situation) currently used in taekwondo and Thai-boxing, we can clearly see the preferences and difference favored by both systems. In modern taekwondo, the roundhouse-kick is usually executed by lifting the knee straight in front toward the target. The hip is turned late, while extending the lower part of the leg with a 'snap' motion. The snap gives extra speed and acceleration. The loud 'bang' sounds when hitting the body protector this way became an indicator for a point and is partly a product of the snap.

This is in sharp contrast to Thai-boxing, where the roundhouse-kick is executed mostly in a wide swinging circle. In this regard, the roundhouse-kick of early taekwondo and karate looked rather similar to the Thai-boxing roundhouse-kick. In Thai-boxing, the snap is also much less pronounced when executing a roundhouse-kick. In addition, because of the wide, round motion, the extra swing allows greater projection of the bodyweight toward the target, which makes the kick more powerful. The main goal in Thai-boxing is to project maximum force toward the target because the opponent mostly blocks or covers and only sometimes moves out of the way (which is often impossible when standing close to the ropes). The Thai kick is also usually kicked with the shin instead of the instep, because the distance to the opponent is frequently shorter, especially when kicking after a punch. Power is clearly favored over speed.

This is also reflected in the choice of the preferred target during practice. In Thai-boxing training, power kicks are mostly trained on heavy targets and the

122 The evolution of sparring technique

Traditional roundhouse-kick
(wide swinging motion)

Modern roundhouse-kick
(straight forward motion, the hip is turned late, only after a straight knee lift)

Figure 6.3 The evolution of the roundhouse-kick
Source: Courtesy of Michael Han

heavy bag. On the other hand, in taekwondo, fast snap kicks are mostly practiced against (coaching) *mit*-targets (flexible, leather paddles), which are the best tools for speed training; these devices are absent in Thai-boxing training.

Taekwondo kicks have adjusted to a speed game within a large competition area without any physical restraints, not to a power game in close confinement. This is also the reason why many taekwondo kicks do not work in a Thai-boxing setting, and vice versa. Many of the kicks developed in taekwondo have not been developed, nor could they develop, in Thai-boxing.

A similar development happened over time with all kicking techniques; powerful, wide swinging motions were naturally substituted with straighter and faster movements in order to accrue as many points as possible in a round (see Figure 6.4). A shorter way to the target is faster, albeit at the expense of power. As a consequence of the shift from power to speed, athletes had to adjust to the new circumstances. Once they could no longer score with their conventional techniques, they had to adapt a new style of kicking.

The evolution of sparring technique 123

Traditionally frequently used back-kick (turn-side-kick, wide swinging motion)

Modern back-kick (narrow, straight backward motion)

Figure 6.4 The evolution of the back-kick
Source: Courtesy of Michael Han

The introduction of direct counterattack kicks

The size of a taekwondo competition court, 8 × 8 meters, is rather large compared to a square boxing ring, which ranges from 5.5 to a maximum of 7.5 meters (similar dimensions are used in kick- and Thai-boxing). According to K-1 ring size regulations, a 7.2 × 7.2 meter ring is standard, which is rather small considering the size of the athletes. Training rings in gyms used in many of these martial arts are often as small as 4 × 4 meters.[21] Yet, commercial taekwondo has been taught in many small gymnasiums as well. However, most taekwondo teams in Korea that engaged in competitions and spearheaded the technical development of taekwondo have been training mostly in large public school or university gyms. As a result, the large size of the competition area and the gymnasiums had a strong influence on training and technique.

The relatively large fighting arena in taekwondo and the lack of any physical constraints (for instance, ropes) caused, in combination with the rules, several fundamental tendencies in the use of sparring technique and tactics. Above all, speed emerged as being more important than power, because athletes needed to cross a longer distance to hit a fast stepping opponent in a fairly large fighting area. Moreover, since the fighting area did not have any physical restrictions, blocks and body cover against attacking opponents could be frequently neglected;

instead, athletes were able to avoid blows by simply moving out of the way, or as a last resort, leaving the fighting area, or diving to the floor. Moreover, in early taekwondo sparring, padded equipment was limited to the body protector only; padding gear to provide cover, such as boxing gloves, or protectors to soften the impact of blows, was typically not applied. For instance, shin and forearm guards were not permitted in most WTF sanctioned international competitions until the early 1980s. As a consequence, blocking in early taekwondo matches caused many bruises and injuries. These combined circumstances contributed almost certainly to the tendency to avoid an attacker's strikes.

As a result, some athletes started spontaneously executing techniques almost at once, without applying blocks. They intuitively grasped that it was possible to skip the sequence of a block as used in traditional taekwondo and karate; instead, counterattacking directly with a kick.[22] During such clashes, the force of the forward moving attacker collides with the force of the counterattacking defender, which increases the energy of the impact. This situation produces the strongest blows in sport taekwondo and partially explains the majority of knockouts, especially from kicks to the head. According to Ko Eui Min, counter-attack kicks (or counter kicks) appeared first in sparring around the late 1960s and early 1970s, in the form of counter back-kicks (see Figure 6.5).[23] This was no coincidence,

Figure 6.5 The counter back-kick against a roundhouse-kick attack
Source: Courtesy of Peter Bolz

because the back-kick is the natural counterattack motion for the newly introduced (at that time) instep roundhouse-kick. In contrast, the back-kick, as a counterattack, is almost impossible to execute against straight kicking techniques, such as front-, push-, and side-kicks. But these techniques were, prior to the introduction of the instep roundhouse-kick, the most popular kicking techniques in sparring.

The counter back-kick had likely been executed in a round, circle-like, back-spinning motion first, which essentially constituted a modified side-kick. This movement is easier to adapt than a straight motion, and most beginners make the mistake of executing the back-kick this way. Moreover, the back-kick was often called by authors at that time, '*twi-dora-yŏp-ch'agi*' ('back-turn-side-kick'), or '*mom-dora-yŏp-ch'agi*' ('body-turn side-kick'); although, some of them also distinguished between a 'back-side-kick' and a conventional 'back-kick.' A kicking technique that follows similar principles, the 'counter spinning-back-kick,' was introduced shortly after (see Figure 6.6).[24]

Figure 6.6 The counter spinning-back-kick against an attack
Source: Courtesy of Peter Bolz

According to Ko Eui Min, the kick that turned out to become the most popular counterattack technique, the 'under-kick,' was first intentionally trained and executed during the mid-1970s.[25] During that time, the kick was called, '*bitch'agi*' or '*bit*-kick.' The term was borrowed from Hwang Kee, who introduced a self-styled technique that he described as a "between a front- and roundhouse-kick;" although referring only to a conventional technique.[26] The under-kick became fully advanced to its present form by the late 1970s, as illustrated throughout Ko Eui Min's sparring manual, *Taekwondo competition* (1980). The few master's theses about taekwondo sparring written at Korean universities during that time, focused to a great extent on this kick. Kim Hyŏng-mok (1977) explained, it is as "a middle one between a Front-kick and Turning-kick [roundhouse-kick]," and called it in English, "slant kick."[27] Following, Yu Yŏng-kwŏn (1980) demonstrated with a series of photographs its function as a counterattack kick in detail. He described its use against a front-, roundhouse-, push-, axe-, back-, and spinning-back-kick. In his conclusion, Yu remarked that trainers and athletes stress counterattack kicks as a "quite necessary skill" and work "more than half of their whole training" perfecting these techniques.[28] Lastly, Yi Kang-hŭi (1981) analyzed scoring frequencies in matches. He grouped scoring techniques into "kicking techniques, *bit*-kicks, counterattack kicks and hand techniques," but with a great emphasis on the *bit*-kick or under-kick.[29] In succeeding studies, the name '*bit*-kick' has not been used any longer and was later replaced with the term '*mit-pada-ch'agi*' or 'under-(counter)-kick.' During the 1980s, the under-kick was perfected by many athletes against push-kicks, and chiefly against all kinds of high kicks (see Figure 6.7). This led to an increasing avoidance of using high kicks in sparring, and also caused a persistent defense-oriented game style for many athletes.

General trends and tendencies in taekwondo sparring history

Historical developments and directions in taekwondo technique were often triggered by changes in the competition rules. Any given set of rules in competition naturally manipulates the game style, the tactics used, the preferred techniques, and the biomechanical execution of techniques. The techniques that are leading potentially to victory are naturally favored. In addition, the scoring behavior of judges and various fashionable trends by athletes also played some role in the development of technique.

International competitions began with the inauguration of the First Taekwondo World Championships in 1973, which led to a growing number of sport taekwondo athletes as well as regional and local tournaments. More participating athletes resulted in a higher skill level and a diversification of kicking techniques.[30] However, the instep roundhouse-kick gradually advanced as the favorite kicking technique in sparring. The 1980s can be seen as the age of counterattack kicks; above all, the under-kick. Moreover, it was the last period for the innovation of truly new kicking techniques; even though, most of the newly introduced techniques constituted a type of variation of the roundhouse-kick. In general,

Figure 6.7 The under-kick against a roundhouse-kick attack
Source: Courtesy of Michael Han

during this era, counterattack kicks dominated attack kicks, and kicks to the body were chosen over high kicks.[31] Moreover, punches were used less frequently, because judges seldom awarded points.

Subsequently, 1990s taekwondo sparring was dominated by the use of a small number of roundhouse-kick varieties. Most attacks were initiated with the fast-kick (front leg roundhouse-kick). Kim Sei Hyeok concluded in his Master's thesis (1993): "In comparing the number of attempts of various Balnolrim [foot steps] patterns[,] Ap-nolim [front step] initial attack recorded the greatest frequency."[32] In addition, double- or multiple-kicks, which are executed very rapidly one after another, were used extensively during this period (for general sparring trends, see Table 6.2).

As a result of the general trends of the late 1980s and 1990s, taekwondo matches were often perceived as boring to watch by the audience. Therefore, a radical revision of scoring rules was considered necessary. The trend of not using

Table 6.2 General trends in the use of taekwondo sparring techniques

1960s	- A reliance on **power**. - Attack: Mostly the **use of front-kicks**. - Counterattack: Use of blocks and punches.
End of 1960s	- The development of a variety of **steps** leads to an increase in **speed**. - The introduction of the **instep roundhouse-kick.**
Late 1960s and early 1970s	- The **large court** and the **absence of protective equipment** lead to an **avoidance of contact** (blocking) with the opponent. - **Combined factors:** A variety of steps, more speed, the instep roundhouse-kick and the avoidance of contact (blocking) with the opponent lead to the introduction of **direct counterattack kicks**.
1970s	- A **diversification** of steps and kicking techniques. - A lesser use of the punch.
Late 1970s	- The elimination of multiple point scores leads to an increased **reliance on roundhouse-kicks** to the trunk, and a lesser use of high kicks.
Early 1980s to mid-1980s	- A reliance on and **perfection of counterattack kicks** leads to **a defensive game style** and a lesser use of high kicks. - An increased **use of front leg kicks** leads to an increase in **speed** and to the introduction of **double-kicks**. - Seldom scoring for punches leads to a neglect of punches.
1990s	- Scoring awards for relatively weak kicks leads to a frequent **use of front leg** and **double-kicks**, the near disappearance of high and turning kicks, and a **focus on speed** at the expense of power. - The persistent use of counterattack kicks. - The near disappearance of punches.
After 2001	- An initial **refocus on power**, because of the introduction of the electronic body protector. - A general trend to use **high and turning kicks** again, because of the reintroduction of multiple point scores. - The game style becomes more **attack oriented** again, because of a variety of rule changes.
After 2010	- An **overreliance on front leg kicking techniques** to the head, as a result of the policy of awarding points for any degree of head contact. - An overreliance on front leg **cut- and side-kicks to the trunk**, because of the shortcomings of the Protector Scoring System /PSS (electronic body protector).

high and turning kicks was reversed with the reintroduction of multiple scoring points, which started in 2001.

In addition, the introduction of the electronic body protector led to a drastic change in preferred techniques. A few companies introduced slightly different functioning body protector systems over the past decade; however, athletes and coaches usually identified the weak points of a system very quickly, and adjusted their training and strategy accordingly. For instance, when kicking at a certain angle, some systems tend to register a scoring point easier; therefore, athletes adjusted their kicking angles. During the first years after the introduction of the first generation electronic body protector, there was a reverse trend toward an emphasis on power again. In particular, the formerly-used Adidas system[33] required strong force for scoring points. A system that is based on force and not merely on contact makes it generally more difficult to score with roundhouse-kicks to the body, especially with the front leg. However, the re-emphasis on power was short-lived and drastically reversed with the introduction of other electronic body protectors. Since straight kicks, such as push- and side-kick-like kicking techniques, seem to score easier on the electronic body protector, they became fashionable again. As a result, most athletes now rely extensively on front leg cut- and side-kick-like kicking techniques to the trunk, which are usually very weak, but sometimes score easily, possibly as a result of the shortcomings of the electronic body protector systems. In addition, high, front leg kicks to the head are used primarily to score multiple points, because they are the easiest high kicks to execute. They are not very powerful kicking techniques, but score anyway because of the newer policy of rewarding points to the head after any degree of contact.

As a general consequence of these developments, taekwondo sparring has partially regressed from a full-contact sport, evaluated by expert, experienced corner judges (who also evaluated the environment and 'art' of the technique), to an electronically measured point game which uses simple, legal, predetermined threshold-level contact as the criterion for scoring a point. Moreover, the instep roundhouse-kick, which used to be the hallmark of taekwondo sparring, may have lost its appeal as the foremost scoring technique. In any case, during the past decade, there has been a radical transformation of necessary skills for athletes and their preferred techniques.

The evolution of specific techniques in sport taekwondo

As in other combat sports, the permitted techniques in taekwondo sparring are regulated and limited by the current WTF competition rules. However, the prospective and permitted striking techniques in taekwondo have never been exactly defined and cataloged, such as the existing punches in boxing. Taekwondo scoring techniques are only defined by permitted striking areas and allowed contact points of the foot and fist. Since there is no satisfactory vocabulary and exact definitions regarding taekwondo sparring techniques, this study seeks to provide an overview and history of these techniques.

The punch

The most profound influence on taekwondo technique came from the rule banning punches and strikes with the hands to the head and face of the opponent. In addition, punches, executed swiftly one after another (or punch combinations), have always been awarded a single point only, or more often, with no points at all. This seems to be an indirect by-product of the original non-contact karate rules, where a fight is stopped after a point is scored, and combination-point aggregations are, therefore, not possible. These combined factors considerably accelerated the development of more kicking techniques, but at the expense of punching techniques.

Stepping, feinting, and blocking an incoming kick with the extended front arm, quickly followed by a strong downward hooking punch to the chest was very popular during the early 1970s.[34] Subsequently, the only punches used in taekwondo sparring since the 1970s, have been the single, straight or downward, oblique hook punches. In attacks, punches are seldom used in combination after a kick – usually only after a roundhouse-kick. In defense/counterattack, they are typically combined with an opposite arm block-cover, and generally used mostly against roundhouse-kick offenses. As a result of the selected rules, taekwondo developed into the only full-contact combat sport in which the punch is not used as a direct attacking technique (punching first), but mostly as a tool for counter-attack (see Figure 6.8). Nowadays, taekwondo is a combat sport that almost exclusively employs kicking techniques; this was probably unintended and just something that gradually evolved over time.[35]

The front-, push-, and side-kicks

The front-, push-, and side-kicks are all straight kicking techniques that eventually disappeared from sparring as a consequence of the introduction of the instep roundhouse-kick. The powerful straight kicks were largely replaced by the fast

Figure 6.8 The punch
Source: Courtesy of Peter Bolz

snap roundhouse-kick as a result of rule modifications and scoring behavior by judges over time.

During the 1960s, when the skill level of competitors was low, the front-kick was the most popular kicking technique in sparring. However, it was increasingly replaced by the push-kick during the 1970s. The push-kick is more suited for full-contact sparring than the front-kick since it applies a larger part of the sole as contact area with the target. The front-kick bears similarities with the traditional roundhouse-kick by using the ball of the foot as a contact point with the target; as a result, the front-kick is also prone to injuries of the toes, especially, when the opponent blocks. Moreover, it is impossible to project one's full body weight behind a traditional snap front-kick. In contrast, the push-kick allows for a powerful 'thrust-blow' by making efficient use of one's body weight. The side-kick was replaced by the push-kick as well, because the side-kick is not suited for smooth combination kicking. The popular instep roundhouse-kick, in particular, is difficult to execute after a side-kick since during a side-kick motion the upper body leans back and turns too much to the side. In contrast, the roundhouse-kick is a smooth and efficient combination technique after a push-kick.

Lastly, after the appearance of direct counterattack kicks, the push-kick proved to be effective as an attack technique by knocking opponents down or off balance, once they tried to counter with a back-kick (see Figure 6.9). However, by the 1980s, athletes had perfected the art of countering push-kicks with under-kicks. Consequently, the usefulness of the push-kick diminished completely during the

Figure 6.9 The push-kick
Source: Courtesy of Peter Bolz

1990s, because even after knock downs, points were no longer awarded for it. All straight kicks lost out to the roundhouse-kick, and eventually vanished over time. However, this trend was thoroughly reversed over the past decade as a result of the introduction of the electronic body protector and the introduction of new scoring rules. Push- and side-kick-like strikes, mainly with the front leg, have become one of the most often used kicking techniques in current taekwondo competitions again.

The axe-kick

Choi Hong Hi (1958) and Hwang Kee (1958), both illustrate a 'front-rising-kick' among other kicking techniques. However, Nishiyama (and Brown, 1960) and Son (and Clark, 1968) clearly state that the technique is thought of as a tool for warming-up and stretching only.[36] The front-rising-kick is basically only a leg swing and not a proper kicking technique, yet. However, during the early 1960s, the technique was modified and found some application in sparring. Ch'oe Yŏng-nyŏl recalled that as early as 1964, a kind of new technique similar to the modern axe-kick had emerged in sparring, even though no points were awarded for its use, yet.[37] Kim Sei Hyeok stated that he began to use the modern axe-kick between 1972 and 1973 (see Figure 6.10). Shortly before, feint motions started to appear in sparring. As a result, when standing in parallel, lateral opposition, athletes begun to trick their opponents by lifting their knee similar to initiating a

Figure 6.10 The axe-kick
Source: Courtesy of Peter Bolz

push-kick, but instead of completing the push-kick movement, they simply extended their leg with a whip-like motion to the face of the opponent.[38] Thus, the modern axe-kick, with its distinctive whipping motion, was invented. Ko Eui Min stated that a front leg version, a jump-axe-kick, was first used by athletes during the late 1970s.[39] Both, the rear leg version and the jump-front leg adaptation, are analyzed by Sŏng Nak-chun in detail in 1984.[40]

The crescent- or half-moon-kick, a relative of the axe-kick, bears some biomechanical resemblance in execution of technique. However, the crescent-kick was, in karate and early taekwondo training, usually used as a blocking technique only, and not as a striking technique. Until recently, when a crescent-kick-like striking technique was executed in taekwondo matches, it was usually not awarded with points, since its impact is very weak and most corner judges did not consider the slap to be a 'real' kicking technique. However, with the introduction of multiple point scores for head kicks, and the policy of awarding points by mere contact, a crescent-kick-like axe-kick has become very popular. The technique is relatively easy to learn and execute, and scores three points. Both varieties, the 'inside-out' and 'outside-in' types, can be classified as axe-kick variations.

The spinning-back-kick and hook-kick

Choi Hong Hi and Yi Kyo-yun both display the spinning-back-kick for the first time in their respective manuals in 1965.[41] According to some anecdotal evidence, the first one to use the kick in Korea was Im U-chong (Lim Woo Jong, a member of *Odo Kwan* in the military) during the early 1960s. Subsequently, Choi Hong Hi named the kick, '*pandae-tollyo-ch'agi*' or 'reverse turning- [roundhouse] - kick.'[42] Yet, Nakayama Masatoshi claimed to have originally invented the kick, inspired by his Chinese boxing instructor in Beijing, once he returned to Japan from China in 1946. Nakayama simply called it, 'reverse roundhouse-kick,' and Choi, aware or unaware of, copied the term.[43] Henry Cho was the first to illustrate an alteration of the spinning-back-kick (1968). Instead of turning backward and executing a full circle spinning kick, he simply performed a similar leg swinging motion, in forward direction, with a half circle-spin. He called both versions by the same name, 'hook-kick.'[44]

However, this study distinguishes between the back-swinging version as 'spinning-back-kick,' and the front-swinging version as 'hook-kick.' The hook-kick never had any great importance in sparring since the kick is not powerful enough and very difficult to execute. However, again, because of the multiple point scores to the head, some athletes started to include the hook-kick into their training routines. On the other hand, the most spectacular kicking technique in taekwondo sparring, the spinning-back-kick, has always been trained by athletes to some extent. The kick is very difficult to execute successfully in sparring (see Figure 6.11), and therefore of minor importance, overall. However, when properly applied (and with some good timing), the spinning-back-kick has resulted in several stunning knockouts over the years, showcasing the sport's controlled violence as well as its pyrotechnical magnificence.

Figure 6.11 The spinning-back-kick
Source: Courtesy of Peter Bolz

The front leg kicks: the cut kick[45] (front leg push-kick) and fast-kick (front leg roundhouse-kick)

Jump kicks, in the form of front- and side-kicks, were probably already used during the 1930s in Japanese karate. The jump roundhouse-kick is mentioned in a variety of early Korean publications and was probably also known in Japan. Traditional jump kicks all follow the same sequence in their execution: after one or several steps, the rear leg is airborne first by lifting the knee and passing the other leg successively. The second leg follows by jumping off the ground, passing the alternate leg, and fully executing the kicking technique. However, these kinds of jump kicks were never widely used in sparring because they are too slow, predictable, and leave the kicker extremely vulnerable. They can be seen only sometimes when an athlete chases the opponent. For effective use in sparring, a quicker and shorter motion with the front leg was necessary.

Ko Eui Min already trained a simple knee lift motion with the front leg, as a tool for feinting or covering distance, during the 1970s.[46] However, the first kicks, with the front leg, were simply executed in connection with a basic 'one-step,' which developed into a jump-like, skipping motion.[47] Side-kicks, especially, and also some front- and roundhouse-kicks, were used this way already during the late 1960s.

During the 1970s, athletes consciously trained and learned to directly counter the instep roundhouse-kick executed after a one-step. Since the attacker aims with the roundhouse-kick to the open side (or front side), the defender simply counterattacks with a direct back-kick. Kim Sei Hyeok presented the following explanation regarding the evolution of tactics and kicking techniques during the 1970s and early 1980s:

1 Athletes learned to counter one-step roundhouse-kicks with counter back-kicks.
2 Therefore, athletes introduced, in anticipation of a counter back-kick, one-step push-kicks. When the opponent turns for the back-kick, the push-kick hits the backside of the opponent and knocks him off balance.
3 Sometime later, athletes introduced the quicker fast-kick (a short and fast front leg jump-like roundhouse-kick) as an attack technique to score before the opponent is able to react with a back-kick.
4 However, athletes adjusted again and learned to beat fast-kicks with counter back-kicks.
5 Finally, athletes introduced the cut-kick (a short and fast front leg jump-like push-kick) to beat anticipated counter back-kicks; again, by knocking opponents off balance once they turn for the back-kick.[48]

The principle motion for the fast- and cut-kicks existed all along in the shape of traditional high jump kicks, which is however not effective in sparring. For the fast- and cut-kicks, the motion was modified by applying a much shorter, fast and low jumping movement. Moreover, the jump motion applies a single step in which the back leg does not pass the front leg during the movement.

Most publications and studies of the 1970s and 1980s are challenging to analyze because their authors frequently apply personalized, self-styled terms and out-of-date language. The modern fast- and cut-kicks are not mentioned yet in a study by An Yong-kyu (1983), in which he examined the First Taekwondo World Games in 1981, and a few national tournaments in Korea in 1982.[49] The first to mention a an "*ap'-pal tollyŏ-ch'agi*" ('front leg roundhouse-kick') was Lee Sung Kook in his master's thesis of 1983. He illustrates the use of the front leg roundhouse-kick as an attack and counterattack technique, and describes the "left foot spinning kick [roundhouse-kick] as a most effective attacking [technique to] target [the]...op[p]onent's body." Furthermore, front leg executions are possible as a "direct attack," but are more frequently completed by using "quick foot steps, with drawing [feinting] steps and jumping steps."[50] The next year (1984), Lee published an article in which he classified and evaluated the frequency of steps in connection with kicking techniques as attack and counterattack techniques. This study uses, for the first time, a wide range of modern taekwondo terminology such as "*pparŭnpal step*" ('fast leg step') and "*ap'pal cut*" ('front leg cut').[51] In the following year (1985), Lee co-authored (Chŏng, Lee, and Sin) an extensive study about taekwondo scoring patterns and variables. This article provides the first nearly comprehensive account of modern sparring technique.[52]

The modern front leg jump-axe-kick follows the same biomechanical principles as the fast- and cut-kicks in terms of executing the jump motion. It likely existed before the fast- and cut-kicks, using a less sophisticated way of jumping. Front leg counterattack roundhouse-kicks appeared at the same time as a tool to counter the front leg attack kicks. They are also first described by Lee Sung Kook in 1983.[53] The increasing use of the front leg as an attack technique was connected to the ever-increasing sophistication in the use of counterattack kicks during the 1970s and 1980s. In order to avoid counterattack kicks, speed became more important in attacking, which the front leg kicks provided. Athletes in contemporary taekwondo competitions often rely almost exclusively on kicking techniques with the front leg (see Figure 6.12), because of the previously discussed changes to the competition rules.

Figure 6.12 The cut-kick
Source: Courtesy of Peter Bolz

The turn-kick[54] (a variation of the roundhouse-kick)

The advance of the turn-kick was probably an accidental result of athletes who executed a strong back-kick, but could not hit the target. The strong momentum of the spin kept the athlete's body turning further, and the athlete unconsciously executed a roundhouse-kick while trying to hit the opponent. The first record of the turn-kick is on film during the Sixth Taekwondo World Championships in Copenhagen, in 1983. Ko Chŏng-ho defeated Reinhard Langer in the flyweight division during a preliminary match by using the turn-kick (see Figure 6.13).[55] Kim Sei Hyeok identified Ko and Chung Kuk Hyun as likely being the first athletes to use the turn-kick in sparring.[56]

The double-kick (a variation of the roundhouse-kick)

Although a variety of double and twin-(jump)-kicks existed in early karate and taekwondo, they were unrealistic for application in sparring. The introduction of a double-kick to sparring was the final result of the ever-increasing importance of

Figure 6.13 Reinhard Langer (left) against Ko Chŏng-ho (right) in 1983. Ko is executing a roundhouse-kick

Source: Courtesy of Reinhard Langer

speed. During the early 1980s, athletes mastered counterattacking the fast- and cut-kicks with a front leg counter roundhouse-kick. Consequently, with an increase in speed, athletes started rapidly executing second roundhouse-kicks, but without putting the initial kicking leg down; this was the birth of the double-kick. Kim Sei Hyeok recalled that this motion was first executed as a counterattack technique by Han Chae-ku.[57] Subsequently, the double-kick was recorded on film for the first time during the Seventh Taekwondo World Championships in Seoul, in 1985. Han scored with double-kicks against Ahmet Ercan from Turkey during the final match in the featherweight division to win the tournament. Han also won the previous 1983 World Championships in Copenhagen, but did not use the technique yet. Therefore, its invention can likely be placed in the period between 1983 and 1985. The double-kick led to the use of triple- and multiple-kicks, which do not represent a distinctive technique since they follow the same principles. Therefore, the double-kick might be considered as being the last distinctive kicking technique developed in taekwondo sparring. However, for the exact classification and history of kicking techniques, additional research and discussion will be required (see Table 6.3).

Summary

In early East Asian martial arts, including Okinawan karate, there was very limited use of kicking techniques. In addition to knee strikes, front- and a sort of side-kick were used as low kicks or strikes to the trunk. After the introduction of karate to Japan, the range of kicking techniques expanded, which was related with the expansion of training activities. The inclusion of free, non-contact sparring during the mid-1930s was essential in this development. Early taekwondo techniques and kicking range were similar to karate until the introduction of full-contact competitions during the 1960s. However, for application in full-contact sparring, most of the kicking techniques had to first be modified.

During the tournaments of the 1960s, the front-kick was the most-widely used kicking technique. In addition, athletes mostly used punches and blocks. However, in the absence of flexible stances and steps, taekwondo sparring still mimicked karate sparring. Over time, the chosen competition rules in taekwondo sparring triggered the introduction of a variety of short stances and swift steps, which in turn led to an increase in speed and agility in sparring. As a result of a rule amendment in 1967, the instep roundhouse-kick to the trunk became more popular, which generated a greater diversification of kicking techniques and combinations. When the instep roundhouse-kick was combined with steps, new fighting tactics, style, and strategies emerged. Due to the selected rules and the large fighting area, combined with the body protector, the use of punches as strikes and arms as block for cover was, by and large, discouraged. The combination of these factors triggered the development of direct counterattack kicks during the early 1970s, which again stimulated the introduction of feint motions and fast stepping methods. These innovations represented the beginning of modern taekwondo sparring and greatly differentiated the art from karate.

Table 6.3 Estimated timeline for the evolution of kicking techniques

Before 1925	Low kicks, front-kick
Early 1930s	Side-kick (mostly **low kicks**, some **body kicks**)
1935	**Introduction of non-contact free sparring in karate training, diversification of kicks, introduction of high kicks**
1940s, 1950s	Roundhouse-kick (ball of foot) Back-kick Push-kick (a variety of the front-kick) Crescent-kick Front-rising-kick (axe-kick-like, used for stretching only) A variety of jump kicks (front-, side-, roundhouse-kick, twin-foot-kicks) A variety of low kicks
KARATE	**(No direct counterattack kicks)**
1963	**Introduction of full-contact taekwondo competition**
TAEKWONDO is still KARATE-like	**1965** Spinning-back-kick (possibly developed during late 1940s, in karate) **1968** Hook-kick
Use of wide static stances, no steps, power; use of mostly front-kicks, blocks and punches in sparring	
Late 1960s	**Introduction of short stances, agile and flexible steps**
TAEKWONDO **1967**	**Instep roundhouse-kick**
Late 1960s, and early 1970s	**Direct counterattack kicks:** 1) Back-kick 2) Spinning-back-kick 3) Under-kick (mid-1970s)
Early 1970s	Modern axe-kick
Late 1970s	Increased use of front leg, possibly jump-axe-kick
1981–82	Turn-kick
1982–83	Fast-kick, cut-kick
1984	Modern double-kick (last new technique introduced in sparring)

Note: See also Table 6.4 in Appendix E for English and Korean terminology of kicking techniques.

Subsequently, a variety of new technical innovations and trends were caused by further rule amendments, scoring behavior by corner judges, the introduction of improved equipment, and an increasing number of athletes and tournaments. A second especially important period for the innovation of new kicking techniques was the early 1980s. During that time, front leg kicking techniques became increasingly important as a result of the continuing increase of speed during matches. This situation triggered the introduction of the fast- and cut-kicks. The development of the double-kick was the final result of the speed game. The double-kick might be considered the last truly new kicking technique adopted in taekwondo sparring. In demonstration taekwondo, which has become very popular lately, a great range of acrobatic and gymnastic jump kicks have been developed, but these theatrical kicking techniques are unrealistic for use in full-contact sparring and are not considered in this study.

The evolutionary development of taekwondo kicking techniques resulted from a combination of naturally gifted, young athletes and smart coaches who tried to adapt to changing rules and circumstances. Moreover, an increasing number of contestants and tournaments required individual athletes to continuously search for new ways to outsmart their opponents. This is a natural cycle that favors new inventions and skills, which in turn stimulates adaptation and innovation once again.

The creative evolutionary process of taekwondo technique was possible only because of the introduction of full-contact competition, which shaped taekwondo's technique and distinguished taekwondo from karate. However, only half of taekwondo's training activities transformed away from karate. The remaining half, which includes forms and self-defense training, retained the technical framework and spirit of karate. This incomplete transformation and the problems which subsequently developed will be addressed in the next chapter.

Figure 6.14 Modern taekwondo training for competition. Winter training at Youngsan University, sparring with different teams, 2010

Notes

1 Funakoshi, *Tōdi (karate) arts: Polish your courage for self-defense*, pp. 155; 164 (or see the English translation titled, *To-te jitsu*). Funakoshi's, as well as later publications by other karate instructors, included parts of the classical China-based combat manual *Bubishi* (武備志), which was known by Funakoshi and other famous *karateka* (see

McCarthy, *Bubishi – The classic manual of combat*, p. 27). The Okinawan *Bubishi* seems to be a collection of a number of manuals, partly based on the Chinese military manual *Jixiaoxinshu* (McCarthy, *Bubishi – The classic manual of combat*, pp. 63–4), just as the classical Korean martial arts publications discussed in Chapter 1, p. 15. All display only low kicks and some front-kicks to the trunk (see illustrations of the *Bubishi* in McCarthy, *Bubishi – The classic manual of combat*). Compare Funakoshi's early books also to some corresponding video footage recorded in 1924. See *Gichin Funakoshi – 1924 Vintage footage*, (n.d.). [Retrieved from www.youtube.com/watch?v=6fyG0-ygmxY].

2   Both of Motobu's early publications are reprinted in Koharu, [*Research in early Ryukyu karate*], see photographs of kicking techniques pp. 23; 85.
3   See Mabuni, *Karatedo kempo*. This work was first published in 1934.
4   Taekwondo language uses the term '*chayu daeryŏn*' (自由 對鍊).
5   Hassell, *Shotokan karate – Its history and evolution*, pp. 43–5.
6   Clayton, *Shotokan's secret – The hidden truth behind karate's fighting origin*, p. 49.
7   Funakoshi, *Karate-dō kyōhan – The master text*, p. 23.
8   Choi, *Taekwondo – The art of self-defence*, p. 88. Yi, [*Taesudo textbook for the masses*], p. 43.
9   Cho, *Korean karate – Free fighting technique*, p. 235.
10 Funakoshi, *Karate-dō kyōhan – The master text*, p. 25; Nishiyama, and Brown, *Karate – The art of "empty hand" fighting*, pp. 134–5; Choi, *Taekwondo – The art of self-defence*, p. 90; Cho, *Korean karate – Free fighting technique*, p. 210.
11 Pieter, and Heijmans, *Taekwondo technique-training-self-defense*, pp. 137–8.
12 As cited in Kim, "A study on how the taekwondo games rules can [have] influence on the changes of game skills [sic]," p. 42.
13 Ko Eui Min, personal interview, January 13, 2010.
14 Kim, "A study on how the taekwondo games rules can [have] influence on the changes of game skills [sic]," p. 40.
15 Kim Sei Hyeok, personal interview, March 23, 2010.
16 Ibid. According to Kim, Ko had several boxers as friends; see also Ko, *Taekwondo competition*, pp. 40–58. The stances are clearly copied from boxing; Choi, and Yoo, *Historic taekwondo-do instructional film*. See the sparring scenes toward the end of the video.
17 Ko Eui Min, personal interview, January 13, 2010.
18 Kim Sei Hyeok, personal interview, March 23, 2010.
19 Ibid.
20 Choi, and Yoo, *Historic taekwondo-do instructional film*. See the sparring scenes toward the end of the video; for the general form of kicking techniques during that time see also Bower, *Original ITF taekwon-do inception, 1966 and (Steve Cheah?) 1972*.
21 See for example, Kraitus, and Kraitus, *Muay Thai*, p. 237; "Boxing rings," (n.d.). [Retrieved from www.boxing-ring.eu/en/web/boxing-rings].
22 Capener, "Problems in the identity and philosophy of *t'aegwondo* and their historical causes," p. 89.
23 Ko Eui Min, personal interview, January 13, 2010; see also the sparring scenes toward the end of the video, which was produced by Choi, and Yoo, *Historic taekwondo-do instructional film*.
24 Ibid.
25 Ibid.
26 See Hwang, [*Tangsudo textbook*], p. 64.
27 Kim, "A study of the influence of the slant kick in tae kwon do," pp. 8; 46.
28 Yu, "A study on the influence of counter-kicking to victory in tae kweon do [sic]," pp. 15–6; 63–4.
29 Yi, "A comparative study on [the] performance of the game in tae kweon do with the member[s] of the national team [sic]."

30 Kim, "A study on how the taekwondo games rules can [have] influence on the changes of game skills [sic]," p. 40.
31 Ibid, p. 40.
32 Kim, "The analysis of the frequency of attempts and the success ratio according to the attacking and bal-no-rim patterns of Taekwondo patterns [sic]," p. 35.
33 The Adidas PSS system was never recognized by the WTF, but was widely used in Europe.
34 Email communication with Gregory S. Kailian, October 25, 2013.
35 Lee Chong Woo claimed: "I decided we should develop Taekwondo as a sport emphasizing foot techniques" (as cited in Yook, "Kukkiwon Vice President Chong Woo Lee's shocking confession of Olympic competition result manipulation!", p. 309). However, it appears that the development was more gradual than deliberately planned.
36 Nishiyama, and Brown, *Karate – The art of "empty hand" fighting*, p. 41; Son, and Clark, *Korean karate – The art of tae kwon do*, p. 49.
37 As cited in Kim, "A study on how the taekwondo games rules can [have] influence on the changes of game skills [sic]," p. 44.
38 Kim Sei Hyeok, personal interview, March 23, 2010.
39 Ko Eui Min, personal interview, January 13, 2010.
40 Sŏng, "Cinematographic analysis of jig eo cha gi in tae kwon do [sic]."
41 Choi, *Taekwondo – The art of self-defence*, p. 88; Yi, [*Taesudo textbook for the masses*], p. 43.
42 As cited in Gillis, *A killing art – The untold history of tae kwon do*, p. 62.
43 As cited in Hassell, *Shotokan karate – Its history and evolution*, p. 66.
44 Cho, *Korean karate – Free fighting technique*, pp. 234–5.
45 Some use the term 'cut kick' for (illegal) intentional low kicks to the legs. Many young Korean athletes nowadays refer to the front and back leg push-kick-like kicks simply as 'cut-.'
46 Ko, *Taekwondo competition*, p. 47.
47 The side-kick combined with a step, can already be seen in the Bruce Lee movies of the early 1970s, which he may have learned from Rhee Jhoon.
48 Kim Sei Hyeok, personal interview, March 23, 2010.
49 An, "Study for numbers used and scoring ability of each kicking [sic]."
50 Lee, "Technical analysis of spinning kick [roundhouse-kick] and study of scoring targets [sic]," p. 36; see photographs on pp. 9–11.
51 Lee, "Research analyzes of taekwondo game stepping patterns."
52 See Chŏng, Lee, and Sin, "Analysis of scoring and losing-score variables by attack patterns in tae kwon do competition."
53 See photographs in Lee, "Technical analysis of spinning kick [roundhouse-kick] and study of scoring targets [sic]," pp. 9–11.
54 This study distinguishes between the 'turn-kick,' which is a variation of the roundhouse-kick, and the 'turning kicks,' which include the turn-kick, back-kick, and spinning-back-kick.
55 Yang, *Art of competition* [Videocassette]. See minutes 7–8.
56 Kim Sei Hyeok, personal interview, March 23, 2010.
57 Ibid.

Bibliography

[An Yong-kyu] (안용규). 태권도 경기의 각 발차기 사용 빈도수와 득점력에 관한 조사연구 "Study for numbers used and scoring ability of each kicking [sic]." Unpublished master's thesis, Dongguk University, 1983. [In Korean only].
Bower, Scott (Poster). *Original ITF taekwon-do inception, 1966 and (Steve Cheah?) 1972* [Video]. [Retrieved from www.youtube.com/watch?v=LlEd7bwHKh0].

Capener, Steven D. "Problems in the identity and philosophy of *t'aegwondo* and their historical causes." *Korea Journal*, 35, 4 (1995): 80–94. [Retrieved from www.eagletkd.com/images/STUDENT%20FORUM%20from%20Korea%0Journal.pdf].
Cho, Sihak Henry. *Korean karate – Free fighting technique*. Rutland and Tokyo: Charles E. Tuttle Company, 1968.
Choi, Hong Hi [Ch'oe Hong-hi] (최홍희). 跆拳道教本 [*Taekwondo textbook*]. Seoul: Sŏnghwa Munhwasa, 1958. [In Korean only].
_____. *Taekwondo – The art of self-defence*. Seoul: Daeha Publication Company, 1965.
Choi, Hong Hi (Supervisor), and Yoo Hyun-mok (Director). *Historic taekwondo-do instructional film* [Video]. Seoul: The Dea Yeong Film Co [probably produced 1968]. [Retrieved form www.youtube.com/watch?v=Ik-j2Cdbd9U].
[Chŏng Rak-hŭi], Lee Sung Kook [Yi Sŭng-guk], and [Sin Hyŏn-cho] (정락희, 이승국, 신현조) 태권도 경기의 공격유형에 따른 득점변인과 실점변인 분석 "Analysis of scoring and losing-score variables by attack patterns in tae kwon do competition." *Journal of The Research Institute of Physical Education and Sports Science*, 4, 1 (1985): 105–133. [In Korean only].
Clayton, Bruce D. *Shotokan's secret – The hidden truth behind karate's fighting origin*. USA: Ohara Publications, Inc, 2004.
Funakoshi, Gichin. 錬膽護身 唐手術 *Rentan goshin tōde-jutsu* (*Tōdi arts: Polish your courage for self-defense*). Tokyo: Airyudo, 1996. [In Japanese; original work published 1925].
_____. *To-te jitsu*. Trans. Shingo Ishida. Hamilton: Masters Publication, 1997. [Original work published 1925].
_____. *Karate-dō Kyōhan – The Master Text*. Trans. T. Ohshima. Tokyo: Kondansha International Ltd, 1973. [Translation of revised edition of 1957; first edition published 1935].
_____. *Karate-dō kyōhan – Master text for the way of the empty-hand*. Trans. Harum Suzuki-Johnston. San Diego: Neptune Publications, 2005. [Original work published 1935].
Gillis, Alex. *A killing art – The untold history of tae kwon do*. Toronto: ECW Press, 2008.
Hassell, Randall G. *Shotokan karate – Its history and evolution*. Los Angeles: Empire Books, 2007.
Hwang, Kee [Hwang Ki] (황기). 唐手道教本 [*Tangsudo textbook*]. Seoul: Kyerang Munhwasa, 1958. [In Korean only].
[Kim Chong-min] (김종민). 태권도 규칙이 경기기술의 변화에 미치는 영향에 대한 연구 "A study on how the taekwondo games rules can [have] influence on the changes of game skills [sic]." Unpublished master's thesis, Kyung Hee University, 2002. [In Korean only].
[Kim Hyŏng-mok] (김형묵) 태권도 경기에서 빗차기가 승부에 미치는 영향 "A study of the influence of the slant kick in tae kwon do." Unpublished master's thesis, Kyung Hee University, 1977. [In Korean only].
Kim, Sei Hyeok [Kim Se-hyŏk] (김세혁). 태권도 경기의 공격 및 발놀림 유형에 따른 시도횟수와 성공도 분석 "The analysis of the frequency of attempts and the success ratio according to the attacking and bal-no-rim patterns of taekwondo patterns [sic]." Unpublished master's thesis, Inha University, 1993. [In Korean only].
Ko, Eui Min. *Taekwondo Wettkampf* (Taekwondo competition). Munich: Schramm Sport, 1980. [In German only].
Koharu, Iwai (ed.). 本部朝基と琉球 カラテ [*Research in early Ryukyu karate*]. Tokyo: Airyudo, 2000. [In Japanese only].

Kraitus, Panya, and Pitisuk Kraitus. *Muay Thai*. Bangkok: Asia Books, 1988.

Lee, Sung Kook [Yi Sŭng-guk] (이승국) 태권도 경기의 돌려차기 기술분석과 득점부위에 관한 조사연구 "Technical analysis of spinning kick [roundhouse-kick] and study of scoring targets [sic]." Unpublished master's thesis, Kyung Hee University, 1983. [In Korean only].

_____. 태권도 경기의 스텝 유형별 분석에 관한 연구 "Research analyzes of taekwondo game stepping patterns [sic]." *Quarterly Taekwondo*. 49 (1984): 106–15. [In Korean only].

Mabuni, Kenwa. *Karatedo kempo*. Trans. Michael Robinson. New York: Shorei-ha Publication, 2007. [Original work published 1934].

McCarthy, Patrick. *Bubishi – The classic manual of combat*. North Clarendon, VT: Tuttle Publishing, 2008.

Nishiyama, Hidetaka, and Richard C. Brown. *Karate – The art of "empty hand" fighting*. Vermont and Tokyo: Charles E. Tuttle Company, 1960.

Pieter, Willy, and John Heijmans. *Taekwondo Technik-Training-Selbstverteidigung (Taekwondo technique-training-self-defense)*. Aachen: Meyer and Meyer Verlag, 1995. [In German, but also available in English].

Son, Duk Sung [Son Tŏk-sŏng], and Robert J. Clark. *Korean karate – The art of tae kwon do*. New York: Prentice-Hall, Inc. Englewood Cliffs, 1968.

[Sŏng Nak-chun] (성낙준). 태권도 찍어차기의 역학적 분석 "Cinematographic analysis of jig eo cha gi in tae kwon do [sic]." Unpublished master's thesis, Seoul National University, 1984. [In Korean only].

Yang, Jin Bang (양진방). (Director). *Art of competition* [Videocassette]. Seoul: WTF, 1987. [Retrieved from www.youtube.com/watch?v=3Rc9SsnpQUg].

[Yi Kang-hŭi] (이강희). 태권도 경기내용에 관한 비교연구 "A comparative study on [the] performance of the game in tae kweon do with the member[s] of the national team [sic]." Unpublished master's thesis, Kyung Hee University, 1981. [In Korean only].

[Yi Kyo-yun] (이교윤). 百萬人의 跆手道敎本 [*T'aesudo textbook for the masses*]. Seoul: T'op'ik Ch'ulp'ansa, 1965. [In Korean only].

Yook, Sung-chul [Yuk Sŏng-ch'ŏl] (육성철). 이종우 국기원 부원장의 '태권도 과거'충격적 고백! "Kukkiwon Vice President Chong Woo Lee's shocking confession of Olympic competition result manipulation!". Trans. Lee Soo Han. *Shin Dong-A*, (2002, April). 290–311. [Retrieved from http://tkdreform.com/yook_article.pdf].

[Yu Yŏng-kwŏn] (유영권). 태권도 경기에서 받아차기가 승부에 미치는 영향 "A study on the influence of counter-kicking to victory in tae kweon do [sic]." Unpublished master's thesis, Kyung Hee University, 1980. [In Korean only].

7 The philosophical roots of taekwondo

> To the traditionalists and to those who regard classical bujutsu from the viewpoint of actual combat, the modern disciplines are nothing but an ass in a tiger's skin.
>
> Don F. Draeger[1]

Taekwondo is not just the offspring of karate in terms of technique and general training activity, but also of its philosophy and dogma. Therefore, a better understanding of the general evolution of the Japanese martial arts, to which taekwondo is intimately related, is useful.

The development of some form of structured methodology for conflict and combat is a practice that has occurred, to some extent, in all cultures and societies which employed warriors or soldiers. In ancient times, structured combat training mostly involved exercising with weapons for military and battle purposes. In addition, the display of combat games, with some religious or ritualistic connotations, and/or for purposes of entertainment, has a long tradition in many societies, as well. Various kinds of wrestling games were especially popular throughout the Middle East and Asia, and in ancient Greece and Rome, a variety of systematic boxing and wrestling styles were also practiced and performed.

Geographically, the term 'martial arts,' as understood in modern times, is mainly associated with East Asia, and represents a collection that groups Japanese, Chinese, Korean, and Okinawan fighting methods, military arts, and boxing styles "inappropriately" together.[2] In contrast, the modern Western activities associated with combat, like boxing, wrestling and fencing, are perceived merely as sports. Moreover, for many educated, middle-class Westerners, boxing has become a deplorable sport, because of the effects of concussion on the brains of competitors and its perceived 'violent nature.' On the other hand, training in certain Oriental martial arts, which are essentially similar activities, has become fashionable and culturally approved of. These superficial classifications, distinctions, and attitudes are likely the results of an inadequate understanding of the nature and history of martial arts and combat.[3] In reality, any activity that serves to improve battle or fighting skills is, by definition, a form of 'martial art.'[4]

The Japanese were the leaders in transforming classical martial arts into activities connected with a philosophical character suited for modern society. Don F.

Draeger was among the first to explain the historical and cultural circumstances in Japan which made the transformation of the classical martial arts from combat to modern martial sports, possible. He explained the transformation from the classical '*bugei*' (武藝) or 'martial arts,' which represented at that time the different '*bu-jutsu*' (武術 'martial skills') arts, to the modern '*bu-dō*' (武道 'martial ways') arts. Draeger distinguished between classical (*ko*) *bujutsu* and *budō*, and modern (*shin*) *bujutsu* and *budō*.

For hundreds of years Japanese warlords battled each other for power and territory. In this long, war-like atmosphere, highly effective fighting systems and distinct warrior codes of conduct and behavior developed, because each provincial lord (*daimyo*) maintained his own, personal military contingent. The purpose and spirit of classical *bujutsu* was to battle with the enemy to the death for power, property, and wealth. However, that original purpose could not be realized anymore during the relatively peaceful Tokugawa or Edo period (1603–1868), which featured a consolidated central government under the emperor. As a result, classical *bujutsu* had to transform its original martial character and purpose into some alternative activities suited for peacetime. The new objective of the martial arts came to emphasize some spiritual and aesthetic aspects of training, which resulted in the formation of classical *budō*. Moreover, from a practical perspective, the classical *bujutsu* arts were rendered increasingly useless with the introduction of Western firearms in the sixteenth century. During the following centuries, the classical *bujutsu* art forms and its gradually distorted *bushi* (warrior) traditions experienced a steep decline because of social, cultural, and political changes.

In 1868, the Meiji government was established and its rulers considered the traditional Japanese feudal society and social structure, with the aristocratic samurai on top, to be anachronistic. Instead, modern ideas and technology from the West were favored and introduced. As a consequence of these modernizations, the aristocratic samurai lost their privileges, ended up in dire financial straits, and had to open their '*ryū*' ('schools' or 'styles') to the general public in order to earn a living. The result was that an even larger number of commoners started *budō* training. This was the time when the purpose of *budō* training necessarily diversified. This was also the era when classical *bujutsu* and *budō* ended, and modern *bujutsu* and *budō* began. Nowadays, modern *bujutsu* is mostly associated with police work, whereas modern *budō* (such as kendo, judo, *karate-dō*, *aikidō*, and some others) transformed into activities mostly associated with recreation and sports.[5] According to Draeger, the transformational process of Japanese martial arts was:

Combat (classical *bujutsu*) → art (classical *budō*) → sport (modern *budō*)

More recent studies, however, suggested that the distinction between classical *bujutsu* and classical *budō* requires redefinition. Rather, both terms had been perceived as identical or interconnected in spirit, manifestation, and content by the samurai warriors; a distinction between *bujutsu* and *budō* was only introduced and articulated by the modern judo founder Kanō Jigorō during the late nineteenth century. That said, most ordinary Japanese martial arts practitioners do not distinguish between the terms at all.[6]

Steven D. Capener[7] applied parts of Draeger's theory, but mostly disregarded the distinction between classical and modern *bujutsu* and *budō*. Instead, he emphasized the evolution from classical *bujutsu* to modern *budō*, with the significance of this process being the transformation from the practical '*jutsu*' (術 'skill') to the focus on the spiritual '*dō*' (道 'way'). In addition, Capener analyzed the philosophical relevance of this process in relationship to modern taekwondo.

The principal objective of martial arts in ancient societies was combat. Initially, Capener compared the historical development of martial arts in Japan and Korea. Japan was ruled by the samurai, who were independent warriors. In contrast, Korea was governed by the *yangban*, a scholarly, Confucian class, which employed soldiers and civil servants. As the Tokugawa period brought peace to Japan, the samurai transformed themselves into scholars and bureaucrats. Their practical warrior skills were suddenly rendered useless and, as a result, these skills became tools for "self-cultivation or sport." On a philosophical level, the training value shifted from the pursuit of combat skills (*jutsu*) to the pursuit of personal spiritual development (*dō*). The first art which accomplished this transformational process was sword fighting, which transformed from '*ken-jutsu*' (剣術) to '*ken-dō*' (剣道 'kendo').[8] Originally, the main training methodology for *kenjutsu* was *kata* (forms or patterns), which became ritualized and fossilized through the absence of warfare. Because of the use of live blades, other methods were not possible until the introduction of protective gear and the bamboo sword during the seventeenth century. These innovations led to sparring-based kendo with a sports character, just as in the case of the transformation of '*jū-jutsu*' (柔術) into '*jū-dō*' (柔道 'judo').

In contrast, military arts in Korea almost disappeared in the Neo-Confucian atmosphere of the Chosŏn Dynasty. Korea's first contact with a "systemized martial art" took place with kendo and judo during the Japanese colonial period. Originally, first-generation taekwondo, being an offshoot of karate and also imported from Japan, relied on the traditional values of self-defense and fighting as its core philosophy. However, with the introduction of full-contact sparring competitions, taekwondo followed in the footsteps of "kendo and judo in re-adjusting its training objectives away from real fighting." In reality, "the new objective became, as in kendo and judo, the development of superior technique."[9] In tandem with these developments, new and modern sports training methods were introduced to taekwondo. However, this transformation was not recognized or articulated on a philosophical level by taekwondo leaders, who did not formulate new objectives and values. Instead, they relied on the old karate ideology, seeing taekwondo as a martial art for practical self-defense and fighting (see Table 7.1).

According to Capener's theory, the correlations between karate's objectives, values, and training methodology are questionable because, by merely training *kata*, which is a solo-performance by a practitioner, development of a proficient fighting skill is not realistically attainable. While the ancient samurai had real

148 The philosophical roots of taekwondo

Table 7.1 The correlation between objectives, values, and training methodologies in martial arts

	Traditional kenjutsu *and* jūjutsu	*Modern* kendo *and* judo
Training objectives	Combat	Technical perfection
Training values	Combat skills (*jutsu*)	Self-cultivation (*dō*)
Training methodology	*Kata*	Sparring

	Karate	*Taekwondo*
Training objectives	Self-defense and fighting	Self-defense and fighting
Training values	Technical skills and behavioral norms	Technical skills and behavioral norms
Training methodology	*Kata*	Sparring

battles to test their skills, modern martial artists have no practical exposure to real fighting. In the case of taekwondo, its training objectives and values are out of step with its training methodology, because taekwondo's training values and objectives have become disconnected to the realities of modern societies, in which martial arts for fighting have no real purpose. Capener believes that taekwondo's objectives and values should be readjusted to modern times, in line with its training methodology (sparring). As in kendo and judo, taekwondo should not be seen as a martial art, but a sport and a means for achieving technical perfection in the quest for self-cultivation.[10]

However, contrary to Capener's portrayal, in the case of taekwondo, the transformation into a purely sparring-based system in terms of training methodology was never completely accomplished. In reality, taekwondo's training activities, from the introduction of sparring competitions during the 1960s onwards, has always consisted of two distinct main training components. One is the more recently introduced sparring/competition sport-based element, and the other is the conventional forms/self-defense karate-based component. Both systems have been practiced as a blend in commercial taekwondo schools and recreational clubs. That being said, the sparring/sport-based component was favored by officials and leaders during the 1970s and 1980s with their push to promote taekwondo as an Olympic sport. However, the forms/self-defense-based system was preserved, and gained renewed importance during the 1990s with the introduction of forms contests and other related activities such as the *Hanmadang*, a kind of 'taekwondo-festival.' As a result, there seems to exist two parallel, yet essentially opposed systems present in modern taekwondo under a common name, with essentially two conflicting training methodologies – forms versus sparring. On a philosophical level, the fundamental contradiction lies in taekwondo's presentation, on one hand, as a deadly martial art for self-defense with various supposedly 'traditional' and 'ancient' Korean cultural values attached to it while, on the other hand, taekwondo is portrayed as a modern, 'scientific' Olympic sport, contributing allegedly to world peace.

This chapter discusses the inconsistent presentation of taekwondo philosophy in connection with its training methods. This inconsistency is the result of taekwondo's historical development, as well as the desire of Korean leaders to establish an indigenous 'national' identity and history for taekwondo, along with the establishment's reluctance to recognize its Japanese karate elements.

The philosophical aspects of East Asian martial arts

Since early taekwondo was a product of karate in not only technical, but also in philosophical terms, the origin of these elements requires clarification. An academic survey revealed that American martial arts literature mostly treats martial arts as a "spiritual discipline," and tends to reject "the practically oriented perspective of martial arts, and competitive or sport oriented modern versions."[11] Therefore, the discussion of spiritual and esoteric characteristics in martial arts training seems to be an important focal point. The same study also found little correlation between the presentations of American martial arts literature and the concrete interpretation of "ordinary American practitioners" in their martial arts activities:

> Whereas American martial arts literature conceptualized martial arts as [a] spiritual, philosophical, [and] educational discipline, ordinary American practitioners defined their training in practical, physical, and personally meaningful ways. The spiritual version of martial arts framed by literature was not accepted by the ordinary practitioners.[12]

This suggests that the philosophical discussions and theoretical interpretations presented by martial arts authors and experts might be quite irrelevant (at least in the West) to the ordinary practitioner.

Nevertheless, many instructors find it essential to provide a philosophy in connection with history, which is also supposed to explain the educational values and benefits of martial arts.

The combat and self-defense aspects

The most ancient of all reasons for training in martial arts is self-defense, combat, and war. Ancient martial arts training dealt mostly with techniques and exercises using weapons, such as bows and arrows, swords, spears, knives, clubs, and other types of arms; and this was mostly found in the domain of hunters, soldiers, and warriors. Until recent history, martial arts were considered a purely "physical..., manual skill" for survival in combat, without any associations with self-cultivation, philosophical doctrines, or religious practices.[13]

In Chinese mythology and history, next to soldiers and warriors, martial arts are often associated with the Shaolin monks. Chinese monasteries frequently served as a refuge for all kinds of troublesome individuals, and the distinction between monks and bandits was not often obvious. Moreover, the fabled Shaolin Monastery represented, in fact, a large landowner who needed to protect his wealth and interests by military means, thus contributing to its legendary, fighting reputation.[14] While monks were, at times, enlisted by rulers as mercenaries during military campaigns, monks were only one of many groups of mercenary parties, whose central role in the development of Chinese martial arts seems to be a modern exaggeration.[15] Apart from monks, secret societies and bands of outlaws were also connected to various martial arts activities in Chinese legends.

In Chinese history, folklore, and mythology, there have been a wide range of military and civil groups associated with martial arts. In Japan, the predominant association was independent samurai warrior factions, and in Korea, martial arts were generally tied to the regular armed forces.[16] Thus, throughout history, the foremost practitioners of combat and war were soldiers and warriors, not monks and bandits. At the same time, the distinction between soldiers and civilians was frequently also blurred since commoners were often forced into military service in times of war.

Ancient warriors and soldiers practiced primarily with weapons as a preparation for general battle and warfare. In such an environment, unarmed striking was not effective against professional, armored opponents carrying lethal weapons. "It is [always] better to be armed in a fight."[17] Martial arts training without weapons was only considered as a means of improving the general physical fitness and strength of soldiers, and grappling or wrestling served this purpose much better than striking.[18] However, during festivities, wrestling matches and contests, especially, were often performed as games for entertainment, ritual, and/or religious activities.

In contrast, the original objective of karate practitioners in Okinawa was personal self-defense because of their limited access to weapons. The Ryūkyū Islands, the birthplace of Japanese karate, unified for the first time in the early fifteenth century. From Okinawa, the crown's main island, the king officially banned the possession of all weapons by commoners throughout the islands through fear of rebellion. Later, in the seventeenth century, the islands were conquered and colonized by a group of Japanese samurai, who kept and enforced the weapons ban for the general population and nobles, alike. These circumstances encouraged the development of weaponless martial arts.[19] In addition, a variety of farm weapons and daily instruments were converted for self-defense, such as the *bō* (a staff), the *kama* (a farming sickle), and the *sai* (a three-pronged truncheon). Naturally, any available weapon-like tool was utilized as a striking device. As a result, there existed no clear distinction between armed and unarmed combat. Nevertheless, the original systems for unarmed combat were imported from China and then modified in Okinawa.

Thus, original Okinawan karate was not perceived as a purely weaponless art.[20] This association was only made with its introduction to Japan. The concept of a purely weaponless martial art for personal self-defense seems to be a rather modern idea, because the very idea could only develop in a relatively peaceful society which had no more practical need for traditional martial arts as a tool for real combat. Only fairly civilized societies have the luxury of associating martial arts with 'practicing' restrained self-defense or sports. Likewise, the connection between martial arts and self-cultivation is also a quite modern notion.

The health, self-cultivation, and religious aspects

The health and self-cultivation aspects of the martial arts often seem to overlap, and are at times indistinguishable from its esoteric and spiritual aspects. In Chinese martial arts, there is a long tradition of associating herbal and homeopathic medicine, acupuncture, acupressure, bone setting, and specific diets harmonized with exercising, as a method for health and long life. The roots of this relationship seem to go back to the introduction of Buddhism to China from India, since India had a long tradition of herbal remedies and physical health exercises in the form of yoga.[21] Besides, wandering street vendors, selling Oriental medicines, often conducted martial arts demonstrations and feats of strength as proofs of vitality and the related benefits of their products.[22]

Internal Chinese martial arts styles, especially, are associated with Daoist health exercises and traditions, for instance, breathing, stretching, muscle strengthening, meditation, and the stimulation of '*qi*' energy (氣 'vital energy;' Japanese: '*ki*'; Korean: '*ki*').[23] Although many of the esoteric concepts attached to the Chinese martial arts, such as the notion of *qi*, were not only reserved for the martial arts, but to the contrary, these beliefs represented in fact a reflection of the general Chinese cosmological awareness and metaphysical world-view found in all walks of life.[24]

In the Chinese martial arts, there was a fusion between spiritual, health-related, and combat aspects; although this synthesis is likely a rather modern representation, only introduced during the last centuries. Associations between Daoism, the Chinese martial arts, and Buddhist practices were probably not made prior to the late Ming (1368–1644) or early Qing Dynasty (1644–1912). In reality, Chinese martial arts styles, such as *taijiquan* and weaponless Shaolin fighting methods are fairly modern inventions which emerged only during the seventeenth century. Unarmed fighting methods in China appeared primarily as health-related and religious exercises and not as a means for real battle.[25]

It is highly unlikely that in Japan similar associations between health and martial arts developed prior to or independently from Chinese martial arts, especially since there always had been exchanges with the mainland and subsequent assimilations. Although the development of the modern Japanese *budō* arts, and their often-made associations with moral and spiritual self-cultivation, emerged separately from the Chinese martial arts, as a result of Japan's relative early modernization drive in East Asia.

Okinawan karate instructors emphasized the conventional health aspects and longevity benefits on frequent occasions, as well. For example, Funakoshi Gichin stated:

> My esteemed teachers, the late masters Shishu (in Japanese, Itosu) and Asato, were both very weak in their childhood, but after starting to train in karate as a means of improving their health, they developed so much that they seemed to be different people... [Both of them and many other karate experts] have all lived to be over eighty.[26]

Funakoshi admitted to being weak and sickly in his childhood and youth. Kanō Jigorō had also been physically very small and weak.[27] Martial arts training helped them overcome their limitations in terms of physical and mental strength. It seems that many martial arts practitioners often started training out of some inferior physical or social condition. This is confirmed by the fact that many martial arts practitioners in modern times, at least in Western countries, tended to come from minority groups and often lower social classes. The goal of gaining self-confidence through martial arts training is not simply confined to minority groups, but seems to be one of the major reasons why today women and children practice martial arts.[28] Thus, nowadays, the traditional, medicinal-related health aspects are less emphasized in most modern martial arts, having been replaced by the fitness aspect, to include associations with self-confidence building. In contrast, esoteric practices in relationship to martial arts are still highly fashionable and reinforced through popular marketing materials, media, and culture.

The spiritual, religious, and esoteric aspects of Japanese martial arts

The Zen (禅) aspect of Japanese martial arts seems to be one of the main focal points in Western martial arts literature. Draeger stated, "The atmosphere of classical bujutsu is that of Zen."[29] Elements present in Zen teachings, like self-discipline, asceticism, and liberation from attachment helped to prepare the *bushi* (warrior) mentally for battle.[30] These attitudes in regards to Zen-Buddhism, generally, had great influence on classical Japanese martial arts writings.[31] However, while certain *ryū* or schools sought "enlightenment and transcendence," and were strongly influenced by some Buddhist practices, the actual goal of warriors in attaining this frame of mind was to enhance their performance in battle.[32]

Eugen Herriegel, a German philosophy professor living in Japan during the late 1920s, was one of the first Westerners to introduce the Zen aspect in connection with the martial arts in his book, *Zen in the Art of Archery* (1936). But, he admitted that this presentation was influenced largely by his prior readings of D. T. Suzuki.[33] Some modern studies suggested that the strong association between Zen and the martial arts, at least in the case of archery, was only introduced after the Second World War, and Herriegel actually initiated this process by accident through faulty interpretations. The irony is that the Japanese themselves fell in love with Herriegel's presentation.[34] This suggestion might have some validity, because the influential Kanō Jigorō, the founder of modern judo, did not emphasize any Zen aspects in the presentation of his judo philosophy. Moreover, several modern studies accused Draeger, Suzuki, and others of exaggerating and/or misinterpreting the Zen aspect in association with martial arts.[35]

Overall, however, it appears that Draeger did not overemphasize the Zen aspect; he stated that the underlying philosophical principles in Japanese martial arts (classical as well as modern) were, rather, mostly derived from Neo-Confucianism and Daoism. For example, Draeger wrote that Confucian cosmology is reflected in the many training rituals of kendo. Moreover, Confucian and Daoist notions of morality are part of the "metaphysical foundations" of modern *budō*, especially.[36] Originally, Confucian concepts were introduced by the Tokugawa rulers to foster and control the social structure by establishing a rigid hierarchy. Besides, Confucianism also found expression in pedagogical methodologies such as rote learning and repetition, which is especially pronounced in *kata* training.[37] Repetition is the essential method for mastering the Chinese writing system, and this is also reflected in traditional approaches to learning martial arts through *kata*.[38] Obviously, *kata* training is filled with Confucian traditions and rituals.[39]

Furthermore, a variety of other virtues and traditions are generally associated with the samurai. Their practice of an ascetic lifestyle, meditation, and the cultivation of the self, bears relation to Daoism and Buddhism, as well as Confucianism. The mystic *Shintō* beliefs, which were essentially a blend of ancient shamanistic and animistic cult practices, embraced all of these doctrines and traditions; combined, these ideas were attached to the *bugei*.[40] Above all, a central concern of the *bushi* was that of death. The constant contemplation and anticipation of death was the warrior's fundamental state of mind.[41] In association with this condition were the classical virtues of '*bushidō*' ('way of warriors'), namely loyalty, honor, bravery, self-sacrifice, discipline, and obedience, all present and encouraged in the Japanese martial arts.[42]

Since none of the samurai were a part of a 'national army' with its vast supply of soldiers, their tight allegiance and sacrifice to the death, was a necessary and highly valued virtue. Subsequently, during the time of Japanese aggression and war in the twentieth century, these virtues were increasingly directed toward nationalistic ends in a cult-like fashion with an emphasis on "self-sacrifice" in the name of the nation.[43] Lastly, the idea of *dō* (道), viewing martial arts as a 'way of life,' emerged as the symbolic expression for the collective spiritual and philosophical aspects of the modern Japanese martial arts and *budō* sports (see also Chapter 2, p. 37).

On the other hand, the entire esoteric discussion and spiritual attributes that modern literature bestows on the samurai, and other idolized Asian warrior groups, appears to be predominantly modern, romanticized fiction and exaggeration. During the Meiji Restoration (1868–1912), the samurai found themselves without clear purpose and essentially powerless, but they experienced, at the same time, a 'restoration' when their values, traditions, and history began to be idolized and romanticized. In this political and social atmosphere, the '*Dai Nippon Butoku Kai*' (DNBK, 大日本武徳会 'Greater Japan Martial Virtue Society') was established with the support of the Japanese government in 1895. The organization aimed for uniform standards of Japanese martial arts, and above all, a restoration of the 'traditional' virtues of the samurai. In the realm of ideology, Nitobe Inazō's (1862–1933) publication, *Bushido – The Soul of Japan* (1900), is regarded as one of the first, and most influential, works idolizing the warrior code, or '*bushidō*' (武士道 'the way of the warrior'). Ironically, his presentation of *bushidō* was influenced by Western ideas of chivalry. Nitobe's book was originally written in English for a Western audience. It became highly popular and was later on translated into Japanese. Subsequent Western literature and martial arts enthusiasts accepted his romantic accounts largely without question.

In reality, the medieval samurai were close to ruthless mercenaries, aligned solely to a feudal landlord; they represented a hereditary caste on top of an antiquated society. The samurai fought predominantly for personal gain and seldom for 'honor.' By killing their opponents, the samurai could pillage and accumulate spoils of war. Their behavior was largely predatory in nature, without consideration of any higher spiritual ends. However, during the Tokugawa period (1603–1868), this lifestyle ended and the samurai turned into an idle ruling caste; instead of pursuing higher spiritual goals and self-cultivation, they tried desperately to cling to their privileges as members of a ruling elite.[44] Their association with Buddhist, Daoist, and Confucian ideals and values is largely modern fiction.

Science, education, and ethics in modern **budō**

In contrast to the earlier esoteric teachings of the classical *bugei*, modern *budō* arts started to emphasize a scientific approach which was a reflection of the Meiji era. During this period, Western methods of education were adopted by the martial arts for the very first time. Kanō Jigorō, the founder of modern judo, had a Western-style, academic upbringing and embraced modern educational methods.[45] Kanō was not satisfied with the traditional system of martial arts teaching, and realized its inefficiency. Therefore, he reformed martial arts education by structuring, systemizing, and introducing a rational Western approach to judo training.[46] Reasoning, and theoretical instruction and discussions were adapted to judo education. Moreover, because of his scientific outlook, Kanō disregarded the esoteric teachings and beliefs of the traditional *bugei*, eliminated the teaching of dangerous and crippling techniques, and instead emphasized the ethical characteristics. The principle of "maximum efficiency" in judo training as in everyday life became his central premise.[47] Kanō recalled a story of how he was taught *jūjutsu*, the martial art that he learned in his youth:

> Fukuda [his teacher] threw me down repeatedly. I immediately picked myself up the first time and asked him to explain how he did the throw. He merely said, "Attack again", which I did, and he threw me down once more. I faced him and repeated the question. Fukuda would only say: "Come on!" and yet again I was thrown. He then shouted, "Do you think you will learn jujutsu by mere explanations each time? Attack again."[48]

In classical East Asian martial arts, the teacher guided and did "not tutor" the students. Students were expected to copy the teacher and acquire knowledge ultimately by themselves, from "within."[49] Generally, a 'teacher' was usually a skilled practitioner who never really learned how to teach. In contrast, Kanō was probably enamored of Western education because there actually was a methodology of instruction. To a certain extent, however, the classical approach to 'teaching' is still found in many modern martial art schools.

Kanō, a life-long school teacher and professor, considered judo first and foremost an educational tool for self-improvement, with the ultimate goal of benefiting society and mankind.[50] This represented the 'spiritual *dō*' for him, which included intellectual and moral education for application in daily life. The idealistic goals articulated by Kanō greatly influenced many later instructors and martial art systems, including taekwondo.

On the other hand, a less cheerful assessment of the modern Japanese *budō* arts suggests that by incorporating Western ideas, they displayed a "blending of European militarism and physical culture with Japanese neo-Confucianism, militarism, and physical culture."[51] Another downbeat view is that the Japanese "managed to pick up some of the worst, most bellicose aspects of the Western world for emulation."[52]

The extension of Japanese philosophical ideals to karate

Karate differed from other traditional Japanese martial arts because it was imported only at the beginning of the twentieth century from Okinawa and, therefore, had no direct link to the classical Japanese *bugei*. In general, traditional karate is associated foremost with self-defense and forms training, as well as a variety of spiritual values, certain ceremonial formalities and rituals. However, at first glance, when combined, these aspects do not appear to be connected, but can be explained in the following manner: karate training in Okinawa consisted mostly of physical conditioning and forms or *kata* training. This method of training was inherited from the Chinese martial arts through a variety of diverse contacts and exchanges with the mainland. Initially, training in Okinawan karate was foremost conceived as a practical art for self-defense, with no philosophical or spiritual foundations, yet. Moreover, karate was not organized, did not have any structured teaching methods, and instead was taught individually without any consistent approach. However, this changed when karate was introduced to Japan. In order to gain acceptance, the Okinawan karate masters 'Japanized' karate by attaching some of the philosophical concepts of the classical Japanese *bugei*. In addition, karate training received structure and a formal character modeled on the modern *budō* sports.[53] In summary, the original and sole objective of karate was self-defense; its original and only training method was repetition in the form of *kata*, and its emphasis on certain spiritual values and training formalities is a result of its introduction to Japan.

Japanese *karate-dō* is presented by Funakoshi as having a strong connection to Zen-Buddhist teachings – a relationship he established, which did not exist in the original teachings of *Okinawa-te*. Historically, Funakoshi tried to link modern karate to Bodhidharma, the mythological founder of Zen-Buddhism and supposedly the Shaolin fighting arts.[54] On a spiritual level, he would associate the meaning of *kara-te*, in connection with the newly introduced '*kara*' or 'empty' (空) logogram, with various esoteric Zen-Buddhist concepts of "emptiness of form" and "emptiness of mind."[55] These Zen-Buddhist ideas are linked with Japanese karate throughout all classical karate literature.[56] In addition, the Okinawan karate masters associated karate with Confucian ethical and behavioral norms, as well as some other traditional spiritual aspects, such as the warrior ethos of the Japanese *bugei*.

In Okinawa, Funakoshi was a public school teacher before he went to Japan in 1922, to introduce karate. Therefore, he often described the objectives of karate from an educational and ethical point of view. He emphasized that karate "as spiritual training... is fostering the traits of courage, courtesy, integrity, humility, and self-control."[57] 'Spiritual karate training' was supposed to be practiced in all actions and daily life activities. Funakoshi, who befriended Kanō Jigorō, shared with him similar convictions; students ought to be educated for the betterment of society and mankind.

The ideological 'Japanization' of karate was necessary to gain acceptance among Japanese audiences. However, as in Kanō's judo, karate ideology was less associated with Shintō ideas and esoteric teachings,[58] instead emphasizing rationality and science. This was a reflection of the times.

The most important period for the development and formation of Japanese karate seemed to have been the 1930s, in which karate reached its present form.[59] All of the founders of the first Korean 'taekwondo' schools, except Hwang Kee, studied karate during that time in Japan (see Chapter 2, pp. 39–43), and subsequently introduced not only the technical framework but also the philosophical values of karate to Korea. However, during the course of time, and as a consequence of a turbulent history, Koreans considered it necessary to 'Koreanize' the art and introduce certain modifications to the philosophical value system inherited from the Japanese *karate-dō*.

The philosophical foundations of taekwondo

In contrast to the Japanese martial arts, during the period of the Chosŏn Dynasty (1392–1897), Koreans had no philosophical concepts or virtues associated with warriors in their culture. Koreans did not glorify the warrior; on the contrary, the symbol of the Chosŏn period was the Confucian scholar. During the Japanese occupation of Korea (1910–1945), the Japanese warrior ethos and spirit had been introduced in connection with Japanese martial arts to Korea, but these concepts were originally foreign to Korean culture at that time. Koreans first came into contact with Japanese martial arts ideas with the introduction of judo in 1906, and later kendo. Therefore, when karate was introduced towards the end of the Second World War, there was already some familiarity with these ideas.[60]

Tangsudo and *kongsudo* (or *karate-dō*) slowly began to spread during the post-colonial years in Korea. The masters associated their art fully with Japanese karate traditions. However, any link with the Japanese past encountered resentment in the increasing nationalistic political environment of the times. Therefore, with the slow formation of the various schools under a guiding umbrella organization, taekwondo was presented increasingly, over time, as an indigenous Korean martial art with an ancient lineage and history, spanning almost two thousand years.

Continuation and modification of ideology

Early Korean martial arts literature focused on the fundamental and practical notion of martial arts as a means for battle and self-defense. In relation to this, the alleged scientific nature of taekwondo instruction was a major fixation of Choi Hong Hi.[61] Conversely, esoteric concepts are mentioned less by Korean martial arts authors.[62] For instance, Choi rejected the use of animal and other mystical names for techniques, and embraced Korean historical names and rational terms, instead. The so-called, 'scientific' aspect was supposed to demonstrate the superiority and modernity of taekwondo, and probably also was a reflection of the fixation with scholarly affiliation held by Koreans in general. In their presentation of taekwondo's educational philosophy and merits, the Korean instructors could readily accept the Confucian values and norms (behavioral rules) of Japanese karate, which were also innate to Korean culture. However, the Zen aspects of karate were mostly ignored, because it was foreign to Koreans in association with martial arts. Moreover, the significance of the '*do*' was not much explained either, other than its literal meaning.[63] An essential function of ideology in taekwondo was, however, its use as a tool to focus on nationalistic education.

Nationalism

A main focus of Choi Hong Hi was the nationalistic glorification of the Korean nation and its history, as expressed in the names of his *Ch'anghŏn hyŏng*, or forms (see also Chapter 3, p. 68). Choi mostly named them after mythical or historical Korean heroes (for instance, "*Tan-Gun*," "*Ch'ung-Mu*," "*Se-Jong*"), modern nationalists (for example, "*Chung'-Gŭn*"), or patriotic events ("*Sam-Il*").[64] Moreover, with nationalism in mind, Korean leaders adopted and connected the Japanese warrior ethos with Korean heroic figures and events.

The *hwarang* myth began to be propagated for nationalistic reasons by the Korean government and military (see also Chapter 1, p. 15). Likewise, the '*hwarang* spirit' was embraced as a central theme in the presentation of taekwondo's ideology. In this context, the claim was made of the existence of taekwondo in the form of '*hwarangdo*' exercises.[65] However, the rather modern Japanese concept of '*dō*' attached to a supposedly historic Korean martial art is a curious, cobbling together of anachronistic ideas and convoluted mythology. The concept of '*do*,' in association with martial arts, did not even exist at the time of the *hwarang*, and is thus unworthy of further consideration. Although an alternative suffic '*do*' (徒 'crowd or group of followers') in connection with the *hwarang* was used and appeared in literature as *hwarang-do* (花郎徒), which means 'fellows of the *hwarang*.' This linguistic confusion certainly contributed, deliberately or by accident, to the claim of the existence of an 'ancient' martial art called *hwarang-do* (花郎道). In general, the ideological presentation of taekwondo literature directed toward Korean readers seems to have had the main goal of fostering nationalism, often in connection with historical accounts of past greatness; the directed aim toward foreign audiences was to gain recognition, respect, and admiration for Korea's history, traditions, and culture.[66]

Education and ethics

Educational and ethical elements always played an essential role in the presentation of taekwondo's philosophy and ideology. In his early publications, Hwang Kee was especially keen on educating the youth and establishing behavioral rules, which represented essentially Confucian behavioral norms.[67] Choi Hong Hi also emphasized educational and ethical goals, just as his Japanese predecessors. Choi stated that the aim of taekwondo was "to cultivate the noble character of the person."[68] But Choi and other taekwondo leaders were not able to present a philosophical system as thorough and reflective as Kanō's or Funakoshi's.

Confucian values, innate to East Asian societies, which concern the relationships between humans, such as filial piety, respecting seniority, one's elders, and teachers, had always played a central role in the philosophical body of karate and taekwondo education. These traditional Asian cultural values, omnipresent in Japanese and Korean daily life, behavior, language, and culture, were naturally adopted by regimented martial arts training. Most parents, who send their sons and daughters to taekwondo classes, expect their children will learn discipline and acceptable social, group behavior, as well as practical self-defense. These educational aspects represent the noble goals and values that karate and taekwondo training is supposed to teach.

In reality, however, the constant attempts to dignify the 'art' by associating it with lofty, noble principles and fabricated heritage often appear like a desperate corporate attempt to hastily validate an insecure profession. Moreover, there is another dimension to martial arts education. The authoritarian and hierarchical nature of taekwondo is as much a product of Confucian culture as Japanese and Korean militarism. Taekwondo teachings and training are conducted with a healthy dose of militarism and fascism, characteristics already present in the karate of pre-war Japan, and only reinforced through the Japanese military. Discipline, devotion, and loyalty were always part of the classical Japanese martial arts; however, the bellicose Meiji rulers and Imperial Japanese governments channeled these traits toward nationalistic ends. During that period, the modern Japanese martial art forms became a tool for fostering nationalism and militarism through physical education.[69] In a similar fashion, taekwondo was applied to cultivate the patriotic spirit, self-confidence, nationalism, discipline, and courage of young Koreans. The militaristic aspect was nothing new for Koreans, since many had served in the Japanese colonial army. After all, the late military dictator and president Park Chung Hee was a Japanese officer, and Choi Hong Hi served as a soldier in the Japanese army, as well. Moreover, from the period following the Korean War, virtually all Korean corporate heads and business leaders came from the ranks of former high-ranking, retired ROK military or diplomatic officers.

From the mid-1950s, taekwondo spread widely with its introduction as mandatory training for the South Korean military, and many of the militaristic components are still visible today. The whole structure of karate and taekwondo classes as a remnant of its militaristic past can be seen, for example, in the military style language and student lineups during training. In addition, every Korean *dojang* or gymnasium displays the Korean flag to which all students bow when entering and leaving the training hall, at the beginning and end of the workout. The flag was possibly considered a way of attracting 'national endorsement' from the government and public; bowing to the flag might have been an indirect means of validation and control as well as a way of assuming authority by means of a symbol. This practice has been exported all over the world and the custom in taekwondo training (and other Korean based martial arts like *hapkido*) of expecting foreigners to salute the Korean national flag is a special peculiarity of Korean nationalism.[70] This ritual is also a copy of pre-war Japanese martial arts practices and expectations, where students used to salute the national flag and protecting deities of their gymnasium. Martial arts from other Asian countries have no such practices, and the Japanese mostly abandoned it after the Second World War.

Furthermore, the strict hierarchy among students, according to age and belt grades, is as much a reflection of the hierarchical structure of East Asian societies as its militaristic components. Until the late 1980s, many Korean taekwondo teams at public schools used to salute military style, instead of bowing to their instructor. Corporal punishment, in the form of hitting students with sticks and bats, was common practice in all Korean sport teams and schools, but especially in taekwondo teams until very recently. Unquestionable obedience to the teacher is also an aspect of traditional martial arts and taekwondo education. In addition, strict rules and behavior were expected in every situation of life. The "courtesy norms" of the Korea Taekwondo Association, in 1971, went so far as to tell taekwondo students how to behave in detail during meals and telephone calls.[71] The historical record of the educational benefits of taekwondo and other martial arts certainly includes questionable aspects, contrary to popular descriptions which tend to emphasize merely the positive.

Embracing new ideas and dogma

During the late 1960s, next generation Korean leaders began incorporating domestic esoteric and metaphysical concepts into the general philosophical body of taekwondo. In order to trump the karate legacy, as well as to cement its political victory over deviant *kwan* leaders, the Korea Taekwondo Association introduced new forms and terminology. With the creation of the *P'algwae p'umsae* in 1968, and the *T'aegŭk p'umsae* a few years later, associations with Chinese cosmological concepts akin to Korean culture blended with nationalist elements, took place. The *T'aegŭk* (太極 Chinese: '*Taiji*,' the source of the dual principle of Yin and Yang), or the 'Great Absolute,' which is also the central symbol of the South Korean national flag, became the collective name of the forms used in modern taekwondo. The movement patterns of the *T'aegŭk p'umsae* were supposedly derived from the divine hexagrams of the *Yŏkkyŏng* (易經 Chinese: *Yi-Ching* or *Book of Changes*).[72] No such metaphysical associations existed for Funakoshi's karate patterns, which were considered purely from a practical nature.

Esoteric associations with taekwondo were also a result of Korean instructors learning quickly to exploit the taste of Westerners for such Oriental teachings. Therefore, taekwondo was portrayed in connection with ancient, mystical Oriental philosophies and doctrines.[73] Indeed, with taekwondo's proliferation in foreign countries and the resulting diversification of styles and organizations, new ideas and a variety of Oriental philosophies became newly associated with taekwondo, although these ideas often vary among schools and organizations. The World Taekwondo Federation (WTF) describes 'taekwondo's philosophy' with a confusing blend of China-based Daoist and Confucian ideas. On top of this, the WTF connects the "history of taekwondo philosophy" to intangibles such as the ancient "*hwarangdo* spirit" and Korean foundation myth. Moreover, the emphasis on aspects such as 'traditional,' 'ancient,' and more recently also 'peace,' has become one of the main themes in taekwondo's representation.[74] The content of the World Taekwondo Federation homepage is particularly puzzling, and a good example of how farfetched so-called, 'taekwondo philosophy,' history, and spiritual traditions have become.

The philosophical concepts and values presented in connection with early taekwondo were:

- Self-defense and combat as the fundamental objectives of training.
- The supposedly scientific nature of taekwondo.
- Nationalism in connection with martial heroes and tales of past greatness.
- The samurai warrior spirit, now presented in the form of the *hwarang* ethos.
- Militarism as an educational tool.
- Strict Confucian behavioral rules and values as an educational tool and norm.
- The concept of '*do*' attached to the newly adapted name '*taekwon-do*,' though *do* was mostly only defined literally.

The leaders of the next generation attached the following additional ideas:

- Obscure metaphysical concepts of Chinese cosmology connected to taekwondo's forms and form training.
- Taekwondo's alleged ancient Korean origin, associated with the nationalistic foundation mythology of the Korean nation, blended with Chinese cosmological and philosophical ideas and concepts.

- Retro-association with values such as 'peace and sportsmanship,' as a means of validating taekwondo's value to the Olympics.

Indeed, many taekwondo schools and instructors present taekwondo in a semi, cult-like fashion. There is considerable power and mystery associated with being the priest of an ancient religion. Acolytes and beginners are not permitted to challenge the authority of the 'Master.' Extreme reverence and obedience are the norm. Periodic rituals and ceremonies permit selective access to graduated levels of rank – all adjudicated by higher level priests, or taekwondo 'grandmasters.' Promotion up the ranks promises increasing amounts of respect and reverence, with the ultimate prize being entry into the ranks of the 'masters.'

The various philosophical and educational ideas offered over time in connection with taekwondo reveal an often confusing and inconsistent picture. Regardless, the majority of the Korean taekwondo elite fiercely refuses to present taekwondo simply as a modern 'sport.' By presenting it as a mere sport, they might be forced to abandon many of the esoteric and educational claims they attribute to taekwondo, and which supposedly makes it different to Western sports. However, under scrutiny, the whole esoteric presentation of taekwondo's philosophy appears superficial and contrived, unrelated in any way to taekwondo's actual evolutionary process and history.

The introduction of a sports character to the East Asian martial arts

The Japanese were the first to introduce a modern sports character to the Asian martial arts, beginning with '*kenjutsu*,' which transformed into 'kendo,' the most essential and most highly regarded discipline among the modern Japanese *budō* arts.[75] During this process, the kendo establishment instigated an ongoing controversy among advocates of the traditional forms/self-defense and modern sparring/sport systems. The debate is as old as sparring in martial arts training. When kendo first introduced free sparring with protective gear and restricted rules in the early 1700s, the following arguments shaped the controversy:

> Proponents of sparring and the competitions that developed concomitantly argued that pattern practice alone cannot develop the seriousness of purpose, the courage, decisiveness, aggressiveness, and forbearance vital to true mastery of combat. Such skills, they said, can be fostered only by contesting with an equally serious opponent, not by dancing through a kata...Kata purists, on the other hand, retorted that competitive sparring does *not* produce the same state of mind as real combat and is not, therefore, any more realistic a method of training than pattern practice. Sparring also inevitably requires rules and modifications of equipment that move trainees even further away from the conditions of duels...The controversy persists today, with little foreseeable prospect of resolution.[76]

Similar arguments shape the discussion in most East Asian martial arts.

The history of the modern *budō* sports starts with the end of the Tokugawa period in 1868 and the beginning of the Meiji Restoration. The new leaders embraced Western values, weapons, and technologies for war, and considered classical *bujutu* as anachronistic for actual combat.[77] Kanō stated: "The uniquely Japanese physical education [in the form of martial arts] fell in disfavor" during this period.[78] In contrast, the new style of kendo sparring became a very poplar practice compared to the old style *kata* training at that time. In addition, participation by commoners was allowed and many schools started to operate on a commercial basis, which paved the way for the introduction of public sporting matches.[79]

Kanō Jigorō (1860–1938) had a profound influence on the modern Japanese *budō* arts. As a young university student, he started to study '*jūjutsu*' (柔術 'gentle technique'), which was originally a generic term for a variety of different bare-handed and short weapon combat methods.[80] Later on, when Kanō decided to establish his own style, he chose the name '*jūdō*' (柔道 'judo,' 'gentle way'), because he wanted to avoid the lower-class and violent associations that *jūjutsu* had at that time. He eventually managed to unify most of the remaining *ryū* or schools under his *Kōdōkan jūdō*. In addition, Kanō introduced a method of safe, free sparring, because he realized that traditional *kata* practice was "monotonous" with "little mental benefit," whereas free sparring "becomes enjoyable as well as beneficial" in terms of mental activity and creativity.[81] In order to guaranty safety in sparring, Kanō introduced the *tatami* (畳), a straw mat that used to be a floor cover in luxurious residences of the nobility, to prevent injuries after throwing and falling. Previously, the traditional *jūjutsu* schools trained on hardwood floors. It was precisely these methods of training, in addition to the elimination of dangerous techniques such as eye-gouging, groin attacks, and crippling attacks that allowed judo to transform into a sport. Even though Kanō advocated, "students should practice judo not for the purpose of competition but rather to become able to use it to attain a greater purpose in life,"[82] he was nevertheless a pioneer and promoter of Japanese and international Asian sports in general. Kanō formalized and structured judo and also influenced kendo training, and helped introduce both to the public school curriculum of Japan in 1911. Moreover, he was directly responsible for the introduction of many of the modern aspects present in Japanese and Korean martial arts training, such as the uniform, the belt-ranking system (colored belts and the *dan*, or black belt levels), and structured training sequences. The karate instructors copied these methods and formalities and later, they were naturally assimilated by the Korean taekwondo community.[83] Furthermore, as the first Asian International Olympic Committee member, Kanō paved the way for judo's eventual acceptance as an Olympic demonstration sport in 1964, an achievement which later motivated and inspired future Korean taekwondo leaders.

Although it took considerably longer, the trend to incorporate martial arts into the mainstream Japanese education system also occurred with karate. In 1901, Okinawan karate had already been adopted by the public school education curriculum in Okinawa. Subsequently, Funakoshi Gichin introduced karate to Japan in 1922. Initially, karate found its way to Japanese universities in the form of karate clubs. The first club was established by Funakoshi at Keiō University in 1924. By the early 1930s, most universities had a karate club, affiliated with a variety of schools and styles.[84] However, karate was considered by the Japanese initially as an "incomplete discipline" due to its lack of teaching consistencies, formalities, and unified organization. Therefore, karate was structured according to the formalities already used in kendo and judo. However, because of the beginning of the Second World War and Japan's subsequent defeat, which changed the role of the Japanese martial arts, karate was not able to develop "a universal set of standards" regarding a training curriculum and single unified organization.[85]

In addition, during this process karate did not develop a well-defined sports character; karate leaders failed to introduce a recreational, enjoyable, and playful component in the form of free sparring and competitions until very late. Instead, they adhered to traditional self-defense and combat values and objectives, and insisted continuously on the practice of *kata* as the main training methodology. Non-contact sparring was only reluctantly introduced by Funakoshi as a daily training activity around the mid-1930s, because the Japanese youth longed for some competitive activity, which they were accustomed to, through kendo and judo.[86] During the onset of the Second World War, regular karate training often included brutal training sessions to harden students as a preparation for war, and as a last-ditch means to defend against the enemy,[87] which only reinforced karate's perception as a means for battle and self-defense.

The first nation-wide organized sport competition did not take place until 1957, with the 'All Japan Karate Championship.' Despite the introduction of free, non-contact karate sparring and competitions, its philosophy continued to uphold the central focus of the self-defense aspects. Karate leaders were unable to articulate and incorporate genuine sport principles in karate's philosophy. The various modifications introduced to traditional karate did arguably not greatly influence its fundamental character and value system until the present day.

The inconclusive transformation of taekwondo into a sport

Shortly before Korea's liberation from Japanese colonial rule, when first introduced to Korea, karate's function was thought of primarily as a means for self-defense, and combat, with only very limited sport associations, a view which was greatly reinforced during the Second World War. Funakoshi wrote that karate was seen as a last stage of battle at that time, in case of "hand to hand encounters with an...enemy."[88] The training methodologies and framework, as well as the dogma connected to this attitude, were assimilated without modifications into early taekwondo.

Early taekwondo philosophy inherited from karate the focus on the lethal self-defense aspect in its doctrine. The concept of 'one blow – certain death' (一拳必殺 '*ikken hissatsu*') is an essential characteristic of traditional karate philosophy, which rejected full-contact sparring. Many instructors upheld the belief that since one strike might kill the opponent, free full-contact sparring was impossible and too dangerous; hence, the insistence on the training of forms as a necessary substitute. This attitude was adopted by many early taekwondo leaders.[89] The conviction that one blow actually might be enough to kill an opponent came originally from the traditional Japanese *bugei*, where one blow with a sword or other weapon could actually carry a lethal consequence. However, the same conviction applied to bare-handed fighting is a rather questionable assumption.

The problem of serious injuries in taekwondo sparring was, however, resolved by limiting the allowed techniques (punches and kicks only) and scoring areas (as in judo), and the introduction of padding devices (as in kendo). As a consequence of the introduction of full-contact, sparring/competitions during the 1960s, a split took place, dividing taekwondo's training activities into a traditional, self-defense/forms based training element, and the modern full-contact sport, sparring/competition component. However, this division was not formalized and the different activities were thought of as compatible in daily training routines. In fact, the split was just a continuation of the rivalry, already in its infancy in early karate, between Funakoshi Gichin and Motobu Chōki and their different philosophies and training methodologies. However, unlike karate, full-contact sparring became gradually mainstream in taekwondo.

Over time, the sport-based sparring component developed completely independent training methodologies, technical frameworks, and skills; as a result, sparring/sport taekwondo became more and more disconnected from traditional style training. In modern times, both systems are not complementary at all, but opposed in terms of technical framework, biomechanical execution of technique, and training methodologies. However, this division and the related philosophical contradictions are not clearly recognized; instead, both systems are still considered one under the single name 'taekwondo.' Classes are blended in most commercial schools and recreational clubs, which seems contradictory in terms of training methodology.

Whereas the fundamental objective in traditional taekwondo is self-defense, in sport taekwondo training, the objective is participation in competitive events. The sole focus of training and conditioning is to increase the level of stamina and sparring skill to win matches. Apart from Spartan training for victory, few real educational values or positive sports goals have been adapted to sparring/sport taekwondo. "Taekwondo competitors are extremely adept at the knocking down, but not so quick to embrace the picking up."[90] Taekwondo leaders failed to articulate new philosophies with broader values for modern sparring/sport taekwondo. Taekwondo has only partly followed the transformation as accomplished in kendo and judo; instead, taekwondo continues to rely on karate's fighting mentality, and partly on its training methodology in terms of forms instruction. By failing to develop a complete sporting character, taekwondo is in danger of becoming at odds with itself. By clinging to the traditional karate martial arts dogma, taekwondo leaders have rendered sport taekwondo ideologically inferior to traditional taekwondo.

As a result, sparring/sport taekwondo is mostly only seen as an element among various taekwondo activities (forms, self-defense, breaking, and a variety of newly established activities such as aerobics, performance, and demonstration training), and as a subdivision under the guiding hand of traditional taekwondo. Even though sparring/sport taekwondo represents taekwondo at the Olympic Games, traditional taekwondo is viewed by great parts of the establishment as the keeper of taekwondo's real spirit, values, and traditions. This inferior status is also reflected in the belt/grade promotion tests where traditional components outweigh and outnumber sparring elements. To this day, these contradictions and inconsistencies in taekwondo's philosophy and training methodologies are not clearly identified or resolved. In general, proponents of traditional taekwondo have hijacked the discussion about taekwondo's values, educational direction, and philosophy while, at the same time, presenting common East Asian and Korean cultural norms and dogma as taekwondo's intrinsic values and philosophy.

The diversification of taekwondo training activities

In 1973, the newly founded World Taekwondo Federation began the international promotion of sparring based taekwondo with biannual world championships that same year. The ultimate goal was taekwondo's inclusion into the Olympic Games. This process started to diminish the popularity of traditional training elements in taekwondo schools affiliated with the World Taekwondo Federation, since the only kind of existing contests at this time were sparring competitions. However, traditional taekwondo, which was always seen on a philosophical level as the keeper of taekwondo's true values and traditions, continued to dominate the content of promotional belt tests and training in many commercial schools. In this way, students who focused on competitions were obligated to practice the traditional elements to some extent, as well.

On a practical training level, Korean high school, university, and military teams have always represented the elite, and the driving force behind advancements and innovations in taekwondo; and, they increasingly started to focus exclusively on sparring training for competitions during the 1970s. The relatively uniform, standardized development of domestic Korean taekwondo was possible solely because of Korean government support to the Korea Taekwondo Association, which excluded and suppressed other organizations. The sports-based taekwondo element was increasingly used as a tool to promote Korea's international standing and cultural recognition. However, in other countries, traditional taekwondo flourished through alternative organizations unconnected to the then-newly established World Taekwondo Federation. This was partly a result of the purge of many non-conforming instructors by the KTA during the late 1960s, and early 1970s, when many emigrated overseas and strongly opposed the WTF and the modern sport taekwondo movement (see Chapter 2, p. 53). Another explanation for the resistance might have been the possibility that many of these instructors were simply unable, incapable, or unwilling to learn the newer, faster style of continuous fighting which modern sport taekwondo competition demanded.

The height of sparring/sport taekwondo's popularity in Korea reached, perhaps, a peak with its introduction to the 1988 Seoul Olympic Games as a demonstration sport. However, soon after this event, taekwondo leaders began the process of diversifying taekwondo activities and events, which subsequently provided practitioners an alternative focus in training. In 1992, the Kukkiwon introduced the *Hanmadang*, a theatrical, community demonstration event with a focus on board-breaking, self-defense, "*Taekwon chejo*" ('*taekwon* gymnastic exercises'), and *p'umsae*.[91] Such an event was not entirely new, since martial arts have historically been associated with folk festivities through exhibition fights and demonstrations of fighting skill for centuries. The Kukkiwon homepage states that it was introduced as a way of "promoting Taekwondo as a cultural and tourism resource,"[92] underscoring the commercial aspects of the expansion process. The financial rewards and the desire for cultural recognition seemed to be, once again, the driving forces for expansion. In addition, decision makers probably saw it as a way to increase taekwondo's membership and powerbase.

The first 'World Taekwondo Poomsae Championships' was held in 2006. Then, in 2009, the Kukkiwon promoted the first official 'Demonstration Contest,' introduced on its homepage with the goal of creating a "new demonstration culture and turn[ing] it into art." A further reason given for its introduction was, again, the promotion of tourism.[93] The commercial and cultural aspects were again important in this process of diversification, and taekwondo leaders envisioned taekwondo as an activity or sport for all. For example, with taekwondo leaders' drive to embrace as many students as possible in some kind of taekwondo activity, the WTF also adopted a 'para-taekwondo' program, for handicapped practitioners. The first 'World Para-Taekwondo Championships' was held in 2009. In addition, a 'Taekwondo Peace Corps' was established to spread taekwondo to underdeveloped countries. The taekwondo leadership seems to believe that taekwondo can be a tool to rid the world of all social ills, poverty, and hostility. In reality, the Taekwondo Peace Corps' stated goals appear to be more of another way of promoting corporate Korea and gaining access to developing countries and emerging markets on behalf of the Korean government.[94]

Lastly, taekwondo found its way into the domain of theatrical performances and fitness aerobics. Taekwondo aerobics were modeled after '*Tae Bo*,' a successful American commercial fitness product. It has been added to the general taekwondo activities in many commercial gyms and fitness clubs. The differentiation between taekwondo aerobics, demonstrations, and dancing is often blurred and some activities seem to be strongly influenced by Korean K-Pop, a popular music and dance movement (for the diversification process, see Table 7.2).

As a consequence of diversification, taekwondo became extremely decentralized and there seem to be few standards for curriculum development, promotion, fee-structures, and educational purposes. Nowadays, the vast majority of taekwondo practitioners worldwide are school-aged youngsters. In many taekwondo schools, taekwondo is neither a martial art nor a sport; instead, these schools have almost become day-care centers, catering to children as an after school, or weekend activity, even going so far as to pick them up after school and drive them

Table 7.2 Time periods for the taekwondo diversification process

	Training methodology	Foremost training objectives
1945–1960s	Forms, prearranged exercises.	Self-defense, real fighting.
1960s–1990s	Shift to sparring exercises, but the traditional form elements are maintained.	Self-defense, real fighting, sport contests (as practiced in reality by many athletes and promoted internationally).
1990s–present	Re-emphasis on forms, diversification of activities.	Diverse or unclear. Not well defined.

home after taekwondo class. Most of these schools are run on a highly commercial basis and offer any activity which can charge a fee and attract revenue. Many boast that everyone will receive a medal during tournaments and, instead of genuine competition, events become exercises in building self-esteem and confidence for parents, as well as children. The result of taekwondo's expansion is an ever widening pool of diverse activities associated with taekwondo, making taekwondo's core training activity and purpose increasingly diffuse and difficult to define.

Taekwondo's success as a street corner, cottage industry for the martial arts business community may have outpaced the influence and oversight of any central authority. Once outside the confines of the Confucian homeland, many emigrating instructors almost immediately assume themselves independent of the corporate leadership back in Korea. In addition, these instructors often resist joining their peers, preferring to operate their schools according to their own vision of what taekwondo 'is.' As a result, there appears to be little oversight and few standards in teaching activities, curriculum, promotion criteria, and general taekwondo policy in offshore taekwondo schools. This situation strongly contributes to the lack of a clear, consistent taekwondo 'identity.'

Summary

There are multiple reasons for practicing martial arts, although the oldest is combat, which, in the case of modern civilians, has been largely replaced by personal self-defense. In the past, popular martial arts were often linked to longevity and gaining physical strength; in modern times, it has become mostly connected to conditioning, general health and fitness, and self-confidence building. Conventional martial arts have served (and still serve) as a tool for educational purposes, in a negative way for militarism and nationalism as in pre-war Japan and post-war Korea, but also as a means for some idealistic educators to improve society. The philosophical and esoteric aspects of martial arts are strongly emphasized in Western literature, but the practical implications of this discussion for the common practitioner are questionable. Furthermore, in the case of taekwondo, many of the esoteric and philosophical systems presented have no connection to any actual historical context. Therefore, taekwondo's philosophical presentation appears superficial and shallow under scrutiny.

Many of the supposedly 'traditional' and 'ancient' Korean cultural elements attached to taekwondo are really, in fact, remnants of East Asia's modernization drive during the beginning of the twentieth century. Moreover, taekwondo's traditions are largely inherited from the Japanese martial arts. For early karate and taekwondo leaders, sports were considered on a philosophical level as mostly irrelevant and perceived as a purely physical activity without spiritual merit. This was also one of the reasons why taekwondo leaders were unable to discard the traditional philosophical framework of karate, and probably what stopped taekwondo from developing into a truly 'martial sport.' As a result, multiple inconsistencies regarding taekwondo philosophy and training methodologies developed.

These days, because of the inclusion of many new activities in taekwondo training, it has become nearly impossible to define the term 'taekwondo,' or its core activity. A wide range of activities has been included for the main purpose of attracting as many students as possible. Money, influence, and the drive to spread Korean culture and recognition are most likely the main motivational forces. The result of the ever widening range of activities included under the name of

Figure 7.1 Taekwondo training in Korea (Youngsan University team)

taekwondo suggests an uncertain core identity, as well as the absence of any meaningful philosophy and direction.[95]

The sport aspect of the martial arts seems to be the most controversial. While traditional oriented practitioners see it as a regression of the martial arts, those oriented toward sport and sparring see it as the essence. Of all the traditional martial arts, only modern judo transformed almost completely into a sport, which was certainly not the intent of its founder, Kanō Jigorō. The schism between the traditional oriented forms/self-defense systems and the modern sport/ sparring oriented systems was never completely resolved in any of the modern martial arts;[96] however, this is especially evident in taekwondo. Hence, a reconsideration of taekwondo's training methodologies and philosophy is overdue.

Notes

1 Draeger, *Modern bujutsu and budo*, p. 55.
2 Friday, and Seki, *Legacies of the sword – The Kashima-Shinryū and samurai martial culture*, pp. 5–6.
3 Lorge, *Chinese martial arts*, p. 5.
4 Ibid, p. 3.
5 Draeger developed his theory in three connected volumes: *Classical bujutsu – The martial arts and ways of Japan*; *Classical budo – The martial arts and ways of Japan*; and *Modern bujutsu and budo*.
6 Friday, and Seki, *Legacies of the sword – The Kashima-Shinryū and samurai martial culture*, pp. 8; 63; 163–4; Bittmann, *Karatedô – Der Weg der Leeren Hand*, pp. 47 (see footnote); 191; Watson, *Judo memories of Jigoro Kano*, p. 16.
7 See Capener, "The modern significance of taekwondo as sport and martial art: Overcoming cultural and historical limitations in traditional thinking," pp. 321–54.
8 This part of Capener's presentation might require reconsideration in terms of historical accuracy, as discussed in Draeger's case, since the traditional *bugei* did not really distinguish between *kenjutsu* and *kendo*.
9 Capener, "The modern significance of taekwondo as sport and martial art: Overcoming cultural and historical limitations in traditional thinking," p. 345.
10 Ibid, pp. 321–54.
11 Yang, "American conceptualizations of Asian martial arts – An interpretive analysis of the narrative of taekwondo participants," p. 191.
12 Ibid, p. 192.
13 Kennedy, and Guo, *Chinese martial arts training manuals – A historical survey*, p. 16.
14 Shahar, *The Shaolin monastery*, p. 2.
15 Lorge, *Chinese martial arts*, pp. 106–8.
16 Kim, *Principles governing the construction of the philosophy of taekwondo*, pp. 118–9.
17 Lorge, *Chinese martial arts*, p. 5.
18 Ibid, p. 45.
19 Funakoshi, *Karate-dō nyūmon*, pp. 18–9; Hassell, *Shotokan karate – Its history and evolution*, p. 3.
20 Hassell, *Shotokan karate – Its history and evolution*, p. 6.
21 McCarthy, *Bubishi – The classic manual of combat*, pp. 111–3. One should also keep in mind the broader meaning of the term 'kungfu' (see Appendix B). For example, in Korea, *Jido Kwan* held seminars instructing self-defense, but also bone setting (see "History of Jidokwan," [n.d.]. Retrieved from www.taekwondojidokwan.com/page6.html). In Japan, when Kanō first was looking for a *jūjustu* instructor, he went

to a bone-setter, because they had the reputation of knowing *jūjustu* (see Watson, *Judo memories of Jigoro Kano*, p. 3).
22 Lorge, *Chinese martial arts*, p 201.
23 McCarthy, *Bubishi – The classic manual of combat*, p. 187; Lorge, *Chinese martial arts*, pp. 195–202; Shahar, *The Shaolin monastery*, pp. 137–81.
24 Kennedy, and Guo, *Chinese martial arts training manuals – A historical survey*, p. 15.
25 Lorge, *Chinese martial arts*, pp. 5–6; 195–202; Shahar, *The Shaolin monastery*, pp. 3; 200.
26 Funakoshi, *Karate-dō kyōhan – The master text*, p. 12.
27 Watson, *Judo memories of Jigoro Kano*, p. 1; see also Funakoshi, *The essence of karate*, p. 18. The same is true for many taekwondo practitioners, such as for instance Choi Hong Hi, who admitted to having been bullied by others (Choi, *Taekwondo – The art of self-defence*, pp. 195–6).
28 Yang, "American conceptualizations of Asian martial arts – An interpretive analysis of the narrative of taekwondo participants," p. 192.
29 Draeger, *Classical budo – The martial arts and ways of Japan*, p. 41.
30 Capener, "The modern significance of the transformation of training values in martial arts," pp. 18–33.
31 Bittmann, *Karatedô – Der Weg der Leeren Hand*, p. 66.
32 Friday, and Seki, *Legacies of the sword – The Kashima-Shinryū and samurai martial culture* , p. 156.
33 As cited in Yamada, "The myth of Zen in the art of archery," p. 79.
34 Ibid, p. 71.
35 Friday, and Seki, *Legacies of the sword – The Kashima-Shinryū and samurai martial culture*, p. 163; Donohue, "Kaho: Cultural meaning and educational method in kata training," p. 12.
36 Draeger, *Modern bujutsu and budo*, pp. 62–3.
37 Capener, "The modern significance of the transformation of training values in martial arts," p. 121.
38 Donohue, "Kaho: Cultural meaning and educational method in kata training," p. 13.
39 Friday, and Seki, *Legacies of the sword – The Kashima-Shinryū and samurai martial culture*, p. 105; Donohue, "Kaho: Cultural meaning and educational method in kata training," p. 13.
40 Friday, and Seki, *Legacies of the sword – The Kashima-Shinryū and samurai martial culture*, p. 60.
41 Draeger, and Smith, *Comprehensive Asian fighting arts*, pp. 86–7; Friday, and Seki, *Legacies of the sword – The Kashima-Shinryū and samurai martial culture*, p. 91.
42 Draeger, *Modern bujutsu and budo*, p. 105.
43 Draeger, *Modern bujutsu and budo*, p. 105; Bittmann, *Karatedô – Der Weg der Leeren Hand*, p. 36.
44 Buruma, *Inventing Japan 1853–1964*, pp. 21; 39; Kure, *Samurai – An illustrated history*, p. 10.
45 Watson, *Judo memories of Jigoro Kano*, p. 1.
46 Kanō, *Mind over muscle*, p. 34.
47 Ibid, p. 20.
48 As cited in Watson, *Judo memories of Jigoro Kano*, p. 4.
49 Friday, and Seki, *Legacies of the sword – The Kashima-Shinryū and samurai martial culture*, p. 100.
50 Kanō, *Mind over muscle*, pp. 94–5.
51 Madis, "The evolution of taekwondo from Japanese karate," p. 189.
52 Buruma, *Inventing Japan 1853–1964*, p. 24.
53 Draeger, *Modern bujutsu and budo*, pp. 128–9; Bittmann, *Karatedô – Der Weg der Leeren Hand*, pp. 92–3.
54 See Funakoshi, *Karate-dō kyōhan – The master text*, p. 7.

55 Ibid, p. 4.
56 Bittmann, *Karatedô – Der Weg der Leeren Hand*, p. 250.
57 Funakoshi, *Karate-dō kyōhan – The master text*, p. 13.
58 Bittmann, *Karatedô – Der Weg der Leeren Hand*, p. 253.
59 Ibid, p. 254.
60 Capener, "The modern significance of taekwondo as sport and martial art: Overcoming cultural and historical limitations in traditional thinking," pp. 335; 337.
61 Choi, *Taekwondo – The art of self-defence*, pp. 16–7.
62 Only Hwang Kee ([*Hwasudo textbook*], pp. 1–4) talks briefly about the principles of the cosmos in relationship to health, and body and mind, in the introduction of his 1949 book. The other authors do not mention esoteric ideas.
63 Hwang Kee talks about '*do*' in various ways, like for example training '*do*' and its relationship to drinking and smoking (see Hwang, [*Hwasudo textbook*], pp. 9–12).
64 See Choi, *Taekwondo – The art of self-defence*, pp. 174–5.
65 See for example, Hwang, [*Hwasudo textbook*], pp. 17–8; [*Tangsudo textbook*], pp. 3–7; Choi, [*Taekwondo textbook*], p. 8; *Taekwondo – The art of self-defence*, p. 22; Son, and Clark, *Korean karate – The art of tae kwon do*, p. 3.
66 See for example Hwang, [*Hwasudo textbook*], p. 16; [*Tangsudo textbook*], 1–9; Ch'oe, [*Kwŏnbŏp textbook*], p. 8.
67 See for example Hwang, [*Hwasudo textbook*], pp. 12–4; 19; [*Tangsudo textbook*], p. 4; Pak, [*Kwŏnbŏp association – Kongsudo textbook*], pp. 18–9.
68 Choi, *Taekwondo – The art of self-defence*, p. 18.
69 Draeger, *Classical budo – The martial arts and ways of Japan*, p. 122; McCarthy, *Bubishi – The classic manual of combat*, p. 86.
70 Gu believes that the origin of the display of the Korean national flag in taekwondo schools is the result of the opening of so many new schools by ex-soldiers during the 1960s, when many returned from service in Vietnam. These instructors did not question the practice, but considered it as natural (see Gu, "Aggression, nationalism and combat sport in East Asia," pp. 55–7).
71 Lee, [*Taekwondo textbook*], pp. 285–7.
72 See Kukkiwon, "Taekwondo Techniques; Poomase; Description of Taeguek Poomsae," (n.d.). [Retrieved from www.kukkiwon.or.kr/viewfront/eng/data/technique_trunk1.jsp].
73 Capener, "Problems in the identity and philosophy of *t'aegwondo* and their historical causes," p. 88.
74 See World Taekwondo Federation, "Philosophy," (2013). [Retrieved from www.worldtaekwondofederation.net/philosophy]; Kukkiwon, "Taekwondo philosophy," (n.d.). [Retrieved from www.kukkiwon.or.kr/viewfront/eng/data/taekwondo_mind.jsp].

  The emphasis on tradition and national culture in taekwondo was greatly encouraged by Park Chung Hee's state sponsored campaigns of "spiritual training," with the aim of fostering nationalism and pride. Ironically, these campaigns were modeled after pre-war Japanese campaigns, which were greatly inspired by Nazi-Germany (see Park, "The paradox of postcolonial Korean nationalism: State-sponsored cultural policy in South Korea," pp. 67–94).
75 Draeger, *Modern bujutsu and budo*, p. 77. Archery was the oldest among the traditional martial arts.
76 Friday, and Seki, *Legacies of the sword – The Kashima-Shinryū and samurai martial culture*, p. 119.
77 Draeger, *Modern bujutsu and budo*, pp. 55–6.
78 Kanō, *Mind over muscle*, p. 64.
79 Draeger, *Modern bujutsu and budo*, pp. 97–101.
80 For a detailed discussion of *jūjutsu*, see Mol, *Classical fighting arts of Japan – A complete guide to Koryū jūjutsu*.
81 Kanō, *Mind over muscle*, p. 24.

82 Ibid, p. 132.
83 See footnote in Friday, and Seki, *Legacies of the sword – The Kashima-Shinryū and samurai martial culture*, p. 52; Bittmann, *Karatedô – Der Weg der Leeren Hand*, pp. 35; 37; 99–100; Madis, "The evolution of taekwondo from Japanese karate," pp. 188–90.
84 Bittmann, *Karatedô – Der Weg der Leeren Hand*, p. 100; Madis, "The evolution of taekwondo from Japanese karate," p.187.
85 McCarthy, *Bubishi – The classic manual of combat*, pp. 87–90. On the other hand, taekwondo in Korea unified eventually under one umbrella organization (the Korea Taekwondo Association), supported by the Korean government. Through this single powerful and well-financed organization, taekwondo was able to spread much more systematically worldwide and eventually gain Olympic recognition. Karate never had such structure and support in place.
86 Hassell, *Shotokan karate – Its history and evolution*, pp. 43–5.
87 Funakoshi, *Karate-dō – My way of life*, p. 88; Noble, "Master Funakoshi's karate – The history and development of the empty hand art part II," p. 144.
88 Funakoshi, *Karate-dō – My way of life*, p. 88.
89 See for example, Choi, *Taekwondo – The Art of self-defence*, p. 292; Son, and Clark, *Korean karate – The art of tae kwon do*, p. 269.
90 Kailian, *Sport taekwondo referee primer*, p. 403.
91 See Kukkiwon, "World Taekwondo Hanmadang," (n.d.) [Retrieved from www.kukkiwon.or.kr/viewfront/eng/pr/hnmadang.jsp].
92 Ibid.
93 Ibid. This information was deleted during the last home page modification (no dates are given).
94 See World Taekwondo Peace Corps, "TPC Foundation – Introduction," (2010). [Retrieved from http://tpcorps.org/html_eng/01/01.php].
95 See as an example the content of the official homepages of the World Taekwondo Federation (2013) and Kukkiwon (n.d.), and their interpretations and presentations of taekwondo history, philosophy, and taekwondo in general.
96 Next to the sport oriented *budō* arts remain the modern, but traditionally oriented, *bujutsu* arts. For example, next to kendo exists '*iai-jutsu*' or '*batto-jutsu*' ('the art of drawing a sword'), and there are still mostly self-defense oriented *jūjutsu* styles. Moreover, arts like *aikidō* never adapted to sparring and sport competitions (see Draeger, *Modern bujutsu and budo*).

Bibliography

Bittmann, Heiko. *Karatedô – Der Weg der leeren Hand* (*Karatedô – The way of the empty hand*). Ludwigsburg: Verlag Heiko Bittmann, 1999. [In German, but also available in English].
Buruma, Ian. *Inventing Japan 1853–1964*. New York: The Modern Library, 2004.
Capener, Steven D. "Problems in the identity and philosophy of *t'aegwondo* and their historical causes." *Korea Journal*, 35, 4 (1995): 80–94. [Retrieved from www.eagletkd.com/images/STUDENT%20FORUM%20from%20Korea%0Journal.pdf].
_____. 동양 무도 수련관의 변천과 현대적 의미 "The modern significance of the transformation of training values in martial arts." Unpublished doctoral dissertation, Seoul National University, 1998. [In Korean only].
_____. "The modern significance of taekwondo as sport and martial art: Overcoming cultural and historical limitations in traditional thinking." *Korean History and Culture*, 30 (2005): 321–54.
[Ch'oe Song-nam] (최송남). 拳法教本 [*Kwŏnbŏp textbook*]. Seoul: Donga Munhwasa,

1955. [In Korean only].
Choi, Hong Hi [Ch'oe Hong-hi] (최홍희). 跆拳道教本 [*Taekwondo textbook*]. Seoul: Sŏnghwa Munhwasa, 1958. [In Korean only].
———. *Taekwondo – The art of self-defence*. Seoul: Daeha Publication Company, 1965.
Donohue, John J. "Kaho: Cultural meaning and educational method in kata training." *Journal of Asian Martial Arts*, 15, 3 (2006): 8–19.
Draeger, Don F., and Robert W. Smith. *Comprehensive Asian fighting arts*. Tokyo: Kodansha International, 1969.
Draeger, Don F. *Classical bujutsu – The martial arts and ways of Japan*. (Vol. 1). New York: Weatherhill, Inc., 1973.
———. *Classical budo – The martial arts and ways of Japan*. (Vol. 2). New York: Weatherhill, Inc, 1973.
———. *Modern bujutsu and budo*. (Vol. 3). New York: Weatherhill, Inc., 1974.
Friday, Karl F., and Seki Humitake. *Legacies of the sword – The Kashima-Shinryū and samurai martial culture*. USA: University of Hawai'i Press, 1997.
Funakoshi, Gichin. *Karate-dō kyōhan – The master text*. Trans. T. Ohshima. Tokyo: Kondansha International Ltd, 1973. [Translation of revised edition of 1957; first edition published 1935].
———. *Karate-dō nyūmon*. Trans. John Teramoto. Tokyo: Kodansha International, 1988. [Original work published 1943].
———. *Karate-dō – My way of life*. Trans. Tokyo: Kodansha International, 1975. [Original work published 1956].
———. *The essence of karate*. Trans. Richard Berger. Tokyo: Kondansha International, 2010. [Original work not published].
Gu, Hyosong. "Aggression, Nationalismus und Kampfsport in Ostasien" ("Aggression, nationalism and combat sport in East Asia"). Unpublished master's thesis, University of Hamburg, 1994. [In German only].
Hassell, Randall G. *Shotokan karate – Its history and evolution*. Los Angeles: Empire Books, 2007.
Herriegel, Eugen. *Zen in the art of archery*. Trans. R. F. C. Hull. New York: Pantheon Books, Inc., 1953. [Original work published 1936].
Hwang, Kee [Hwang Ki] (황기). 花手道教本 [*Hwasudo textbook*]. Seoul: Chosŏn Munhwa Ch'ulp'ansa, 1949. [In Korean only].
———. 唐手道教本 [*Tangsudo textbook*]. Seoul: Kyerang Munhwasa, 1958. [In Korean only].
Kailian, Gregory S. *Sport taekwondo referee primer*. Pennsylvania: Word Association Publishers, 2010.
Kanō, Jigorō. *Mind over muscle*. Trans. Nancy H. Ross. Tokyo: Kodansha International, 2005. [Original work not published].
Kennedy, Brian, and Elizabeth Guo. *Chinese martial arts training manuals – A historical survey*. Berkeley: Blue Snake Books, 2005.
[Kim Yong-ok] (김용옥). 태권도철학의구성원리 *Principles governing the construction of the philosophy of taekwondo*. Seoul: T'ongnamu, 1990. [In Korean only].
Kure, Mitsudo. *Samurai – An illustrated history*. Boston – Rutland, Vermont – Tokyo: Tuttle Publishing, 2001.
Lee, Chong Woo [Yi Chong-u] (이종우). 태권도교본 [*Taekwondo textbook*]. Seoul: Korean Taekwondo Association Publication, 1972. [In Korean only].
Lorge, Peter A. *Chinese martial arts*. Cambridge: Cambridge University Press, 2012.
McCarthy, Patrick. *Bubishi – The classic manual of combat*. USA: Tuttle Publishing, 2008.

Madis, Eric. "The evolution of taekwondo from Japanese karate." In *Martial arts in the modern world*. Eds. Thomas A. Green and Joseph R. Svinth, 185–209. Westport: Praeger Publishers, 2003.

Mol, Serge. *Classical fighting arts of Japan – A complete guide to Koryū jūjutsu*. Tokyo: Kodansha International, 2001.

Nitobe, Inazō. *Bushido – The soul of Japan*. San Bernardino, 2014. [Original work published 1900].

Noble, Graham "Master Funakoshi's karate – The history and development of the empty hand art part II." *Dragon Times*, 4 (n.d.): 6–9. [Retrieved from http://museum.hikari.us/].

[Pak Ch'ŏl-hŭi] (박철희). 破邪拳法 – 空手道敎本 [*Kwŏnbŏp association – Kongsudo textbook*]. Seoul: Kudŏgwŏnsa, 1958. [In Korean only].

Park, Sang Mi. "The paradox of postcolonial Korean nationalism: State-sponsored cultural policy in South Korea, 1965–Present." *The Journal of Korean Studies*. 15, 1 (2010): 67–94.

Shahar, Meir. *The Shaolin monastery*. Honolulu: University of Hawai'i Press, 2008.

Son, Duk Sung [Son Tŏk-sŏng], and Robert J. Clark. *Korean karate – The art of tae kwon do*. New York: Prentice-Hall, Inc. Englewood Cliffs, 1968.

Watson, Brian N. *Judo memories of Jigoro Kano*. Trafford Publishing, 2008.

Yamada, Shoji. "The myth of Zen in the art of archery." In *Martial arts in the modern world*. Eds. Thomas A. Green and Joseph R. Svinth, 71–92. Westport: Praeger, 2003.

Yang, Jin Bang (양진방). "American conceptualizations of Asian martial arts – An interpretive analysis of the narrative of taekwondo participants." Unpublished doctoral dissertation, The University of North Carolina at Greensboro, 1996.

8 Forms versus sparring

Since sparring competitions were introduced to taekwondo in the 1960s, training began to split into two distinct categories: the conventional forms and self-defense exercises of hitherto traditional taekwondo or karate, and the new methodology of full-contact sparring training for sports competitions. This chapter seeks to demonstrate that forms training and sparring are fundamentally different activities. This chapter will show that traditional and sport/sparring taekwondo have distinct differences regarding biomechanical characteristics and principle movement patterns, which are incompatible with one another. The fact that these disparate training styles coexist under the same banner is a fundamental inconsistency in taekwondo's training methodology and philosophy. This chapter will conclude by offering some possible solutions.

The technical inconsistencies in taekwondo

Even though there have been no truly new kicking techniques for sparring developed since the mid-1980s, preferred sparring technique and strategies keep changing with revisions in the competition rules, format, and equipment. Essentially, the techniques and strategies that lead to victory in the context of the rules are correct; hence, the execution sequence or form of specific techniques is not entirely permanent. In addition, individual techniques have to adapt in sparring to shifting fight situations and often also to the physical limitations of individual athletes. Moreover, some concepts, strategies, and even training activities do not fit everyone and have to be adjusted for different personalities. The training of techniques and combinations merely serve as a general framework, a preparation for sparring. The training methods and exact execution of techniques often vary in schools, regions, and countries. Training programs and strategies keep changing as a result of trial and error.

In contrast, traditional taekwondo techniques have not really changed much from the time of the introduction of karate to Korea. Even though every year, there are some minor superficial revisions of techniques, for instance, of how to position one's hand or fingers or feet during a block or strike, these revisions are relatively arbitrary and without any practical purpose related to improving fighting skills. Moreover, these revisions are dictated from the top, that is the taekwondo leadership, whereas technical changes in sparring originate from the bottom, namely from the athletes who actually have to apply the technique in competition.[1] There is a great deal of spontaneous creativity involved in sparring, whereas the goal of traditional forms training is to mimic a movement and the instructor, exactly.[2] The concepts, origins, and purposes of technique in sparring and traditional forms training are at odds with one another.

This section discusses and presents some typical examples of basic techniques used in traditional forms training and sparring, to present a visual contrast showing the incompatibility of these different systems.

Stances

In full-contact taekwondo sparring, the stances are flexible, which allow fast movement, changes of position, and smooth execution of combination techniques, as well as immediate recovery and counterattack, if necessary. The body weight in these stances is often concentrated in a deep, forward direction, and rests more often on the front leg. From this stance, it is easier and faster to project one's weight into a kick or punch toward the opponent. An alternative is a more centered position that especially tall athletes, relative to their weight category, sometimes prefer.

The stances used in traditional karate and taekwondo are impractical for the quick movements necessary in sparring. They are too static and inflexible, and some are too wide. The upper body is too straight and upright. None of these stances is used in any full-contact martial arts sparring systems.

- The forward stance (see Figure 8.1) is the most often used stance in forms training.
- Sparring stances (see Figure 8.2) are flexible and can vary among athletes.
- The upper body in traditional stances is always straight and upright; in sparring stances, often slightly bent in a forward direction, anticipating action.

Punches

Even though kicking is the main activity in taekwondo sparring, punching is occasionally used, as well. And since the traditional straight punch is usually one of the first techniques that a student learns, a comparison between a traditional punch as used in forms training, and one as performed in fighting is useful.

Boxing technique is representative for punching techniques in full-contact martial arts. The taekwondo punch for full-contact sparring had to develop fundamentally according to the same principles (see Figures 8.4 and 8.6). Therefore, it is helpful to the discussion to compare a straight punch in boxing (also called a cross) and a traditional taekwondo or karate punch.

Boxers try to project their maximum body weight toward the target by throwing their shoulders toward the opponent, turning their entire torso, hips, and feet. The upper body bends forward during this process and the muscles are tensed on

Figure 8.1 The traditional forward stance   *Figure 8.2* The sparring stance

impact. The punch does not stop on impact, but rather hits 'through' the target. This is all done while using the second hand as a cover for the body and head.[3] Punching in taekwondo sparring follows the same principles. Although in taekwondo sparring, the cover to guard the head is largely neglected and unnecessary since sport taekwondo competition forbids punching to the head, and kicking techniques to the head are far less frequent and much more difficult to execute. Instead of covering the face, the arm is often used as a low cover or block against mostly roundhouse-kick attacks or counterattacks.

A punch in traditional taekwondo and karate, however, is executed by extending the arm in a straight line in a forward direction while rotating the fist, which comes from the waist. At the same time, the hip and the shoulders are slightly rotated as a counter motion while the other hand is pulled back to the waist, which supposedly "[adds] more force to the punch." Then the arm is fully extended, and in modern taekwondo, the upper body ends up often (depending also on the stance) with almost parallel shoulders in punching direction. "At the moment of impact, all of the muscles of the body…must be momentarily tensed."[4] This point is the end of the punching motion; there is no further extension. During the whole process the upper body stays upright and there is no cover (see Figures 8.3 and 8.5).

Traditional taekwondo and karate are usually described as being 'scientific' in most standard literature. The typical portrayal, for example according to Choi Hong Hi, is that "every movement of Taekwon-Do is scientifically organized."[5] Further, when explaining the punch, "keep the back straight," and "[at t]he moment the striking point reaches the target, pull it back."[6] Henry Cho advised,

Figure 8.3 The traditional punch (I)

Figure 8.4 The punch in boxing and Thai-boxing

Figure 8.5 The traditional punch (II)

Figure 8.6 The punch in taekwondo sparring

"While punching, avoid the mistake of throwing your shoulder toward the opponent as a boxer does, for it endangers the balance and coordination."[7] Nishiyama Hidetaka asserted, "Do not lean forward; otherwise, the twisting of the hips is delayed and the punch weakened."[8] The claims made by these instructors are highly questionable as being 'scientific' in terms of body mass and consequently force projection toward the target. In fact, a punch in traditional karate and taekwondo according to the references quoted above lacks full body mass projection. Nowadays, the punch in modern taekwondo forms training is executed without any hip rotation using merely the power of the arm, and lacking any body weight projection. In addition, this kind of static punch is absolutely impractical against a moving opponent in a free fighting situation. Moreover, the notion of pulling back one's second hand to the hip during a punch or block makes traditional techniques impractical for any full-contact fighting system because of the lack of cover. Actually, there is very little 'punching' in traditional taekwondo. Instead, what you have is a straight *strike* using the fist. The fist is almost never retracted, either before or after impact or extension. The illusion (or delusion) that 'one strike may kill,' is such that repetitive or consecutive punches are almost never taught.

- During punching, the upper body in traditional karate and taekwondo (Figures 8.3 and 8.5) is straight and upright, while in boxing and taekwondo sparring (Figures 8.4 and 8.6) it is bent and forward directed.
- Straight punches in taekwondo sparring follow the same principals as in boxing.

Kicking techniques

The front- and side-kicks are the most used kicking techniques in traditional taekwondo and forms training. The front-kick is only used for basic warm-up exercises in sparring training, but almost never in actual sparring. A traditional side-kick is also not used in sparring; instead, the side-kick in sparring transformed into a fusion between a side- and push-kick. Such side-kick-like kicks are especially popular with the front leg nowadays. However, the instep roundhouse-kick is probably still the most used kicking technique in sparring, but there are only two roundhouse-kicks in all of the *T'aekŭk p'umsae* (namely in *T'aekŭk* 6 *chang*). The roundhouse-kick is a rather seldom trained technique in traditional taekwondo practice. Kicking techniques in sparring are usually executed with a 'snap,' but in traditional and demonstration training the leg is often straightened out and held for a short moment for visual effect. Traditional training prefers wide swinging motions and high jump-kicks, but these are ineffective in sparring because they are too slow and predictable. The focus of kicking techniques in traditional training is to showcase the technique in an aesthetic, theatrical, or spectacular fashion during demonstrations to an audience or in forms contests to judges; in contrast, the focus in sparring is efficiency, power, and speed in order to score points or knock the opponent out. The techniques and their purposes used in both systems are not compatible. Moreover, the kind of kicking techniques that are mostly trained in both systems are not even the same (see Figure 8.7).

- An artificial posture of the arms and foot during the execution of a front-kick in a forms contest; a relaxed and natural movement of arms and foot during the execution of a roundhouse-kick during sparring (see Figure 8.7).
- The front-kick is never used in sparring, but is the technique most often used in forms training. The position of the arms is for aesthetic reasons.
- The roundhouse-kick is the most often used kicking technique in sparring, but it is almost never used in forms training. The motion of the arms and the shoulders serve as a natural counterbalance motion for the kicking technique. This counterbalance motion is greatly ignored in forms training because of aesthetic considerations.
- Kicking with the ball of the foot is not useful in full-contact sparring and not often used.[9] On the other hand, it is frequently used in forms and other traditional taekwondo exercises, such as board breaking.

Figure 8.7 The front-kick versus the roundhouse-kick
Source: Courtesy of Peter Bolz

Most traditional techniques have similar problems when applied to sparring. The problems of striking and blocking techniques in traditional karate and taekwondo when applied to sparring and real fighting can be summarized as follows:

- Problems with weight distribution and therefore lack of force projection.
- Too static and inflexible for changing fight situations.
- No use of cover; body wide exposed.
- Absence of flexible steps.

The technical focus and purpose in both systems are not compatible and do not match. Taekwondo sparring is technically much closer to boxing and other full-contact combat sports than to traditional taekwondo and karate.

Regular instructors of taekwondo often claim that the traditional punch, which usually is one of the first techniques taught to beginners, constitutes the basis for the taekwondo punch in general, and such is the case for other techniques. One has to learn the traditional punch first and then later continue learning the punch used in sparring; like different steps or levels when learning, for example, a language. However contrary to popular belief, learning the former (traditional punch) is actually an obstacle to mastering the latter (punch for sparring), because the technical and biomechanical concepts of both systems are not related to each other. This brings us to the contradictions in the principle training activities of taekwondo – forms versus sparring.

The purpose of forms training

Since forms training is the focus of training activity in traditional taekwondo,[10] its fundamental purpose needs to be closer examined. Karl Friday believes, originally, the true purpose of forms training was as follows:

[P]attern practice is employed as a tool for teaching and learning the principles underlying the techniques that make up the kata. Once these principles have been absorbed, the tool is to be set aside... The eventual goal is for the student to move beyond codified, technical applications... [and] to transcend the kata.[11]

According to this statement, the ultimate purpose of *kata* training has been to go beyond the form in a real free fight situation.

In principle, forms training consists of a sequence of different movements with the aim of simulating various fight situations. The rehearsal of these movements is done to improve and connect the individual techniques and to automate certain movement patterns. Moreover, forms training should also explain the fundamental relationship of certain attack and counterattacking techniques. In essence, forms training represents a preparation for free fighting. However, the exact training method of forms practice differs among martial arts. Forms training in many Chinese martial arts, karate, and taekwondo represents mostly a solo-performance by a practitioner, whereas the traditional Japanese *bugei*, and modern judo and kendo mostly equate forms training with partner exercises where fight situations are rehearsed (see Chapter 3, 66–7).

Kanō Jigorō, the founder of judo, adapted two methods for his judo training: one was *kata* (forms)[12] and the other *randori* (free practice or sparring). The purpose of *kata* training according to Kanō is that students are "better able to grasp more quickly how these throwing techniques should be executed for maximum effect in *randori*."[13] In the case of Kanō's judo, the technical and biomechanical system of movements in *kata* is identical to the system used in free sparring, and is thus a suitable preparation for free sparring. However, in the case of taekwondo, the technical and biomechanical systems of movements used in forms training and sparring are not related, and forms are thus not a preparation for sparring. 'Forms training' or '*kata*,' as understood by Kanō, represent exercises performed together with a partner. Likewise in sparring taekwondo, the element of '*kata*' or 'form' is also really represented by target and *hogu* (body protector) drills with a partner.[14] This kind of 'forms training' comes closer to the original way of how *kata* training is understood in the traditional Japanese *bugei*. The traditional Japanese *bugei*, and especially modern judo and kendo, provide an alternative concept of the meaning of forms training, which is also already existent as a practical necessity for modern sparring training in taekwondo, although it is not formalized and standardized as such.

The purpose of forms training in taekwondo

The fighting purpose of forms training has long been mostly lost in karate and never existed in taekwondo; so, forms training became a formalized ritual without any real practical application. In the traditional Japanese martial arts, this principal development was a consequence of the relatively peaceful Tokugawa period, when most samurai could not test their skills in real battle any longer;

instead, they had to rely entirely on *kata* exercises as a training tool to sharpen their skills.[15] This was the time when the classical Japanese *bugei* introduced aesthetic considerations to *kata* and training; simultaneously, they compromised the practical and realistic features of training for real combat. During the same period, an alternative to exclusively *kata* practice evolved with the then-newly introduced sparring training using padding equipment and mock swords. Proponents of solely *kata* training have been at odds with sparring advocates to some extent ever since. A similar process of 'fossilization' happened in the evolution of karate *kata*. Funakoshi Gichin and other karate instructors embraced educational considerations like simplicity as a learning device, a certain censorship of especially brutal techniques they thought not suited for modern society, and some aesthetic considerations into the design of exercises and *kata*.[16]

The aesthetic aspect is one of the foremost features in forms training and contests of modern-day taekwondo; even though many taekwondo leaders still consider it secondary to its purpose in "real battle."[17] However, in the case of modern taekwondo, most of the founders and practitioners never experienced any 'real' hand-to-hand combat at all, and the modern taekwondo forms are not designed as a system for real and practical fighting in any sense. The emphasis on the aesthetic aspect, formalities, mannerism, and educational considerations on the general training activity and forms, and at the same time the declaration of realism and practicality for self-defense, is a contradiction in taekwondo's and other martial arts' general training philosophy. This is the reason there are so many unrealistic techniques practiced in many self-defense systems and traditional martial arts; because, they have not been tested in any way, and were introduced for all kinds of other reasons than real practicality. Ancient warriors had their test in battle; the modern traditional-minded martial artists have only imaginary opponents. Forms training in karate and taekwondo as a means for real fighting became merely an illusion. The concept of forms training in karate and taekwondo became an end in itself. The whole concept of forms training, as understood in taekwondo, deserves a fundamental rethinking.

While the repetition of movements (combinations and counterattacks) and fighting an imaginary opponent (shadow boxing) exists in all full-contact sparring systems, it is trained with a different purpose than forms in taekwondo. These kinds of mechanical drills of techniques and combinations are a necessary part of sparring preparation. But, these drills are not intended as a goal and end in themselves; they are intended to teach coordination of techniques, timing, and the underlying technical principles of sparring. The ultimate goal is to assimilate and 'transcend' these drills in sparring.

By following taekwondo's current training methodology, learning and training traditional taekwondo technique and forms first is actually an obstacle to mastering sparring technique. The initially learned movements of the traditional taekwondo system, which become increasingly coordinated and automated with repetition, have to be disregarded in order to master the technically different sparring system. Forms training in taekwondo, which uses the technically different system of traditional taekwondo, does not improve sparring skills. The underlying logic of learning technique in taekwondo is neither found in boxing, kick- or Thai-boxing, nor in the very recently introduced mixed martial arts. None of these martial arts consider a system that is not based on actual full-contact sparring as a basis for their techniques. Moreover, no athlete in any full-contact sparring martial art practices forms as understood in taekwondo and karate.

General training activities in taekwondo schools

In reality, the practical implementation of training activities in commercial taekwondo schools and recreational clubs seems to be a confusing blend of traditional and modern sparring exercises. As a result, the training activities and teachings are often at odds. The traditional punch is trained in forms and other traditional exercises, but in sparring, during the same lesson, the punch is changed to a sparring-style punch based on the principals of full-contact sparring. The traditional wide, upright, and static stances practiced during forms training, are completely inefficient in sparring and therefore changed to narrower, deeper, more forward directed, and flexible stances. Front-kicks are practiced during forms training, but almost never used in sparring. Roundhouse-kicks, which constitute the majority of kicking techniques in sparring, are usually not practiced during forms training. All of this is taught during the same lesson. Two fundamentally different concepts and methods of training are usually forced into one single class.

Nowadays, the great majority of taekwondo practitioners worldwide tend to be children. In Korea, most commercial schools or institutes do not even offer classes for adults. The great majority of members are elementary and middle school students, and sometimes a few high school students. These institutes are geared toward the after-school training of this age group. The trend in many of these institutes seems to be toward practicing mostly forms, demonstration taekwondo for performances, taekwondo aerobics often with dancing, and sometimes non-related games. Sparring is largely neglected, because many students are small children and the instructors are worried about losing students if they were to get hurt in sparring.[18] Although most taekwondo classes still tend to be a blend of traditional and sparring-related exercises in some way, the result is that there is little standardization or consistency found in the structure of common taekwondo classes. The most common element in taekwondo classes is the uniformity of forms, which is a required and central part in belt promotion tests. In contrast, martial arts like judo, kendo, boxing, wrestling, Thai-boxing, and mixed martial arts are much more structured and consistent in their training activities, training content, objectives, and methodologies. These martial arts do not blend different concepts of technique; their various training activities are uniform and compatible and make much more practical sense.

Summary

For most ordinary taekwondo practitioners, the clear distinction between traditional and sparring/sports taekwondo is unclear because traditional self-defense and forms exercises, sparring oriented sports exercises, and a variety of new activities like aerobics and demonstration training are often blended together in a confusing manner without a clear system or purpose during single lessons in most commercial schools and recreational clubs. Moreover, the taekwondo establishment maintains the claim in the compatibility of these activities, even though from an educational point of view it makes little sense to blend these activities. The taekwondo curriculum in schools, clubs, and even programs at Korean universities portray taekwondo in such a manner.

Contrary to common belief, the technical and training systems of traditional forms/self-defense and the sport-based sparring/competition taekwondo do not complement each other. Traditional taekwondo techniques are not the foundation for techniques trained and applied in sparring. Both systems are fundamentally different and not connected in terms of biomechanical execution of techniques, training concepts, and purposes. Sparring taekwondo follows with its training methodology and values in the footsteps of modernized Japanese martial arts such as judo, kendo, and Western combat sports like boxing and wrestling; whereas traditional taekwondo represents the remains of traditional karate in terms of ideology, technique, and training methodology. Both systems have little in common in terms of technique, training methodologies, objectives, and values. No other modern full-contact sparring method claims a system that is not technically connected to its actual sparring activity as a technical base for its training activity.

The foremost training methodology for traditional taekwondo is the karate-based solo-form training, which originated from China and was introduced via Okinawa and Japan to Korea. This kind of training consists of repetition with the goal of copying the instructor as closely as possible. While there is also an important element of repetition in modern martial arts such as judo and kendo, this training is mostly performed with a partner and consists of the repetition of certain attack and counterattack combinations. However, in judo and kendo, the practice of prearranged exercises did not become a goal or end in itself, but became their technical basis for free sparring. Therefore, taekwondo leaders should look to judo and kendo for the way these arts resolved the problem of compatibility and synchronization between forms and sparring, and opt for a reinterpretation of the purpose and meaning of forms training.

Notes

1 The leaders on top dictate changes in regulations, but the athletes ultimately adapt to the changes in their own ways. There are many examples when rule changes or other revisions did not lead to desired outcomes (see Chapter 5, pp. 107–8).
2 Even though a relatively new form of *p'umsae* contest, called 'Free Style Poomsae,' is also associated with creativity.
3 Gotay, *Boxing basics*, pp. 68–9.
4 Nishiyama, and Brown, *Karate – The art of "empty hand" fighting*, pp. 70–1.
5 Choi, *Taekwondo – The art of self-defence*, p. 292.
6 Ibid, 44–5.
7 Cho, *Korean karate – Free fighting technique*, p. 81.

Forms versus sparring 185

8   Nishiyama, and Brown, *Karate – The art of "empty hand" fighting*, p. 72.
9   A kind of front-kick is often used in kick- and Thai-boxing sparring. However, this kick is closer to a push-kick than a snap-front-kick.
10 Nowadays, other traditional partner exercise, such as self-defense exercises with a partner and *yaksŏk-taeryŏn*, are seldom part of general training activities in most Korean taekwondo schools associated with the WTF. However, their popularity varies in other countries and organizations.
11 Friday, and Humitake, *Legacies of the sword – The Kashima-Shinryū and samurai martial culture*, p. 107. See also Bittmann (*Karatedô – Der Weg der leeren Hand*, pp. 60–1) for a similar discussion.
12 As a reminder, the Chinese character used for *kata* (形 form) in judo expresses 'form' as something not rigid, in distinction to the character (型) which is mostly used in karate and (formerly) in taekwondo (see Chapter 3, pp. 66–7).
13 Watson, *Judo memories of Jigoro Kano*, pp. 78–9.
14 These drills are exercises, performed with a partner, that teach the underlying logic of how to respond (counter) to certain attack techniques. They teach the logic behind combination techniques and are an exercise to improve timing. Some of these drills also serve the purpose of conditioning and/or technique development.
15 Friday, and Humitake, *Legacies of the sword – The Kashima-Shinryū and samurai martial culture*, pp. 108; 117–18.
16 Funakoshi, *Karate-dō kyōhan – The master text*, pp. 11–12.
17 See for example Lee, *What is taekwondo poomsae? (Theory)*, pp. 68–9.
18 I am not aware of any existing statistic in regards to training activities in general clubs and schools. However, the current taekwondo programs at taekwondo departments of Korean universities are certainly geared toward forms and demonstration training, and employers of commercial schools in Korea often value these skills higher than expertise in sparring training. The diverse activities and content of taekwondo classes in commercial schools would be a good subject for future research.

Bibliography

Bittmann, Heiko. *Karatedô – Der Weg der leeren Hand* (*Karatedô – The way of the empty hand*). Ludwigsburg: Verlag Heiko Bittmann, 1999. [In German, but also available in English].
Cho, Sihak Henry. *Korean karate – Free fighting technique*. Rutland and Tokyo: Charles E. Tuttle Company, 1968.
Choi, Hong Hi [Ch'oe Hong-hi] (최홍희). *Taekwondo – The art of self-defence*. Seoul: Daeha Publication Company, 1965.
Friday, Karl F., and Seki Humitake. *Legacies of the sword – The Kashima-Shinryū and samurai martial culture*. USA: University of Hawai'i Press, 1997.
Funakoshi, Gichin. *Karate-dō kyōhan – The master text*. Trans. T. Ohshima. Tokyo: Kondansha International Ltd, 1973. [Translation of revised edition of 1957; first edition published 1935].
Gotay, Al. *Boxing basics*. Denver: Outskirts Press, Inc., 2008.
Lee, Kyu-Hyung [Yi Kyu-hyŏng] (이규형). 태권도 품새란 무엇인가? (이론편) *What is taekwondo poomsae?(Theory)*. Seoul: Osung Publishing Company, 2010. [The book provides a Korean and English text together].
Nishiyama, Hidetaka, and Richard C. Brown. *Karate – The art of "empty hand" fighting*. Vermont and Tokyo: Charles E. Tuttle Company, 1960.
Watson, Brian N. *Judo memories of Jigoro Kano*. Trafford Publishing, 2008.

9 Conclusion

The incomplete transformation of taekwondo from a 'martial art' to a 'martial sport'

In many societies, the compulsion to invent traditions frequently arises to satisfy a need to quickly adapt to changing social conditions.[1] In modern times South Korea, the need for inventing certain traditions seems, initially, to have resulted from Korea's liberation from Japanese colonial rule, and the accompanying ideological void which followed. In North Korea, a policy of state-sponsored history and cultural reconstruction was implemented from its founding. In South Korea, after the Korean War, and following a decade of chaos, the implementation of a policy of cultural and historical restoration directed by official government guidelines, also became perceived as necessary by the military regime headed by president Park Chung Hee, who assumed power with a coup d'état in 1961.

In general, Korea's strong authoritarian, hierarchical Confucian culture became reinforced by the evolving, and revolving, totalitarian regimes of both nations. The South Korean regime promoted a nationalistic policy asking the population to identify with the country through a "sense" of exceptionalism, common history, and tradition. Official and semi-official state agencies were charged with constructing and propagating "a shared national past" to the general Korean public. A variety of "state-cultural policies" and movements were retrofitted, but styled after former Japanese models, with the goal of mobilizing and directing the general population.[2]

The implementation of these policies should be considered in the context of South Korea's economic and cultural reconstruction efforts, which took place under the continuing threat of annihilation by the North. However, successive South Korean governments have continued to assert strong influence on the presentation of history, culture, and tradition, well into the present, and long after South Korea's transition to a democratic, modern society.

A continuation of a number of these policies happens for political and nationalistic purposes with the aim of influencing domestic opinions, but also to project a strong and splendid image of Korean culture to the international community.[3] Moreover, in the international sphere, the South Korean government and public long for global recognition and appreciation. As a consequence, they aggressively push for the hosting of any international sporting, cultural, and political events, as well as the inclusion of Koreans and Korean events in international organizations and conventions, often regardless of the means to an end. Taekwondo developed and was aggressively promoted in this broader political, cultural, economic, and historical context.

Fact and fiction in Korean martial arts presentations

Only a few early Korean martial arts records have survived from the past, mostly short, scant references, leaving great gaps throughout the centuries. As a result, claims about early Korean martial arts tend to sound speculative and exaggerated, although it is evident that Korea almost completely lost its martial traditions toward the end of the Chosŏn Dynasty. The only surviving semi, fight-like activities were *t'aekkyŏn* and *ssirŭm*. However, *t'aekkyŏn* was most likely just a folk game performed by farmers and commoners, while *ssirŭm* was simply a wrestling game. *T'aekkyŏn* had nearly vanished at the beginning of the twentieth century and the foremost association of *t'aekkyŏn* with martial arts is a fairly recent one, mostly contrived for nationalistic reasons in order to lay the groundwork and help construct a native Korean martial arts tradition.

The general presentation of *t'aekkyŏn*'s past suggests parallels with other cases of 'invention of tradition.' Moreover, *t'aekkyŏn*'s association with taekwondo is an invention by taekwondo leaders, desperate for any link to Korea's past. None of Korea's ancient martial arts or folk games, including *t'aekkyŏn*, has any physical or philosophical connection to modern taekwondo and, with the exception of *t'aekkyŏn*, they all disappeared long ago.

Until now, the absence of evidence to the contrary and available historical records lead to the conclusion that much of the widespread historical portrayal of 'ancient' martial arts in Korea appears somewhat dubious.[4] However, this seems to be the case for the presentation of Asian martial arts in general, where history and mythology are often confused and blended. Nevertheless, this provides little justification for the academic research done by many Korean scholars in the field of taekwondo which, by and large, is strongly biased and driven by nationalistic sentiments with a shared goal of fabricating an ancient, indigenous Korean martial arts tradition.

The original reason for presenting martial arts and, in particular, taekwondo, in such a fashion has to be seen in the broader context of South Korea's devastation and division after the Korean War, which required a comprehensive and internationally sponsored effort of nation building and cultural reconstruction. While such a policy conceivably had a place in the context of 1960s South Korea, it has no place in a modern nation, because it is so blatantly disingenuous. What is perhaps even more puzzling is that academics continue to stubbornly twist the logic and facts of historical research in order to maintain their denial of taekwondo roots in karate.

The formation of modern Japanese and Korean martial arts

Because of the relatively, stable political and social conditions enjoyed by Korea during the five hundred-year Chosŏn Dynasty, the scholar, not the warrior, became the enduring symbol and ideal of Korean society. As a result, martial arts were greatly neglected and largely vanished by the end of the nineteenth century. Japanese society, on the other hand, was initially a warrior culture, mostly due to internal, civil strife, historical circumstances, and the subsequent absence of the type of political stability which existed in Korea. Later, according to popular martial arts literature, in the absence of real opportunities for combat during the relatively peaceful Tokugawa period, some idle samurai focused their energies on self-cultivation and aesthetic activities loosely connected to martial arts. The original purpose of the classical martial arts was combat; however, its function transformed into a tool for art and self-cultivation, and ultimately for sport, in the form of modern *budō*.

In reality, however, the idealized and romanticized depiction of the samurai warrior was initiated only during Japan's modernization drive at the end of the Tokugawa period. Later, Western literature and martial arts enthusiasts kept exaggerating and romanticizing the 'honorable' warrior stereotypes, and their 'noble' martial arts traditions and traits. The systematic presentation of martial arts as a 'spiritual way,' and/or as a sport, is mostly a modern development that began in late nineteenth century Japan. The common assumption that the Asian martial arts (Japanese and Korean) in their present forms have a long and venerable history is, by and large, wishful thinking.

The philosophical foundations of traditional Japanese martial arts were mostly a blend of conventional warrior ideals, traditional East Asian values, ordinary customs, and a variety of ancient, esoteric beliefs. During the Meiji era, these notions were combined and systemized with newly introduced theories of Western enlightenment and scientific models of physical education. Moreover, they were blended with modern ideological concepts of nationalism and militarism. These collective ideas helped to shape and structure the character of modern judo and kendo in terms of training methodology, formalities, and philosophical presentation.

Karate, which was not a classical Japanese *bugei*, but rather an imported martial art from Okinawa, lacked a formal structure or any association with higher philosophical or educational attributes. Originally an assortment of fighting techniques, Okinawan karate was considered simply a tool for practical self-defense. Therefore, in order to gain widespread recognition in Japan, Okinawan karate leaders introduced a formal training structure, as well as some philosophical concepts deemed suitable for Japanese karate audiences, modeled after the standardized methods of kendo and judo. As a result, these technical innovations and philosophical additions might be considered to formally represent the early origins of taekwondo. Whereas Kanō Jigorō was fundamental in formulating the general character and framework of the modern Japanese martial arts, Funakoshi Gichin and several other karate masters copied many of Kanō's innovations regarding training formalities and methods; thus, Funakoshi became greatly responsible for the particular structuring of karate, and subsequently taekwondo.

A reinterpretation of taekwondo's origins

Unlike judo or kendo, early taekwondo lacked a unified organization and uniform training methodology, which represented an inherited problem from karate. When introduced to Korea, karate was propagated through a variety of independent schools using different names, and without a standardized training curriculum.

Nevertheless, the comprehensive picture which emerges from an analysis of existing records, testimonies, and obtainable early Korean martial arts literature, provides evidence that early taekwondo was, by and large, a direct descendent of *Shōtōkan* karate. Early Korean martial arts manuals almost exclusively display Funakoshi's *kata*; although the selection and range of his forms often varies among schools, with a few additional modified or self-styled patterns. Moreover, we can conclude that the main taekwondo training methodology, as in karate, was mostly forms or pattern practice. Supplementary training activities and the specific technical framework of early taekwondo were also mostly assimilations of *Shōtōkan* karate. Free sparring, which at that time was mostly non-contact, played a minor role. As in mainstream karate manuals, it was barely mentioned in early taekwondo literature. Taekwondo was not yet considered a sport; rather, physical conditioning, self-defense, and combat were the objectives of the general training activity. In summary, until the late 1960s, Korean martial arts terminology, ceremonial procedures, attire, training tools, and settings, were virtually identical to that of karate.

Early taekwondo incorporated not only the technical features, framework, and formalities of karate, but also great parts of its philosophy. As with karate, Korean martial arts emphasized the importance of traditional East Asian values, such as etiquette, proper behavior, and formalism. Early taekwondo also exhibited many of its authoritarian fundamentals. In addition, the first 'taekwondo' manuals reveal a variety of chauvinistic characteristics regarding the origins of Korean martial arts. The authors were trying to establish a framework for an indigenous Korean martial arts tradition in association with their particular styles; they would attempt to connect their martial arts with various ancient Korean legends and events. Later, when taekwondo leaders deliberately tried to distinguish themselves from karate, new ideological concepts more native to Korea were introduced to the philosophical body of taekwondo. Moreover, taekwondo was systematically associated with ancient Korean history, mythology, and a fictitious, putative martial spirit. These new components, introduced with increasingly nationalistic motives in mind, have no valid historical, philosophical or even logical precedent or purpose; therefore, they tend to appear superficial, shallow, and contrived. The process of creating a fictional past and philosophy for taekwondo's evolution was in the early years, perhaps, an obvious deception; over the years, however, the establishment started widely to believe its own propaganda.

The origins of taekwondo as a sport

In reality, taekwondo technique only started to gradually develop away from karate technique with the introduction of full-contact competition in the 1960s. Full-contact taekwondo sparring was, at first, a continuation of the existing *bōgu* sparring tradition of Japanese *Shurite* karate students, likely introduced by Yun K'wae-Pyŏng, a student of Tōyama Kanken, when Yun became the *Jido Kwan* leader during the early 1950s. The other *kwan* or schools kept practicing standard-style karate, and it was only sometime later, during the late 1950s, that full-contact sparring became more widespread and popular.

The original format for taekwondo competition, introduced in 1962, was mostly a clone of the judo and kendo-based, Japan Karate Association non-contact system, but with the application of full-contact rules. The use of protective gear and the restriction of allowed techniques and scoring areas were necessary in such a system, because of the potential for frequent injuries. Therefore, the following year, a modified body protector, modeled after kendo equipment, was introduced. From this time on, the evolution of taekwondo as a distinctive martial art began. Sport taekwondo developed into a unique, aggressive combat sport that almost exclusively uses kicking techniques, as a result of the chosen rules.

With an increasing number of athletes and tournaments, many new techniques were developed over the years. The evolutionary process of full-contact taekwondo sparring and competitions provides further proof of its karate origin, but also illustrates how sport taekwondo eventually became such a distinctive art. Whereas, Funakoshi's *Shōtōkan* karate provided the basis for traditional taekwondo in terms of practical training activity, centered on forms, self-defense, and general philosophy, Motobu Chōki and some *Shurite* karate students of Tōyama Kanken (like Yun K'wae-Pyŏng) were the initiators of full-contact *bōgu* sparring, which led directly to the successful development of sport taekwondo.

The cause of inconsistencies in taekwondo philosophy and training activity

While taekwondo leaders introduced a full-contact sparring-based sports element, they also tried to preserve the traditional karate character by continuing to practice forms in general training and keeping them as a requirement in promotion tests. Moreover, many taekwondo leaders never abandoned the notion of declaring taekwondo first and foremost a tool for self-defense and combat. Besides, traditional taekwondo has always been perceived as the 'true' keeper of taekwondo's values and principles; many of which are simply general East Asian cultural norms and traditions. In contrast, sport taekwondo objectives and values have not yet been articulated properly and are perceived as being of subordinate priority. Over the years, sparring/sport taekwondo developed into a completely independent and distinctive system compared to traditional forms/self-defense taekwondo. Nowadays, neither systems have anything in common in terms of technique, training activity, or objectives; furthermore, they are mutually contradictory when combined. Nevertheless, on a club level and in most commercial schools, they are mixed and taught together, in the same lessons, on a daily basis.

The process of the introduction of full-contact taekwondo sparring and competitions was a remnant of the transformation of the Japanese martial arts, which represented a struggle between traditionalists and modernists, and their conflicting training methodologies – forms versus sparring. Over time, these conflicting training activities were associated with different training objectives – self-defense versus sporting contests. Consequently, the roots of taekwondo's current dilemma can be found in the spiritual and practical evolution of the Japanese martial arts. However, the distortions in taekwondo's historical presentation have become a hindrance to a clearer understanding of this evolutionary process and, consequently, of making general training activities more consistent, logical, and effective. In contrast, some of the Japanese martial arts, like kendo and judo, were able to resolve these problems more effectively than taekwondo and mainstream karate. Like kendo and judo, taekwondo has begun the combat sport developmental process, but the transformation has been incomplete. Therefore, taekwondo leaders might also look to these disciplines for possible solutions, such as a reinterpretation of the meaning and purposes of basics and forms training (see the discussion in Chapter 8).

The value of taekwondo as a martial art for self-defense

Critics coming from traditional taekwondo frequently label sparring taekwondo as being merely a sport (in a derogatory sense), while, at the same time, claiming that they practice 'real martial arts' for self-defense and combat. However, this discussion is as old as free sparring in martial arts training, and historical precedents abound. For example, when kendo first introduced free sparring with protective gear and restricted rules in the early 1700s, the following arguments shaped the controversy: proponents of free sparring rejected *kata* by claiming that it was an unrealistic method of training for real combat, because it lacked free interaction with an opponent. Conversely, the advocates of *kata* maintained that sparring is not realistic either, because it introduces rules, padded equipment, and other alterations.[5]

Following the lead of judo pioneer Kanō Jigorō, traditionalists like Funakoshi Gichin and other Japanese karate leaders embraced educational considerations (such as simplicity as a learning device), censored most of the brutal, crippling techniques considered unsuitable for modern society, and also added some aesthetic considerations into the design of exercises and *kata*.[6] Lately, the aesthetic aspect became one of the foremost features in form training and modern-day taekwondo forms contests, even though many taekwondo leaders still consider it secondary to its purpose in "real battle."[7] When the classical *bugei* first introduced aesthetic considerations to *kata* and training, they compromised the practical and realistic features for real combat training. A similar process of 'fossilization' happened in the evolution of karate *kata*. In the case of modern taekwondo forms, most designers and practitioners never experienced any 'real fighting' at all,[8] and modern *p'umsae* are not designed as systems for real and practical fighting in any sense, nor is its principal training method – a solo-performance by the practitioner. The emphasis on the aesthetic aspects of forms and general training, and at the same time the declaration of realism and practicality for self-defense, is a contradiction in taekwondo's general training philosophy. As understood in taekwondo, forms training as a means for real fighting became an illusion; or, more accurately: a comfortable mirage.

The introduction of mixed martial arts competition, a sporting event with almost no rules and regulations,[9] brought seemingly final resolution to the age-old controversy of realism in martial arts training. Currently, all fighters in mixed martial arts have some kind of full-contact, sparring-based striking background (such as Western boxing or Thai-boxing), and a sparring-based grappling background (such as Brazilian *jiu-jitsu*, wrestling, or judo), or they consider their training activity to be a distinct style (a blend of striking and grappling), simply called 'mixed martial arts.' On the other hand, even though many athletes from traditional martial arts tried to win these competitions during the early years, it turned out that they and their training methods (forms) had no place in mixed martial arts fighting. Mixed martial arts is now considered the undisputed, 'most effective' martial art in the world; and it is, very much, a sport.

That being said, neither traditional nor modern sport taekwondo is suited for realistic 'street' self-defense. Because WTF competition taekwondo sparring technique has developed into a very specialized, sports system requiring a high level of skill, this has, ironically, resulted in limited practical applications for self-defense. Due to the influence of the very confined rules, sport taekwondo sparring technique has become narrowly specialized and focused on the earning of points in competition. While sensible in the restricted, limiting framework of the rules and regulations, these skills and strategies are often utterly useless in a broader context with fewer rules; let alone, when defending against a psychotic assailant attacking in the absence of *any* rules. Of course, many individual taekwondo athletes or practitioners are quite able to defend themselves, but the realistic value for the application of taekwondo techniques and training (traditional or sparring) in real 'street' fighting situations is limited and largely a fantasy.[10]

The diversification of taekwondo training activities and the arising contradictions

During the past twenty years, general taekwondo training activity again started to diversify greatly with the introduction of new elements, such as *p'umsae* competitions, demonstration contests, performance activities, aerobics, and other popular novelties. The introduction of *p'umsae* tournaments represents a refocus on traditional karate ideology which centers on forms. Almost thirty years ago, when the popularity of sparring-based taekwondo reached, perhaps, its peak with its 1988 introduction to the Olympic Games, taekwondo leaders failed to discard the legacy of karate training elements based on forms and self-defense training, in favor of an exclusively sparring- and sport-oriented training system. Ironically, since taekwondo is presented as an indigenous Korean martial art with a long tradition, taekwondo leaders were also unable to leave the karate elements behind. On the contrary, taekwondo leaders opted to revive and reanimate the traditional training elements and instructional content.

Apart from a lack of imagination, the main reason for further diversification in taekwondo training activities was, and is, to recruit as many people as possible to participate in some type of activity under the ever-widening taekwondo banner. The financial rewards, the increase in influence, and the desire to spread Korean cultural recognition seem to be the main motivational driving forces behind this movement. Ironically, in order to spread their influence as widely as possible, taekwondo leaders have opted to go 'back to the future,' by investing heavily in the development of traditional taekwondo due to its 'sport-for-all' mass appeal and viewer-friendly nature. Spectators enjoy watching quasi-gymnastic and/or theatrical taekwondo performances and *p'umsae* demonstrations; in contrast, sport taekwondo events often find it difficult to attract even minimal audience numbers.

With the daily-growing activities connected with modern taekwondo, the attempt to offer an integrated, consistent, and meaningful philosophy in terms of purpose and value, in accordance with the diverse training activities, seems an ever-elusive goal. Only some shallow formalities, such as wearing the *dobok* (uniform) during these activities, holds the dubious enterprise called 'taekwondo' together.

Concluding remarks

Many problems and questions remain regarding the identity of taekwondo, because of the general lack of recognition and acceptance of taekwondo's origins in karate. While there are certainly "multiple realities for martial arts training,"[11] and different people train for different purposes, interpreting taekwondo's principles and values in different ways, the general institutional presentation of taekwondo's history, philosophy, and training methodology displays numerous inconsistencies and contradictions.

There is a general tendency in the Asian martial arts to confuse mythology with historical fact, and neither taekwondo nor karate is an ancient martial art. Unlike the taekwondo establishment, however, karate did not hide its origins in Okinawa. Since the Japanese already boasted a valid martial arts history, they had no need to invent tradition, unlike taekwondo's guardians. Modern karate developed only with its introduction to Japan during the 1920s. Likewise, the actual history of taekwondo is only about fifty years old. It was only with the introduction of full-contact competitions in the 1960s that taekwondo's creative training activities, techniques, and purpose started to significantly distinguish itself from karate, leaving an essential contradiction at the heart of taekwondo.

Taekwondo has split into modern sparring/competition taekwondo, an Olympic sport, and traditional forms/self-defense taekwondo, which is presented as a martial art. Traditional forms/self-defense taekwondo is a vestige from traditional karate, and yet it is retained in general taekwondo activity, even though links to a Japanese past are denied. It is as if, by retaining elements of a Japanese past (the *kata* or *p'umsae*), taekwondo acquires historical and cultural legitimacy while, at the same time, the Korean taekwondo establishment attempts to secure greater validity by denying Japanese links while claiming more ancient and indigenous origins.

On the other hand, modern, sport/sparring taekwondo, which has evolved over the past fifty years, actually represents the indigenous Korean taekwondo, but is essentially not recognized as such. The techniques, training methods, focus, and purpose of both systems have no apparent connection whatsoever, and therefore make little sense when combined. As a consequence, instructors can neither present a consistent training methodology or a meaningful philosophy about taekwondo purposes and educational values. As a result, the implementation of taekwondo at the club level has come to resemble a disparate collection of diverse activities (basics, self-defense, forms, sparring), none of which are really linked and, when consolidated, do not seem to make much sense.

The inability to part with Japanese concepts and the contradiction of claiming a long native tradition are obstacles to reforming taekwondo. On the other hand, an honest presentation of taekwondo's evolution from karate might help to resolve the dilemma. By abandoning claims of ancient Korean origins and acknowledging its roots, today's taekwondo establishment would be able to leave the karate elements behind.

However, as a result of the vast diversification of taekwondo's activities, it has become difficult to discard most of the traditional karate elements; doing so would result in the loss of most of the taekwondo training population not to mention the considerable livelihoods of the associated instructor population. In fact, taekwondo practitioners, who focus on sparring, have become a tiny minority in many countries and usually represent a group of elite athletes, only. These days, the vast majority of taekwondo students tend to focus mostly on basics, forms, pattern practice, promotion preparation, and demonstration related activities. The WTF establishment and the national organizations are aware of and endorse this situation, so that they can claim a large, inflated number of practitioners who are practicing 'the Olympic sport taekwondo.' Moreover, these members indirectly finance large tournaments and the leadership through membership and promotion fees.

A feasible solution to taekwondo's inconsistencies would be, however, to divide taekwondo's main training activities, forms and sparring, into clearly separated and distinct entities, which would make structural and methodological sense.

Many taekwondo leaders and instructors have not yet come to realize or accept these issues, leaving traditional and modern sport taekwondo to face each other in an odd and uneasy relationship brought on by a distorted history.

Although, some of these conclusions and suggestions might be considered quite radical or even offensive by many taekwondo leaders and practitioners, I do not seek to offend; rather, I seek to contribute to healthy and open discussions with the goal of encouraging further research and debate and, ultimately, improving taekwondo. And, for many of the issues touched upon in this study, follow-up research and analysis will be necessary. Finally, if any of my conclusions are found to be controversial, I hope to read published rebuttals, and I eagerly look forward to a positive exchange of positions and ideas.

Notes

1 See Hobsbawm, "Introduction," in *The invention of tradition*, pp. 1–14.
2 Park, "The paradox of postcolonial Korean nationalism: State-sponsored cultural policy in South Korea, 1965–Present," p. 76; see also Sîntionean, "Heritage practices during the Park Chung Hee era."
3 See Park's discussion, "The paradox of postcolonial Korean nationalism: State-sponsored cultural policy in South Korea, 1965–Present," pp. 67–93. The constant revisions of public school history text books by incumbent South Korean governments are also a good example of how politicians, through their ideologies, try to influence education and public views.
4 In contrast to the general portrayal of taekwondo, the *kŏmdo* (kendo) and judo associations of Korea avoid any historical descriptions and disputes regarding their Japanese origin. See for example, Korea Kumdo Association, (n.d.). Retrieved from www.kumdo.org/; and Korea Judo Association, (n.d.). Retrieved from http://judo.sports.or.kr:8088/judo2009/guide/greeting/greeting.jsp

With that being said, the unconventional *kŏmdo* associations, as for instance *Haedong Kŏmdo*, draw often connections to ancient Korean martial arts as well. There are several different *haedong kŏmdo* associations. See for example, World Haidong Gumdo Federation, (n.d.). Retrieved from www.hdgd.org/01_federation/ 01_federation_ 02.html

The *Daehan Hapkido Hwe* also does not dispute its Japanese *aikidō* origin, but most of *hapkido*'s splinter organizations, such as *Kuksul Won*, cite the same 'evidence' of their ancient roots as taekwondo does. See Daehan Hapkido Hwe, (n.d.). Retrieved from www.aikido.co.kr/xe15/index.php?mid=basic&document_srl=220; and Kuk Sool Won, (n.d.). Retrieved from www.kuksoolwon.or.kr/
5 See the discussion in Chapter 7, pp. 161–3.
6 See Funakoshi, *Karate-dō kyōhan – The master text*, pp. 11–2.
7 See for example, Lee, *What is taekwondo poomsae? (Theory)*, pp. 68–9.
8 Some of the designers of *p'umsae* possibly served in the Korean War, but most likely did not experience any hand-to-hand battles. And if any of these men indeed had such an experience, it is certainly not reflected in the framework of *p'umsae* techniques.
9 During the first years of competitions of the 1990s, no gloves were used, and no rounds or time limit was applied. Only techniques such as strikes to the groin, pulling hair, and eye-gouging were forbidden. However, for minimum safety and some spectator considerations a few restricting rules were introduced.
10 This is also reflected in the uncomfortable fact that not a single of the leading fighters in the mixed martial arts claims to designate his martial arts background as taekwondo; and, only a few claim also to have studied some taekwondo, among other martial arts.
11 Yang, "American conceptualizations of Asian martial arts: An interpretive analysis of the narrative of taekwondo participants," p. 42.

Bibliography

Funakoshi, Gichin. *Karate-dō kyōhan – The master text.* Trans. T. Ohshima. Tokyo: Kondansha International Ltd, 1973. [Translation of revised edition of 1957; first edition published 1935].

Hobsbawm, Eric. "Introduction." In *The invention of tradition.* Eds. Eric Hobsbawm and Terence Ranger, 1–14. Cambridge: Cambridge University Press, 1983.

Lee, Kyu-Hyung [Yi Kyu-hyŏng] (이규형). 태권도 품새란 무엇인가? (이론편) *What is taekwondo poomsae?(Theory).* Seoul: Osung Publishing Company, 2010. [The book provides a Korean and English text together].

Park, Sang Mi. "The paradox of postcolonial Korean nationalism: State-sponsored cultural policy in South Korea, 1965–Present." *The Journal of Korean Studies.* 15, 1 (2010): 67–94.

Sintionean, Codruta. "Heritage practices during the Park Chung Hee era." In *Key papers on Korea.* Ed. Andrew David Jackson, 253–74. Kent: Global Oriental, 2013.

Yang, Jin Bang (양진방). "American conceptualizations of Asian martial arts – An interpretive analysis of the narrative of taekwondo participants." Unpublished doctoral dissertation, The University of North Carolina at Greensboro, 1996.

Appendix A
Individuals interviewed for this study

The interview participants were selected for their relevance in the development of taekwondo.

Capener, Steven D. Personal interview, January 13, 2011, conducted in Seoul.
   Dr. Capener was a former US national team member, PanAm Champion, and medalist at the 8th World Championships in Barcelona, in 1987. During the early 1990s, he worked for the World Taekwondo Federation and was, from 2007 to 2009, the Special Advisor to the Secretary General for Competition and Refereeing. In 2009, when extra points for turning kicks and head kicks were added, he was the vice-chairman of the World Taekwondo Federation Technical Committee.

Chai, Ik Jin. Email correspondence, October 16, 2013.
   Chai was an early taekwondo pioneer and a member of *Ch'angmu Kwan* and later at *Kangdŏk Wŏn*. He immigrated to the United States. The email correspondence was conducted by Gregory Kailian on my behalf.

Ch'oe, Yŏng-nyŏl. Email correspondence, October 28, 2011.
   Choi was the leading heavy weight champion in Korea during the 1960s, and is a member of *Jido Kwan*. He was the dean of the College of Physical Education and the Taekwondo Department at Kyung Hee University. The email correspondence was conducted by Cho Sungkyun on my behalf.

Kailian, Gregory S. Email correspondence, October 25, 2013.
   Dr. Kailian lived, worked, and trained in Korea, for over ten years, from the early 1970s.

Kim, Sei Hyeok. Personal interview, March 23, 2010, conducted in Suwon, Korea.
   Kim has been one of the most successful trainers in taekwondo history. He held the positions of coach or head coach of the Korean national team for the 1988, 2004, and 2008 Olympic Games, and the 1987, 1989, 1993, and 2011 World Championships. In addition, Kim was the director of the Samsung S-1 professional team, until 2010. From 2011 to 2012, he was the first 'permanent'

national trainer of the Korean national team as well. Lastly, from 2013–2014, he was the 'general director' of the Korea Taekwondo Federation. Kim is a student of Ko Eui Min.

Ko, Eui Min. Personal interview, January 13, 2010, conducted in Munich.
Ko was the Korean national team head coach for the 1975 and 1977 World Championships, Chair of the World Taekwondo Federation Technical Committee until 2008, and the World Taekwondo Federation technical delegate for the 2008, Beijing Olympics.

Kobos, Peter. Email correspondence, January 13, 2014.
Kobos is the director of *Motobu-ryū* and represents the Motobu family in international matters. He is located in Edmonton, Canada.

Nefedow, Eugen. Telephone interview, October 20, 2013.
Nefedow was the leading middle-weight champion in Germany from the late-1970s to the mid-1980s.

Appendix B
General classification and terminology of East Asian martial arts

The physical and technical elements, and the spiritual principles and philosophies associated with diverse martial arts are not uniform, but vary greatly in regions, countries, and cultures. The differences between the more practical (in terms of fighting) and spiritually (in terms of esoteric and/or religious associations) oriented arts are sometimes expressed by the choice of names which also have potentially different connotations in the respective cultures of China, Korea, and Japan. Adding to the puzzle, many of the following concepts overlap, and their interpretations and meanings are often disputed (see Table A.1).

The popular term for Chinese martial arts used in the West, 'kungfu' (*Pinyin*: '*gongfu*' 功夫 literally 'effort, labor, skill'; a skill which is acquired through energy, work, and effort), does not exclusively refer to martial arts but is a

Table A.1 General classifications of East Asian martial arts*

	1. Martial skill	*2. Martial art*	*3. Martial way*
Chinese	武術 wu-shu	武藝 wu-yi	武道 wu-dao (generally not used)
Japanese	bu-jutsu	bu-gei	bu-dō
Korean	mu-sul	mu-yae	mu-do

The character 武 literally means 'stopping violence,' but is usually translated as 'martial.'**

Definitions of the following characters: 術 'skill;' 藝 'art;' 道 'way.'

1. Martial skill: technically oriented.
2. Martial art: aesthetically oriented.
3. Martial way: spiritually oriented in a philosophical, ethical, and/or religious context.

Notes:
* See Jin Bang Yang, (양진방), "American conceptualizations of Asian martial arts – An interpretive analysis of the narrative of taekwondo participants" (unpublished doctoral dissertation, The University of North Carolina at Greensboro, 1996), pp. 49–50.
** The Chinese character for '*bu*' (武) is allegedly a combination of two characters with the original meaning of 'stopping a halberd.' This in turn shows supposedly the 'true peaceful purpose' of the martial arts. This questionable interpretation was already made by Ōtsuka Hironori in 1970. See Heiko Bittmann, *Karatedô – Der Weg der leeren Hand* (*Karatedô – The way of the empty hand*), (Ludwigsburg: Verlag Heiko Bittmann, 1999), p. 188.

"generic term for exercise."[1] 'Kungfu' as an exclusive term for Chinese martial arts began to emerge only during the twentieth century in Western popular culture.[2] Besides the term is also popularly used in Southern China by Cantonese speakers (pronounced '*mouh-seuht*' in Cantonese) to refer to martial artists in an informal manner; in contrast, the name is not frequently used by Mandarin speakers.[3] Nowadays, the term kungfu generally encompasses modern gymnastics exercises, martial arts demonstrations, and fighting contests, as well as the entire spectrum of traditional Chinese fighting styles.

Historically, the first distinction between striking and wrestling arts in China dates back to the seventh century. The boxing art was referred to as '*shoubo*' (手搏 'hand fighting') and wrestling as '*jueli*' (角力 'wrestling').[4] However, distinctive 'martial arts styles' developed likely only during the Ming Dynasty (1368–1644), with individual styles usually originating from lineages generally traceable to a particular, real or mythical founder, or place.[5] Later, under the Qing Dynasty (1644–1912), the distinction between styles and schools became already well established. The most common distinction is between the 'Southern' and 'Northern' (beyond the Yangtze River), and between the 'internal' (more spiritual, health, and/or esoteric-oriented) and 'external' (more practical fight-oriented) styles. However, in general, the classifications seem to be not very reliable and are often disputed.[6]

In the past, among a variety of terms, an often-used generic name for weaponless Chinese martial arts was '*quanfa*' (拳法 'fist' or 'boxing method'). However, traditional names were replaced by the Chinese nationalists during the late 1920s, with the generic term '*guoshu*' (國術 or 国术 'national art' or literally 'national skill'). Following the Communist victory, the term '*wushu*' ('martial skill') was introduced in 1950, which became the most widespread generic term for Chinese martial arts in modern times. The term includes a variety of weapons-based arts as well as weaponless boxing methods and modern sporting styles. Some early Chinese documents refer to martial arts with the term '*wuyi*' (literally 'martial art').[7] In contrast, the name '*wudao*' ('martial way') has usually not been used in connection with Chinese martial arts.

The term '*bugei*' ('martial art') refers to the classical Japanese martial arts. Whether there was any subdivision and differentiation in early times between the practically oriented '*bujutsu*' ('martial skill') arts and the philosophically oriented '*budō*' ('martial way') arts remains controversial among scholars (see a detailed discussion in Chapter 7). The term '*bugei*' is a generic term that originally included a variety of weapons-based arts or, in the case of *jūjutsu*, a mixture of barehanded and weapons-based methods. In modern Japanese martial arts some entirely weaponless arts have developed, as well. The modern Japanese martial arts are divided into the *bujutsu* and *budō* arts. *Bujutsu* is mostly associated with the classical *bugei* and modern systems of self-defense for law enforcement, whereas *budō* is mostly associated with the modern *budō* sports such as judo, kendo, *aikidō*,[8] and *karate-dō*. However, again, the exact classifications seem to be controversial (see the discussion in Chapter 7).

According to Yang Jin Bang, from a cultural point of view, most Koreans associate their understanding of martial arts with '*muyae*' ('martial art'). However, the modern Korean martial arts concepts and terms are mostly assimilations of Japanese ones. The majority of martial arts systems in modern Korea fall under the modern Japanese-based '*mudo*' (Japanese: *budō*, 'martial way') classifications: taekwondo (karate-based), judo, *kŏmdo* (kendo), and *hapkido* (*aikidō*, which is strongly *Daitō-ryū aiki-jūjutsu*-based). While there are a great variety of terms used for martial arts in Korea, they mostly fall into the groups listed above.[9] China-based systems in modern Korea are marginal, with some having been introduced more recently. That said, most martial art practitioners in Korea do not distinguish between the terms *musul*, *muyae*, and *mudo*.

Notes

1. Don F. Draeger, and Robert W. Smith, *Comprehensive Asian fighting arts* (Tokyo: Kodansha International, 1969), p. 12.
2. Peter A. Lorge, *Chinese martial arts* (Cambridge: Cambridge University Press, 2012), p. 9.
3. Patrick McCarthy, *Bubishi – The classic manual of combat* (USA: Tuttle Publishing, 2008), see preface "Note on Romanization."
4. Peter A. Lorge, *Chinese martial arts* (Cambridge: Cambridge University Press, 2012), pp. 46–7.
5. Peter A. Lorge, *Chinese martial arts* (Cambridge: Cambridge University Press, 2012), p. 4; and Brian Kennedy, and Elizabeth Guo, *Chinese martial arts training manuals – A historical survey* (Berkeley: Blue Snake Books, 2005), p. 9.
6. Brian Kennedy, and Elizabeth Guo, *Chinese martial arts training manuals – A historical survey* (Berkeley: Blue Snake Books, 2005), p. 78.
7. Peter A. Lorge, *Chinese martial arts* (Cambridge: Cambridge University Press, 2012), p. 10.
8. The term '*aikidō*' was only used officially from 1942, in Japan.
9. Jin Bang Yang, "American conceptualizations of Asian martial arts – An interpretive analysis of the narrative of taekwondo participants" (unpublished doctoral dissertation, The University of North Carolina at Greensboro, 1996), p. 209.

Appendix C
Martial arts literature in chronological order

Overview of early karate publications

From the 1930s onward, there existed a great variety of subsequent publications that could not all be included into this study for reasons of space (see Hawaii Karate Museum, "Rare karate book collection," for further information).

1922: Funakoshi, Gichin. 琉球拳法唐手 *Ryūkū kempō tōdi*. [First comprehensive karate book, in Japanese only].

1925/1996: Funakoshi, Gichin. 錬膽護身 唐手術 *Rentan goshin tōdi jutsu* (*Tōdi arts: Polish your courage for self defense*). [In Japanese, English translation available].

1926/2000: Motobu, Chōki. 沖縄拳法唐手術組手編 *Okinawa kenpō tōdi jutsu kumite-hen* (*Okinawa kenpō: Karate-jutsu on kumite*). [In Japanese, English translation available].

1932/2000: Motobu, Chōki. 私の唐手術 *Watashi no karate jutsu* (*My karate art*). [In Japanese only].

1935/1957/1973: Funakoshi, Gichin. 空手道教範 *Karate-dō kyōhan – The master text*. [Revised in 1957, translated into English in 1973].

1943/1988: Funakoshi, Gichin. *Karate-dō nyūmon*. [Translated into English in 1988].

1953: Mitose, James M. *What is self defense? Kenpo jiu-jitsu*. [First English karate publication].

1958: Ōyama, Masutatsu. *What is karate?*

1960: Nishiyama, Hidetaka and Richard C. Brown. *Karate the art of "empty hand" fighting*. [Most sold karate book ever].

Overview of early Korean martial arts literature

This is to my best knowledge a complete list of Korean martial arts publications until 1968. All were included into this study.

1949: Hwang, Kee. 花手道教本 *Hwasudo kyobon* [*Hwasudo textbook*]. [First Korean martial arts textbook of modern times, in Korean only].

1955: [Ch'oe Song-nam]. 拳法教本 *Kwŏnbŏp kyobon* [*Kwŏnbŏp textbook*]. [In Korean only].
1958: Hwang, Kee. 唐手道教本 *Tangsudo kyobon* [*Tangsudo textbook*]. [In Korean only].
1958: [Pak Chŏl-hŭi]. 破邪拳法 – 空手道教本 *Pasa kwŏnbŏp – Kongsudo kyobon* [*Kwŏnbŏp association – Kongsudo textbook*]. [In Korean only].
1958: Choi, Hong Hi. 跆拳道教本 *Taekwondo kyobon* [*Taekwondo textbook*]. [In Korean only].*
1965: Choi, Hong Hi. *Taekwondo – The art of self-defence*. [First English taekwondo textbook].**
1965: Read, Stanton E., and Chai Ik Jin. *Taekwondo: A way of life in Korea*.
1965: [Yi Kyo-yun]. 百萬人의 跆手道教本 *Baekmanin-ŭi t'aesudo kyobon* [*T'aesudo textbook for the masses*]. [In Korean only].
1968: Lee Won Kuk. 태권도 교범 *Taekwondo kyobŏm* [*Taekwondo manual*]. [In Korean only; the first edition was probably published around 1965].
1968: Cho, Sihak Henry. *Korean karate*.
1968: Son, Duk Sung, and Robert J. Clark. *Korean karate – The art of tae kwon do*.
1970: Hwang, Kee: 수박도 대감 (唐手) *Subakdo taegam (tangsu)* [*Subakdo encyclopedia –Tangsu*]. [Korean, but translated into English].***
1972: Lee, Chong Woo. 태권도 교본 *Taekwondo kyobon* [*Taekwondo textbook*]. [In Korean only].

Notes

* Most sources state that this book was first published in 1959, but the copy used for this study carries the date, December 31, 4291 (*Tan'gi*), the same year as Hwang Kee's publication. There were several editions. Moreover, the Korea Military Academy released a similar book with the same title.
** The Korean version was published around the same time under the title: 태권도 지침 [*Taekwondo guide*], 1966.
*** An English translation was published in 1977 titled, *Tang soo do (soo bahk do)*.

Overview of earliest modern taekwondo sparring literature

These are only the most important publications. There exist some other publications in other languages from the 1980s.

1980: Ko, Eui Min. *Taekwondo Wettkampf* (*Taekwondo competition*). [First taekwondo sparring textbook; in German only].
1988: [Ch'oe Yŏng-nyŏl]. 태권도 겨루기 論 *Taekwondo kyŏrugi-ron* [*Taekwondo sparring discussion*]. [First Korean taekwondo sparring textbook; in Korean only].
1994: [Yi Kyŏng-myŏng], and Chung Kuk Hyun [Chŏng Kuk-hyŏn]. 태권도 겨루기 *Taekwondo kyŏrugi* [*Taekwondo sparring*]. [Korean, but translated into English: *Tae kwon do kyorugi: Olympic style sparring*].

Overview of critical taekwondo history literature

1986: Yang, Jin Bang. "A study on the history of the modern Korean taekwondo." Master's thesis. [In Korean only].

1990: [Kim Yong-ok]. *Principles governing the construction of the philosophy of taekwondo.* [In Korean only].

1995: Capener, Steven D. "Problems in the identity and philosophy of t'aegwondo and their historical causes." *Korea Journal.*

1997: Burdick, Dakin. "People and events of taekwondo's formative years." *Journal of Asian Martial Arts.*

1998: Capener, Steven D. "The modern significance of the transformation of training values in martial arts." Ph.D. dissertation. [In Korean only].

1999: Kang, Won Shik, and Lee Kyong Myong. *The modern history of taekwondo.* [In Korean, but parts published on the internet in English].

2003: Madis, Eric. "The evolution of taekwondo from Japanese karate." In *Martial Arts in the Modern World.*

2005: Capener, Steven D. "The modern significance of taekwondo as sport and martial art: overcoming cultural and historical limitations in traditional thinking." *Korean History and Culture.*

2008: [Hŏ In-uk]. *Taekwondo's formation history.* **[In Korean only].**

2008: Gillis, Alex. *A killing art – The untold history of tae kwon do.*

Annotation: critical taekwondo history literature

Few critical, compelling studies exist that deal with the history of taekwondo; and then, only partially, but they have provided the basis for many of the enquiries conducted for this study. Yang Jin Bang (former secretary general of the Korea Taekwondo Association and current chairperson of the World Taekwondo Federation Technical Committee) was the first of the modern taekwondo leaders to acknowledge taekwondo's karate history in his Master's thesis, "A Study on the History of Modern Korean Taekwondo" (1986). This thesis formed the basis for many of the later critical discussions about taekwondo history. Even though he served (and serves) as a high KTA and WTF official, his former work had little influence on the general presentation of taekwondo history by the Korea Taekwondo Association or by the World Taekwondo Federation.

In 1990, Kim Yong-ok, a popular Korean philosopher, who wrote various books on a wide range of subjects, published a work about taekwondo, titled, *Principles Governing the Construction of the Philosophy of Taekwondo.* Using his vast knowledge of history and philosophy, Kim analyzed and pointed to many problems in taekwondo's historical presentation. However, the taekwondo leadership in Korea responded mostly with insults, anger, and denial.

Steven D. Capener is the first non-Korean to discuss the inconsistencies in taekwondo's history and philosophy in his article, "Problems in the Identity and Philosophy of *T'aegwondo* and Their Historical Causes" (1995). The article lays out most of the major historical and philosophical problems in taekwondo's general presentation. Capener's Ph.D. dissertation, "The Modern Significance of the Transformation of Training Values in Martial Arts" (1998, in Korean only), discusses the development and problems of East Asian martial arts, in general. His article, "The Modern Significance of Taekwondo as Sport and Martial Art: Overcoming Cultural and Historical Limitations in Traditional Thinking" (2005), is based on one of the chapters of his dissertation. Capener's works, which present the best overall English publications addressing taekwondo's history and philosophy, influenced this study. Even though his principle arguments remain valid, the course that he suggests for the future direction of taekwondo may require further consideration because of the many new developments in taekwondo during the past ten to fifteen years.

The martial arts historian Dakin Burdick also deals critically with taekwondo's formative history in his article, "People and Events of Taekwondo's Formative Years" (1997). The article, however, lacks any in-depth insight into taekwondo. The author does not cite any of the crucial sources discussed above, and relies mostly on questionable sources, rendering his conclusions mostly speculative in nature. Furthermore, his knowledge and perception of taekwondo in general seems to lack practical experience on an advanced level. Nevertheless, the article is one of the first attempts to critically examine taekwondo's history.

The Modern History of TaeKwonDo (1999), by Kang Won Shik and Lee Kyong Myong, represents the most important taekwondo book published from a historical point of view. This is especially so since Kang is a reliable witness to history, having been a part of early taekwondo, and progressing over time into a major taekwondo leader. The last office that he held was as president of the Kukkiwon from 2010 to 2013. His first-hand historical accounts are presented in an honest and unbiased way, and he does not conceal his dislike for Choi Hong Hi, the way all high-ranking members of the World Taekwondo Federation or Korea Taekwondo Association tend to do. The book presents mostly facts and events, but lacks analytical in-depth discussion. All subsequent publications about the origins of the first taekwondo schools rely heavily on this work as a main source. Anyone interested in historical facts about taekwondo formation should read this book which is published only in Korean, with parts available in English on the internet.

Eric Madis is a martial arts historian, and a *tangsudo* and karate expert. His article, "The Evolution of Taekwondo from Japanese Karate" (2003), is probably the best analysis of the original taekwondo *kwan* or schools. The article is rather short, but condensed with vital and original information. Furthermore, the article showcases the author's extensive knowledge of Japanese karate. In 2011, Madis published a series of extended articles on the subject in several internet martial arts magazines and blogs. Anyone wanting to learn about the formation of the early taekwondo *kwan* should read his articles.

In *Taekwondo's formation history* (2008), Hŏ In-uk, a researcher on Korean martial arts, provides some additional information regarding taekwondo's early years, however, the book is not as original as the others. He discusses several of the primary Korean literature publications analyzed in this study, but no English-language books or articles. Some of his conclusions are questionable because he overemphasizes the influence of Chinese martial arts on early taekwondo and ultimately resists giving full credit to taekwondo's karate origins. In fact, several more taekwondo history publications exist in Korean, but they were not mentioned in the review because they do not contribute much new content. Another problem is that Korean publications often do not provide any references. Moreover, most of them lack a critical approach.

Lastly, in 2008, Alex Gillis, a journalist and taekwondo practitioner, published a book titled, *A Killing Art – The Untold History of Tae Kwon Do*. The book concentrates mostly on Choi Hong Hi and partly on Kim Un Yong. Gillis conducted extensive research and many interviews, and the book presents much original information, especially regarding political manipulations and corruption by insiders and leaders. However, Gillis seems to describe taekwondo mostly from the viewpoint of the International Taekwondo Federation and often ignores other schools and styles, largely unaware of the technical development of sport taekwondo through sparring and competition. At times in his writings, Gillis seems torn between admiration and aversion for taekwondo leaders; as a result, in several of the anecdotes, taekwondo leaders appear to be almost 'superhuman.' Apart from some innocent exaggerations, the book makes for worth-while reading.

Publications and discussions in the United States, which deal with taekwondo's history and evolution, are often dominated by adherents of traditional taekwondo. Moreover, these individuals are frequently founders or members of small splinter groups, and they perceive the values and importance of taekwondo from a quite different point of view than say, for example, athletes and coaches with a WTF sparring competition background.

Highly recommended readings and sites

1973: Draeger, Don F. *Classical bujutsu – The martial arts and ways of Japan.* (Vol. 1).
1973: Draeger, Don F. *Classical budo – The martial arts and ways of Japan.* (Vol. 2).
1974: Draeger, Don F. *Modern bujutsu and budo.* (Vol. 3).
1996: Yang, Jin Bang. "American conceptualizations of Asian martial arts: An interpretive analysis of the narrative of taekwondo participants." Ph.D. dissertation.
1997: Friday, Karl F., and Seki Humitake. *Legacies of the sword – The Kashima-Shinryū and samurai martial culture.*
2010: Kailian, Gregory S. *Sport taekwondo referee primer.*
2012: Lorge, Peter A. *Chinese martial arts.*
- Hawaii Karate Museum. Retrievable from www.hikari.us/
- International Ryukyu Karate Research Society. Retrievable from www.koryu-uchinadi.com/about/
- *Journal of Asian Martial Arts.* Retrievable from www.journalofasianmartialarts.com/

Appendix D
Forms in early taekwondo manuals

See Chapter 3 for a discussion about forms and manuals, and for works cited.

Table 3.2 Forms described and/or illustrated in early taekwondo literature (I)

If the forms' names differ from Funakoshi's pronunciation, his original terms are indicated in brackets.

Forms	Hwang Kee 1949 Founder of *Mudŏk Kwan*	Ch'oe Song-nam 1955 Member of *Ch'ŏngdo Kwan*	Pak Ch'ŏl-hŭi 1958 Member of *YMCA Kwŏnbŏp Pu*, and founder of *Kangdŏk Wŏn*
Funakoshi's 13 *Shōrin-ryū* **and 6** *Shōrei-ryū* **kata in** *Karate-dō Kyōhan*	1. *P'yŏngan* 1–5 (*Heian* 1–5, written in Chinese characters. All other forms are written in *han'gŭl*, using the Japanese pronunciation). 2. *Naihantchi* 1–3 *Dan* (*Tekki* 1–3). 3. *Jitte*. 4. *Passai*. 5. *Tchindo* (*Gankaku*). (pp. 82–143)	1. *Heian* 1–5. 2. *Passai*. 3. *Kibadachi Shodan* (*Tekki* 1). 4. *Tekki* 2 5. *Jutte*. 6. *Kongsanggun* (*Kwankū*). 7. *Jion*. (All written using Chinese characters, pp. 57–192)	Uses Chinese characters for the following forms: 1. *Kibon Hyŏng* 1–5 * (*Taikyoku*). 2. *Heian* 1–5. 3. *Kibadachi Shodan* (*Tekki* 1). 4. *Jutte*. 5. *Nohai* (written in Korean; *Rohai* is the Okinawan name, renamed by Funakoshi to *Meikyo*. Not mentioned in *Karate-dō Kyōhan*). (pp. 41–117) Pak mentions a variety of other forms by name.*** (pp. 39–40)
		Tando hyŏng (pp. 192–210), probably developed by Ch'oe.**	*Chŏngch'i* 1 *hyŏng* (pp. 67–71), probably developed by Pak or his instructor Yun Pyŏng-in
***Quanfa* form**	*Solim Changkwŏn*. (pp. 144–54)		

Notes:

* *Kibon hyŏng* is similar to *T'aegŭk hyŏng* or *Taikyoku kata* in *Shōtōkan* karate, but there are originally only three. Funakoshi developed them based on the *Heian kata*. He simplified them and thought of them as a preparation for *Heian*. Only the first of Pak's forms, *Kibon hyŏng* 1, is similar to *Taikyoku Shodan* (1). The *All Japan Karate-dō Gōjū-kai Karate-dō Association* (founded by leaders of *Gojū-ryū*) developed five *Kibon hyŏng* based on Funakoshi's, but only left the first one unchanged. Pak also shows five. However, forms 2, 4, and 5 seemed to be modified, possibly by Pak's teacher Yun Pyŏng-in.

** *Tando hyŏng* is a knife form, but there exist no knife forms in karate.

*** He mentions several Chinese *quanfa* forms by name among about fifty mostly karate *kata*. Six or seven are probably Chinese forms, but it is not exactly clear without illustrations because the Japanese sometimes used the same names for karate *kata* as the Chinese, such as in the case of the *Taikyoku kata*.

Table 3.3 Forms described and/or illustrated in early taekwondo literature (II)

If the forms' names differ from Funakoshi's pronunciation, his original terms are indicated in brackets.

Forms	Hwang Kee 1958 Founder of *Mudŏk Kwan*	Choi Hong Hi 1958 Founder of *Odo Kwan*	Choi Hong Hi 1965 Founder of *Odo Kwan*	Yi Kyo-yun 1965 Member of *Chosŏn Yŏnmu Kwan*, and founder of *Hanmu Kwan*
Funakoshi's 13 *Shōrin-ryū* **and 6** *Shōrei-ryū* **kata in** *Karate-dō Kyōhan*	1. *Kijo hyŏng* 1–3 (*Taikyoku* 1–3). 2. *Ppingang** 1–5 (*Heian* 1–5). 3. *Passai* 4. *Naihantchi*** 1 *Dan* (*Tekki* 1). (pp. 68–163)	Describes all of the *Shōrin* and *Shōrei* forms. He uses Chinese characters, and the Korean pronunciation written in *han'gŭl*. (pp. 123–288)	Admits its Japanese origin (p. 216), and uses the Japanese pronunciation, written in English, for the terms. (pp. 216–239)	1. *Kibon hyŏng* (*Taikyoku* 1). 2. *P'yŏngan hyŏng* 1–5 (*Heian* 1–5). 3. *Naepochin* 1–3 (*Naihanchi* or *Tekki* 1–3). 4. *Panwŏl* (*Hangetsu*). 5. *Kongsanggun* (*Kwankū*). (pp. 62–131) He uses Chinese characters and the Korean pronunciation in *han'gŭl*.
20 *Ch'anghŏn* **school or** *hyŏng*, **developed by Choi Hong Hi.**		Only 5 forms are shown in this book yet. (pp. 123–288)	20 forms. (pp. 174–215)	
	Mentions many mostly karate forms by name. (p. 19)			*Yŏnmu hyŏng* (pp. 132–40), possibly developed by Yi.

Notes:
* '*Ppingang*' (삥앙) written in *han'gŭl* vaguely resembles the Chinese pronunciation '*píng ān*' (平安).
** '*Naihantchi*' is the old Okinawan name for *Tekki*. Hwang wrote the Japanese pronunciation in *han'gŭl*.

Table 3.4 Forms described and/or illustrated in early taekwondo literature (III)

If the forms' names differ from Funakoshi's pronunciation, his original terms are indicated in brackets.

Forms	Son Duk Sung 1968 Successor at Ch'ŏngdo Kwan	Lee Won Kuk 1968 Founder of Ch'ŏngdo Kwan	Lee Chong Woo 1972 Successor at Jido Kwan
Funakoshi's 13 *Shōrin-ryū* and 6 *Shōrei-ryū kata* in *Karate-dō Kyōhan*	Uses the Korean pronunciation, written in English: 1. "*Pyong A[n]*" 1–5 (*Heian* 1–5). 2. "*Chul Gi*" (*Tekki* 1). 3. "*Pal Sek*" (*Bassai*). (pp. 89–218)	Uses han'gŭl and Chinese characters: 1. *T'aegŭk hyŏng* 1–3 (*Taikyoku* 1–3). 2. *P'yŏngan hyŏng* 1–5 (*Heian* 1–5). 3. *Ch'ŏlgi hyŏng* 1–3 (*Tekki* 1–3). 4. *Palsae hyŏng* (*Bassai*). 5. *Sipsu hyŏng* (*Jutte*). 6. *Yŏnbi hyŏng* (*Empi*). (pp. 150–271)	The Korea Taekwondo Association stops using karate *kata*.
P'algwae p'umsae developed late 1960s.	"*Kuk Mu*" 1 and 2. (pp. 64–88) (Developed by Son)	*P'algwae hyŏng** 1–8 (pp. 347–75), only described, without pictures.	*P'algwae p'umsae* 1–8. (pp. 95–152)
T'aegŭk p'umsae developed late 1960s/early 70s.		*T'aegŭk* 1 and 2 *hyŏng**(pp. 341–4), only described without pictures. Only two developed yet.	*T'aekŭk p'umsae* 1–8. (pp. 238–278)
Dan *p'umsae* of the Korea Taekwondo Association. Most developed during the late 1960s and used in promotion tests.		*Koryŏ hyŏng, Kŭmgang hyŏng, T'aebaek hyŏng, Paekje hyŏng, Sipchin hyŏng, Jidde hyŏng, Ch'ŏn'gwŏn hyŏng, Hansu hyŏng,* and *Silla hyŏng*** (pp. 376–413). Only described without pictures.	*Koryŏ p'umsae, Kŭmgang p'umsae, T'aebaek p'umsae, P'yŏngwŏn p'umsae, Sipchin p'umsae, Jidde p'umsae, Ch'ŏn'gwŏn p'umsae, Hansu p'umsae, Ilyŏ p'umsae.* (pp. 144–235)

Notes:
* The term *p'umsae* for forms was not used yet at that time; first used in Lee Chong Woo's book in 1972.
** The *Paekje* and *Silla hyŏng* are not used any longer in modern taekwondo. Some of them, such as the *Jidde hyŏng*, are karate *kata*. Lee Chong Woo (1972) still mentions the karate form as well.

Appendix E

General terminology for kicking techniques in taekwondo

(See Chapter 6 for a detailed discussion about the evolution of kicking techniques).

The following English terms (Table 6.4) are often used among English-speaking athletes. In addition, descriptive clarity and usage of taekwondo language in international literature was considered. Several of the Korean terms were collected by Gwak Taeg Yong.

Table 6.4 Terminology used for kicking techniques and punches

Kicking techniques/punch (modern names)	Other terminology used in past or present*
Ap'-ch'agi (앞차기) **Front-kick**	
Tollyŏ-ch'agi (돌려차기) **Roundhouse-kick****, round-kick	*Ap'-tollyŏ-ch'agi* (앞돌려차기)
Yŏp'-ch'agi (옆차기) **Side-kick**	*Yŏp'-ppŏtŏ-ch'agi* (옆뻗어차기)
Dwi-ch'agi (뒤차기) **Back-kick**	*Dwi-dorayŏp-ch'agi* (뒤돌아옆차기) *Mom-dorayŏp-ch'agi* (몸돌아옆차기) *Mom-tollyŏ-ch'agi* (몸돌려차기)
Dwihuryŏ-ch'agi (뒤후려차기) *Dwihurigi* (뒤후리기) **Spinning-back-kick**, spinning-hook-kick	*Hwech'uk* (회축), *mom-dora-ch'agi* (몸돌아차기) *Dwi-tollyŏ-ch'agi* (뒤돌려차기) *Mom-tollyŏ-ch'agi* (몸돌려차기
Huryŏ-ch'agi (후려차기) **Hook-kick**, whip-kick	Front leg hook: *Ap'-huryŏ-ch'agi* (앞후려차기), *ap'-hurigi* (앞후리기), *ap'pal-hurigi* (앞발후리기) Back leg hook: *Yŏp'-huryŏ-ch'agi* (옆후려차기), *yŏp'-hurigi* (옆후리기), *dwipal-hurigi* (뒤발후리기)

Table 6.4 continued

Kicking techniques/punch (modern names)	Other terminology used in past or present*
Tchiggi (찍기), *tŭrŏ-tchiggi* (들어찍기) **Axe-kick**	*Naeryŏ-ch'agi* (내려차기), *kokkwaengi* (곡괭이) *Tchikŏ-ch'agi* (찍어차기) *Naeryŏ-tchiggi* (내려찍기)
Pparŭn-pal-tchig (빠른발찍) *Rŏnnŏ (-tchiggi)* (런너[찍기]) **(Front leg) Jump-axe-kick**	
Mirŏ-ch'agi (밀어차기) **Push-kick** (back leg push-kick)	*Milki* (밀기), *tŭrŏ-milki* (들어밀기) *Kkŭrŏ-milki* (끌어밀기)
K'atŭ (-ch'agi) (카트[차기]) **Cut-kick**, front leg push-kick	*Ap'-pal-mirŏ-ch'agi* (앞발밀어차기) *K'atŭ(-milki)* (카트[밀기])
Pparŭn-pal-ch'agi (빠른발차기) *Put'igi* (붙이기) **Fast-kick*** *Dolgae-ch'agi* (돌개차기)	*Put'yŏ-ch'agi* (붙여차기) *Palput'yŏ-ch'agi* (발붙여차기) *Pparŭnpal*-ch'agi (빠른발차기)****
T'ŏn (-ch'agi) (턴[차기]) **Turn-kick**, tornado-kick**	*Narabang* (날아방) *Mom-dora-ch'agi* (몸돌아차기)
Narae-ch'agi (나래차기) **Double-kick***	*Ttapŭl (-ch'agi)* (따블[차기])
Pada-ch'agi (받아차기) **(Direct) counterattack kick, counter kick****	
Mit'-pada-ch'agi (밑받아차기) **Under-kick (under-counter-kick)**	*Bit-ch'agi* (빗차기), *mit'ppong-ch'agi* (밑뽕차기) *Mit'pal (-ch'agi)* (밑발 차기), *mit'-ch'agi* (밑차기)
Ap'-chumŏg-ch'igi (앞주먹치기) **Front-fist punch** *Dwi-chumŏg-ch'igi* (뒤주먹치기) **Back-fist punch**	

Notes:
* Different schools and regions often use different terminology or slang in Korea.
** The fast-, turn-, and double-kicks are variations of the roundhouse-kick. Students who studied ITF taekwondo often still refer to the roundhouse-kick as 'turning-kick' in English.
*** '(Direct) counterattack kick' and 'counter kick' are used as similar expressions in this study.
**** The term '*pparŭnpal-ch'agi*' is also sometimes used for a 'one-step roundhouse-kick.'
• Compare Table 6.4 to Taeg Yong Gwak (곽택용), 택권도경기기술용어변천과사용실태 "A study on terminology of taekwondo competition," (unpublished manuscript, n.d., Yongin University). [In Korean only].

Glossary

(Ch.: Chinese, J.: Japanese, K.: Korean)

aikido (J.), *hapkido* (K.) 合氣道	'the way of unifying (with) the life energy,' or 'the way of combining forces'
All Japan Karate Championship	karate tournament held by the Japan Karate Association annually since 1957
All Japan Karate-do Federation (AJKF)	founded by Tōyama Kanken
bōgu (J.) 防具	protective equipment in full-contact sparring for kendo and karate
budō (J.) *mudo* (K.), *wudao* (Ch.) 武道	'martial way'
bugei (J.), *muyae* (K.), *wuyi* (Ch.) 武藝	'martial art'
bujutsu (J.), *musul* (K.), *wushu* (Ch.) 武術	'martial skill'
bushi (J.) 武士	Japanese warrior or warrior class, similar to the term samurai
bushidō (J.) 武士道	'the way of the warrior'
chadō (J.), *dado* (K.) 茶道	'way of tea' or tea ceremony
Ch'anghŏn hyŏng (K.)	forms developed by Choi Hong Hi
Ch'angmu Kwan (K.) (*Chang Moo Kwan*) 彰武館	'rising martial arts school,' successive school of *YMCA Kwŏnbŏp Pu*
chayu daeryŏn (K.) 自由 對鍊	free sparring, compare to *jiyū kumite*
Ch'ŏngdo Kwan (K.) (*Chung Do Kwan*) 青濤館	'blue wave school,' one of the five original taekwondo schools
Chosŏn Yŏnmu Kwan Kwŏnbŏp Pu (K.) 朝鮮研武館拳法部	'the great *Chosŏn* martial art of the *Kwŏnbŏp* division,' one of the five original taekwondo schools

dado (K.), *chadō* (J.) 茶道	'way of tea' or tea ceremony
Dai Nippon Butoku Kai (DNBK) (J.) 大日本武徳会	'Greater Japan Martial Virtue Society,' organization responsible for the Japanese martial arts
dao (Ch.), *dō'* (J.), *do* (K.) 道	'way'
dō' (J.), *do* (K.), *dao* (Ch.) 道	'way'
dobok (K.) 道服	'the clothing for the *do* (way),' the taekwondo uniform
dojang (K.), *dōjō* (J.) 道場	'place of *do*,' training hall or gym in taekwondo and karate
dōjō (J.), *dojang* (K.) 道場	'place of *do*,' training hall or gym in karate and taekwondo
gi 着 or *dōgi* 道着 (J.)	the Japanese martial arts uniform
hapkido (K.), *aikidō* (J.) 合氣道	'the way of unifying (with) the life energy,' or 'the way of combining forces'
han'gŭl	the Korean alphabet
Hanmadang (K.)	a taekwondo festival with athletics and forms competitions
Hanmu Kwan (K.), *Kanbukan* (J.) 韓武館	'Korean martial arts institute'
heian (J.), *p'yŏngan* (K.), *pinan* (used in Okinawa), *píng'an* (Ch.) 平安	'peaceful or calm,' a karate *kata*
hogu (K.) 護具	body protector in taekwondo
hwa (J.) 花	flower
hwarang (K.) 花郎	'flower youth' or 'flower boys'
hwarangdo (K.) 花郎道	'the way of the hwarang'
hwarang-do (K.) 花郎徒	'fellows of the hwarang'
hwasudo (K.) 花手道	'the way of the flower hand,' name of Hwang Kee's martial arts style during the late 1940s
hyŏng (K.), *kata* (J.) 型 / 形	form or pattern
ikken hissatsu (J.) 一拳必殺	'one blow – certain death'
International Taekwondo Federation (ITF)	founded by Choi Hong Hi in 1966, rival organization of the WTF, the ITF was (and is) supported by the North Korean government
Japan Karate Association (JKA), *Nihon Karate Kyokai* 日本空手協会	founded by senior *Shōtōkan* members

jiaodi (Ch.), *kakchŏ* (K.) 角觝	China-based wrestling
Jido Kwan (K.) 智道館	'school of the way of wisdom,' successive school of *Chosŏn Yŏnmu Kwan*
Jixiaoxinshu (Ch.) 紀效新書	'*New book recording effective techniques*,' an early Chinese martial arts manual
jiyū kumite (J.) 自由組手	free sparring
judo (K.), (J.) 柔道	'gentle way'
jūdō (J.) 柔道	judo or 'gentle way'
jueli (Ch.), *kangnyŏk* (K.) 角力	China-based wrestling
jūjutsu (J.), *jusul* (K.) 柔術	'gentle technique or skill'
jutsu (J.) 術	'skill'
kakchŏ (K.), *jiaodi* (Ch.) 角觝	China-based wrestling
kan (J.), *kwan* (K.) 館	lit.: 'hall 'or 'house,' but refers to a martial arts school or style; *kwan* were single institutes that spread out to become distinctive styles
Kanbukan (J.), *Hanmu Kwan* (K.) 韓武館	'Korean martial arts institute'
kangnyŏk (K.), *jueli* (Ch.) 角力	China-based wrestling
karate (J.), *tangsu* (K.), *tōdi* (used in Okinawa) 唐手	'China (Tang) hand'
karate (J.), *kongsu* (K.) 空手	'empty hand'
karate-dō (J.), *tangsudo* (K.) 唐手道	'way of the China hand'
karate-dō (J.), *kongsudo* (K.) 空手道	'way of empty hand'
karate–jutsu (J.) 唐手術	'skill of the *tang* hand,' used before the introduction of the term *karate-dō*
kata (J.), *hyŏng* (K.) 型 / 形	form or pattern
kendōgu (J.) 剣道具	kendo protective equipment
kenjutsu (J.) 剣術	'sword skill,' Japanese swordsmanship
kenpō (J.), *kwŏnbŏp* (K.), *quanfa* (Ch.) 拳法	'fist method' or China-based boxing
ki (K.), *qi* (Ch.) 氣	life force, energy, or principal, lit.: 'breath' or 'air'
kihon kumite (J.) 基本組手	basic sparring, similar to *yaksoku kumite* or prearranged sparring

Kōdōkan (J.) 講道館 — 'school of the study of the way,' judo school founded by Kanō Jigorō, worldwide headquarters of judo

kŏmdo (K.), *kendō* (J.) 劍道 — 'way of the sword,' Japanese swordsmanship

kongsu (K.), karate (J.) 空手 — 'empty hand'

kongsudo (K.), *karate-dō* (J.) 空手道 — 'way of empty hand'

Korea Subakdo Association — martial arts organization founded by Hwang Kee

Korea Taekkyon Federation (*Taehan T'aekkyŏn Yŏnmaeng*) — one of Korea's *t'aekkyŏn* associations

Korea Taesudo Association (*Taehan T'aesudo Hyŏphwoe*) — official name of Korea's martial arts association from 1961 to 1965

Koryŏsa (K.) 高麗史 — '*History of Koryŏ*,' principal surviving history book of Koryŏ Dynasty, composed after the fall of Koryŏ

Kukkiwon [*Kukkiwŏn*] (K.) 國技院 — lit.: 'hall or gymnasium of national skill or sport,' home of the World Taekwondo Academy, the official governing organization established by the South Korean government; responsible for promotions, promotion certificates, and technical matters such as instructor training and certification, since 1973

Kuk Mu [*Kungmu*] *hyŏng* (K.) — forms developed by Son Duk Sung

kuksul (K.), *guoshu* (Ch.) 國術 — lit.: 'national skill,' in South Korea, strongly *hapkido*-based; name derived from modern Chinese martial arts, the term *guoshu* (国术 simplified characters) was used from 1928 to 1948 in China by the Nationalists

kumite (J.) 組手 — lit.: 'grappling hands,' free fighting, sparring

kungfu (*Pinyin: gongfu*) (Ch.) 功夫 — lit.: 'task, work, ability,' generic Chinese term for exercise; generic term for Chinese martial arts in the West

kŭp / dan (K.), kyū / dan (J.) 級 / 段	student (color belts) and master (black belt) ranks
kwan (K.), kan (J.) 館	lit.: 'hall' or 'house,' but refers to a martial arts school or style; *kwan* were single institutes that spread out to become distinctive styles
kwŏnbŏp (K.), kenpō (J.), quanfa (Ch.) 拳法	'fist method' or China-based boxing
Kwŏnbŏp po (K.) 拳法譜	'fist-method documentation'
Kyokushin Kaikan (J.) 極真会館	'combined school of the ultimate truth,' karate style with emphasis on full-contact sparring without protectors, founded by Ōyama Masutatsu
kyū / dan (J.), kŭp / dan (K.) 級 / 段	student (color belts) and master (black belt) ranks
makiwara (J.), kwŏnko (K.) 卷藁	a wooden board and brick wrapped in straw or rope for punching which originates from Okinawan karate
mixed martial arts (MMA)	modern combat sport using grappling and striking in sparring
mudo (K.), budō (J.), wudao (Ch.) 武道	'martial way'
Mudŏk Kwan (K.) (Moo Duk Kwan) 武德館	'school of martial virtue,' one of the five original taekwondo schools
musul (K.), bujutsu (J.), wushu (Ch.) 武術	'martial skill'
muyae (K.), bugei (J.), wuyi (Ch.) 武藝	'martial art'
Muye chepo (K.) 武藝諸譜	'*Martial arts illustrations*,' first early Korean martial arts manual, China-based
Muye tobo t'ongji (K.) 武藝圖譜通志	'*Comprehensive illustrated manual of martial arts*,' early Korean martial arts manual, China-based
National Sports Festival (Chŏn'guk Ch'eyuk Daehwe)	nation-wide annual sports competition held in South Korea
Odo Kwan (Oh Do Kwan) (K.) 吾道館	'the school of my (or our) way,' founded by Choi Hong Hi in the military

P'algwae p'umsae (K.)	forms developed and used by the KTA during the late 1960s
píng'an (Ch.), *p'yŏngan* (K.), *heian* (J.), *pinan* (used in Okinawa) 平安	'peaceful or calm,' a karate *kata*
po (K.) 譜	'record' or 'table'
Protector Scoring System (PSS)	electronic body protector system used in taekwondo
p'umse (K.) 品勢 (품세), *p'umsae* (품새)	lit.: 'set of forms,' name for 'forms' in taekwondo, spelling in Korean 품세 before 1987, after 1987 품새
p'yŏngan (K.), *heian* (J.), *pinan* (used in Okinawa), *píng'an* (Ch.) 平安	'peaceful or calm,' a karate *kata*
qi (Ch.), *ki* (K.) 氣	life force, energy or principal, lit.: 'breath or air'
quanfa (Ch.), *kwŏnbŏp* (K.), *kenpō* (J.) 拳法	'fist method' or China-based boxing
randori (J.) 乱取り	free-style practice or sparring, term used in judo
Renbukan (J.) 練武館	'school of martial arts practice'
Republic of Korea (ROK)	official English name of South Korea
ryū (J.), *ryu* (K.) 流	'school' or 'style' in martial arts
samurai (J.) 侍	usually referred to in Japanese as *bushi*, Japanese warrior or warrior class
Shaolin Changquan (Ch.), *Solim Changkwŏn* (K.) 少林長拳	Chinese form of northern Shaolin style
Shaolin (Ch.), *Solim* (K.) 少林	lit.: 'young bamboo forest,' refers to the Chinese Shaolin kungfu, monks, and monastery
Shōrei-ryū (J.) 昭靈流	karate style in Okinawa, *Nahate* style
Shōrin-ryū (J.) 少林流	karate style in Okinawa, *Shurite*-style
Shōtō (J.) 松	'pine tree,' Funakoshi's pen name
Shōtōkan (J.) 松濤館 or *Shōtōkan-ryū* (J.) 松濤館流	'house of pine-waves' ('*Shōtō*' was Funakoshi's pen name), name of Funakoshi Gichin's karate headquarters and style

shoubo (Ch.), *subak* (K.) 手搏	'hand fighting,' China-based unarmed contest or boxing
Shūdōkan (J.) 修道館	'school for the reform of the way [of karate],' name of Tōyama Kanken's karate school
Shurite (J.) 首里手	'hand of Shuri,' ('Shuri' is an area in Ryūkyū), Okinawan karate style
Solim Changkwŏn (K.), *Shaolin Changquan* (Ch.) 少林長拳	Chinese form of northern Shaolin style
Solim (K.), Shaolin (Ch.) 少林	lit.: 'young bamboo forest,' refers to the Chinese Shaolin kungfu, monks, and monastery
Sŏn (K.), Zen (J.), *Chan* (Ch.) 禪	form of Mahayana Buddhism that developed in China
Songmu Kwan (K.) (*Song Moo Kwan*) 松武館	'pine tree martial arts school,' one of the five original taekwondo schools
ssirŭm (K.)	Korean-style wrestling
subak (K.), *shoubo* (Ch.) 手搏	'hand fighting,' China-based unarmed contest or boxing
subakdo (K.) 手搏道	'way of *subak*,' see *subak*
T'aegŭk (K.), *Taikyoku* (J.), *Taiji* (Ch.) 太極	source of the dual principle of Yin and Yang, name of some forms in Chinese, Japanese, and Korean martial arts
T'aegŭkkwon (K.), *Taikyoku* (J.), *Taijiquan* (Ch.) 太極拳	Chinese form and/or martial arts style
Taegŭk p'umsae (K.)	forms used by the WTF
t'aekkyŏn (K.) 태견/택견	traditional Korean folk game, nowadays described as martial art
taekwondo (*t'aekwŏndo*) (K.) 跆拳道	lit.: 'step on, fist, way,' generally translated as the 'way of kicking and punching'
Taikyoku (J.), *T'aegŭk* (K.), *Taiji* (Ch.) 太極	source of the dual principle of Yin and Yang, name of some forms in Chinese, Japanese, and Korean martial arts
Taiji (Ch.), *T'aegŭk* (K.), *Taikyoku* (J.) 太極	source of the dual principle of Yin and Yang, name of some forms in Chinese, Japanese, and Korean martial arts

t'akkyŏn (K.) 卓見/ 托肩	lit.: 'high view'/'push shoulder,' former pronunciation for *t'aekkyŏn*
Tan'gi (K.)	refers to the foundation of the Korean state by the mythical founder Tan-gun in 2333 BCE, the Republic of Korea numbered books according to this date from 1948–1961
'Tang Soo Do Moo Duk Kwan Federation'	also known as 'Tang Soo Do (Soo Bahk Do) Moo Duk Kwan Federation,' founded by Hwang Kee
tangsu (K.), karate (J.), *tōdi* (used in Okinawa) 唐手	'China (Tang) hand'
tangsudo (K.), *karate-dō* (J.) 唐手道	'way of the China hand'
tatami (J.) 畳	judo mat
Thai-boxing (or Muay Thai)	traditional martial art of Thailand
t'ŭl (K.) 機	'frame,' term introduced for forms in ITF taekwondo
Ultimate Fighting Championships (UFC)	mixed martial arts competition
World Taekwondo Academy (WTA)	Kukkiwon-based, established by the South Korean government; organization responsible for technical and educational matters, as well as world-wide black belt promotions of the WTF
World Taekwondo Federation (WTF)	official taekwondo organization which is recognized by the IOC, promoted by the South Korean government, founded in 1973
wudao (Ch.), *mudo* (K.), *budō* (J.) 武道	'martial way'
wushu (Ch.), *musul* (K.), *bujutsu* (J.) 武術	'martial skill'
wuyi (Ch.), *muyae* (K.), *bugei* (J.) 武藝	'martial art'
yaksŏk daeryŏn (K.) 約束 對鍊	prearranged contest, similar to Japanese *yaksoku kumite*
yaksoku kumite (J.) 約束組手	prearranged fighting or sparring
Yi-Ching (Ch.), *Yŏkkyŏng* (K.) 易經	*Book of Changes*
YMCA *Kwŏnbŏp Pu* (K.) 拳法部	'*Kwŏnbŏp* Division,' one of the five original taekwondo schools
Yŏkkyŏng (K.), Yi-Ching (Ch.) 易經	*Book of Changes*

Zen (J.), Sŏn (K.), *Chan* (Ch.) 禪	form of Mahayana Buddhism that developed in China

Individuals mentioned in this study

Asato (Yasutsune) Ankō (安里 安恒)	Funakoshi's and many other famous karate masters' instructor in Okinawa
Chai Ik Jin [Ch'oe Ik-chin]	member of *Ch'angmu Kwan*, later *Kangdŏk Wŏn*
Cho Sihak Henry [Cho Si-hak]	member of *Jido Kwan*
Ch'oe Song-nam	member of *Ch'ŏngdo Kwan*
Ch'oe Yŏng-nyŏl	Korean heavy weight champion during the 1960s, member of *Jido Kwan*
Choi Hong Hi [Ch'oe Hong-hi]	founder of *Odo Kwan*
Chŏn Il-sŏp	member of *Jido Kwan*
Chŏn Sang-sŏp	founder of *Chosŏn Yŏnmu Kwan*
Chung Kuk Hyun [Chŏn Kuk-hyŏn]	four-time world champion, professor at Korea National Sport University (한국체육대학교)
Funakoshi Gichin (船越 義珍)	considered the 'father' of modern karate, founder of *Shōtōkan*
Funakoshi (Yoshitaka) Gigō (船越 義豪)	Funakoshi's third son
Itosu (Yasutsune) Ankō (糸洲 安恒)	often considered the 'grandfather' of karate, Funakoshi's and many other famous karate masters' instructor in Okinawa
Hwang Kee [Hwang Ki]	founder of *Mudŏk Kwan*
Kang Won Shik [Kang Wŏn-sik]	member of *Songmu Kwan*, former president of the Kukkiwon (2010–2013)
Kanō Jigorō (嘉納 治五郎)	founder of judo, first Asian IOC member
Kim Il Sung [Kim Il-sŏng]	dictator (prime minister and president) of North Korea or Democratic People's Republic of Korea from 1948 to 1994

Kim Sei Hyeok [Kim Se-hyŏk]	multiple Korean national team coach, former director of the Samsung S-1 professional team, former general director of the KTA
Kim Un Yong [Kim Un-yong]	former president of the WTF (1973–2004), and former IOC vice-president
Ko Eui Min [Ko Ŭi-min]	the Korean national team head coach for the 1975 and 1977 World Championships, member of *Mudŏk Kwan*
Lee Chong Woo [Yi Chong-u]	member and successive leader of *Jido Kwan*, former secretary general and vice president of the World Taekwondo Federation, and former vice president of the Kukkiwon
Lee Sung Kook [Yi Sŭng-guk]	several times Korean national team coach, former president of Korea National Sport University (한국체육대학교)
Lee Won Kuk [Yi Wŏn'-guk]	founder of *Ch'ŏngdo Kwan*
Mabuni Kenwa (摩文仁 賢和)	founder of *Shitō-ryū* karate
Motobu Chōki (本部 朝基)	karate pioneer in free fighting, perhaps the first Okinawan karate instructor who settled in Japan
Nakayama Masatoshi [中山 正敏]	*Shōtōkan* student of Funakoshi
Nam T'ae-hŭi	member of *Ch'ŏngdo Kwan*, later co-founder of *Odo Kwan*
Nishiyama Hidetaka (西山 英峻)	member of *Shōtōkan*
No Pyŏng-jik	founder of *Songmu Kwan*
Ŏm Un-kyu	member and successive leader of *Ch'ŏngdo Kwan*
Ōyama Masutatsu (大山 倍達)	founder of *Kyokushin Kaikan karate*, Korean name Ch'oe Yŏng-ŭi
Pak Ch'ŏl-hŭi	member of YMCA *Kwŏnbŏp Pu*, founder of *Kangdŏk Wŏn*

Park Chung Hee [Pak Chŏng-hŭi]	former South Korean military dictator and president from 1961 to 1979
Rhee Syngman [Yi Sŭng-man]	first South Korean president from 1948 to 1960
Son Duk Sung [Son Dŏk-sŏng]	member and successive leader of *Ch'ŏngdo Kwan*, successive leader of *Kungmu Kwan*
Song Tŏk-ki	'last surviving *t'aekkyŏn* player of the Chosŏn Dynasty'
Tōyama Kanken (遠山 寬賢)	founder of *Shūdōkan* karate
Rhee Jhoon (Yi Chun'-gu)	member of *Ch'ŏngdo Kwan*, moved to the United States in 1956, claims of having been the first Korean taekwondo instructor in the U.S.
Yi Kyo-yun	member of *Chosŏn Yŏnmu Kwan/Jido Kwan*, later founder of *Hanmu Kwan*
Yun K'wae-pyŏng	founder of *Kanbukan*, leader of *Jido Kwan*, likely introduced full-contact sparring to Korea
Yun Pyŏng-in	founder of the *YMCA Kwŏnbŏp Pu*

About the author

Professor Udo Moenig was born in Peißenberg, near Munich, Germany. As a young man, he studied various martial arts, and began taekwondo in 1979. During the 1980s, he was once a competition member of the German national taekwondo team, and trained professionally for four years as a member of the German national military team, headquartered at the Sportschule in Sonthofen. In 1988, after finishing military service, he traveled extensively in Asia and, in 1990,

Figure A.1 Foreigners training in Korea at Dongsŏng High School, during the early 1990s. From left: Steven Whittle, Kim Sei Hyeok (at that time, the trainer at Dongsŏng High School), Bobby Clayton, Steven D. Capener, the author, and Todd Johnson
Source: Courtesy of Steven Whittle.

settled for further studies and training in Korea. A B.A. in Asian Studies (University of Maryland) was soon followed by three terms of North Korean Studies (Graduate School for North Korean Studies), culminating in Master's and Ph.D. degrees in Physical Education (Keimyung University), with concentrations in taekwondo, history, and philosophy. In 2005, professor Moenig was appointed by the Youngsan University Department of Taekwondo, in Yangsan, as the first foreigner in Korea to teach taekwondo at university level.

Index

aikidō 37, 58–9, 201 *see also* hapkido
All Japan Karate Championship 88, 94, 100, 108, 163
All Japan Karate-do Federation (AJKF) 93
American martial arts literature 9, 149
Asato (Yasutsune) Ankō 39, 43, 152
axe-kick 132, 139, 212

back-kick 116–17, 123–5, 135
ball of the foot 100, 119–21
bit-kick 73,117, 126 *see also* under-kick
blocks in sparring 118, 138
Bodhidharma 13, 156 *see also* Zen
body protector *see bōgu; hogu*
bōgu 86–93, 190 *see also* hogu
boxing 85, 99, 110, 118, 129, 145, 176–9
boxing gloves 85, 89, 109–10
boxing ring 85, 99, 123
budō 37, 146–8, 154–5, 161–2, 188, 199, 200 *see also mudo; wudao*
bugei 146, 153–6, 66, 188, 199, 200 *see also* martial arts; *muyae; wuyi*
bujutsu 37, 146–8, 162, 199, 200 *see also musul; wushu*
bushi see samurai
bushidō 153–4

Capener, Steven D. 147–8, 197
Chaemulpo 20–1, 26
Chai Ik Jin 7, 75, 91
Ch'anghŏn hyŏng (*Ch'anghŏn* school or forms) 68–9, 209
Ch'angmu Kwan (Chang Moo Kwan) 7, 42, 74–5, 91 *see also* YMCA Kwŏnbŏp Pu
Chinese boxing *see kwŏnbŏp; shoubo; subak*
Chinese cosmology 151, 160 *see also* Confucianism; Daoism; *T'aegŭk*
Chinese forms *see* Shaolin Changquan; *T'aegŭkkwon* form
Cho, Sihak Henry, 7, 76, 117, 133, 177
Ch'oe Song-nam 6, 73–4
Ch'oe Yŏng-nyŏl 9, 118, 132, 197
Choi Hong Hi 6, 7, 14, 43, 46–9, 51, 53–5, 68–9, 74, 77, 89, 108–9, 111, 117, 133, 157–8, 177, 209 *see also* Odo Kwan
Chŏn Il-sŏp 92
Chŏn Sang-sŏp 40–1, 43, 90 *see also Chosŏn Yŏnmu Kwan Kwŏnbŏp Pu*
Ch'ŏngdo Kwan (Chung Do Kwan) 6, 7, 39, 40, 42, 47, 49, 73–6
Ch'ŏnggu yŏngŏn 18
Chosŏn Dynasty 14–16, 18, 21, 23, 25, 27, 147, 187
Chosŏn musa yŏngungchŏn 22–3
Chosŏn Yŏnmu Kwan Kwŏnbŏp Pu 41–2, 44–5, 74–5, 90 *see also* Jido Kwan
Chung Kuk Hyun 9, 137
Chūō University 39, 46
combination kicking 100, 121
Communism 52–3
Confucianism 66, 146, 153, 156–8, 160, 186
counterattack kicks 101, 123–8, 131, 138–9, 212
court for fighting 99–100, 103, 119, 123
crescent-kick 116–17, 133
Culin, Steward 22
Cultural Korea 52
cut-kick 134–6, 212

Dai Nippon Butoku Kai (DNBK) 50, 153
dao 37, 199, 200 *see also do*
Daoism 153
demonstration taekwondo 140, 166

diversification of taekwondo 165–8, 192–3
Dō (*do*) 37, 153, 155–7, 199–201 *see also* dao
dobok 50, 61,193
dojang 50 *see also* dōjō
dōjō 41, 59
double-kick 127–8, 137, 139–4, 212
Draeger, Don. F. 146, 152–3

education in martial arts 154–5, 158, 183–4
electronic body protector 105, 107–8, 127–9, 132 *see also* hogu
electronic scoreboards 103–5
esoteric beliefs 151–4, 188 *see also* Confucianism; Daoism; *ki*; Shintōism; Zen-Buddhism
ethics in martial arts 37, 153–5, 158

fast-kick 134–6, 139, 212
feint motions in sparring 119, 134–5
forms/self-defense taekwondo *see* traditional taekwondo
forms training 66–9, 180–4 *see also* kata; *p'umsae*
free sparring *see* sparring
front-kick 115–17, 130–1, 139, 179–80, 211
front leg kicks 102, 108, 127–8, 134–6
front-rising-kick 116–17, 139, 179–80, 183
full-contact sparring 84–9, 99, 109–10, 118, 164, 182–3, 190 *see also bōgu*; hogu
Funakoshi Gichin, 5, 35, 38–41, 43–7, 67–71, 73–8, 80, 84–5, 87–8, 93, 115–17, 151–2, 155–6, 158, 182, 188–90, 208–10 *see also* Shōtōkan
Funakoshi and health aspects 151–2
Funakoshi and sparring 84–5
Funakoshi's books 5
Funakoshi's *kata* 67–71, 208–10
Funakoshi's Korean students 40–1
Funakoshi's philosophy 155–6
Funakoshi (Yoshitaka) Gigō 39, 43, 116

gaining or loosing points by chance 103–4
gi 40, 50 *see also* dobok
guoshu 42 *see also* kuksul

Haedong chukchi 23
Hanmadang 79, 148, 166
Hanmu Kwan 75 *see also* Kanbukan

hapkido 37, 58–9, 159, 201 *see also* aikido
headgear 101, 109 *see also* protective equipment
Herriegel, Eugen 152
high kicks 101–2, 107–8, 116, 128 *see also* multiple points
hogu 92–4, 99–100, 119 *see also bōgu*; electronic body protector
hook-kick 117, 133, 139, 211
Hwang Kee 4, 6, 42–4, 53, 72–3, 77, 93, 117, 126, 157 *see also* Mudŏk Kwan
hwarang 6, 13, 15, 44, 76, 157–8
hwarangdo 14–15, 157–8
hwasudo 6, 44
hyŏng *see* kata

ikken hissatsu 100, 163
Important Intangible Cultural Asset 18, 24
inside-out-kick 73–4, 78
instep roundhouse-kick 100, 119–21, 138
internal/external martial arts 151, 200
International Olympic Committee (IOC) 4, 54, 101–2, 106 *see also* Olympic Games
International Taekwondo Federation (ITF) 4, 52–4, 69, 108–9, 206
invention of tradition 25–7, 186–7
Itosu (Yasutsune) Ankō 39, 41, 43, 50, 68, 152

Japan Karate Association (JKA) 88, 95, 111
Japanese militarism 38, 158–9, 163, 188
Japanese nationalism 38, 153, 155
Jido Kwan 41, 90–4, 190 *see also* Chosŏn Yŏnmu Kwan Kwŏnbŏp Pu
Jixiaoxinshu 16 *see also* Muye tobo t'ongji
judge/referee 103–6, 129
judo (*jūdō*) 37, 39, 50, 54, 66, 84, 111, 116, 156, 162–4, 181, 184, 188, 191
jūjutsu 146–8, 154, 162
jump kicks 74, 117, 134–6, 139
jutsu 37, 199–201

K-1 kick-boxing 110, 123
kakchŏ 15
kan 39 *see also* kwan
Kanbukan 41, 87–8, 90 *see also* Hanmu Kwan; Renbukan
Kang Won Shik 48, 101, 205
Kanō Jigorō 37, 50, 87, 147, 152, 154–5, 161–2, 169, 181, 188

karate 34–46 *see also tangsu; kongsu*
karate clubs at universities 40–1, 44, 46, 163
karate forms 67–8, 70–1
karate in Okinawa 34–6, 150
karate kicking techniques 115–17
karate literature 5–6
karate philosophy 155–6
karate sparring 84–8, 116, 138 *see also bōgu*; non-contact sparring
karate-dō 37, 155–6 *see also kongsudo; tangsudo*
kata 66–71, 161, 180–2, 191–2, 208–10
Kaya 36
kendo (*kendō*) 37, 39, 84, 86, 89, 90, 92, 111, 116, 146–8, 156, 161, 164, 184, 188, 191
kendo equipment 86, 89, 92
kenjutsu 146–8, 161
kenpō see kwŏnbŏp
ki 118, 151
kicking techniques 115–49, 211–12
Kim Il Sung 53
Kim Sei Hyeok 8, 118–19, 132, 135, 137, 197
Kim Un Yong 52–4, 106, 111
Ko Eui Min 8, 100, 118–19, 124–6, 133, 198
Kōdōkan judo 162 *see also* judo
Koguryŏ Kingdom 13–14
kŏmdo 201 *see also* kendo
kongsu 37, 44 *see also* karate; *karate-dō*
kongsudo see karate-dō
Korea Subakdo Association 93 *see also* Hwang Kee
Korea Taekkyon Federation (*Taehan T'aekkyŏn Yŏnmaeng*) 13
Korea Taekwondo Association (KTA) 49, 51–3, 69, 76, 78–80, 93, 108, 159, 165
Korea Taesudo Association (*Taehan T'aesudo Hyŏphwoe*) 49, 68, 75, 92–3
Korean karate 51, 55, 76 *see also kongsudo; tangsudo*
Korean War 46, 56, 186–7
Korean wrestling *see ssirŭm*
Koryŏ Kingdom 14, 18, 36
Koryŏsa 14
Kŭki taekwondo (movie) 23
Kukkiwon 3, 52, 166
kuksul 42, 53 *see also guoshu; hapkido*
kumite 88 *see also* sparring
kungfu 199, 200
kŭp / dan 50, 53 *see also kyū / dan*
kwan 39–43, 46, 53 *see also kan*

kwan names (taekwondo founding *kwan*) 45
kwŏnbŏp 16–17, 21, 26, 35, 44–5, 200
Kwŏnbŏp po 16; *po*, 67
Kyokushin Kaikan 5, 44, 109–10
kyū / dan, 50

Lee Chong Woo 8, 24, 34, 41, 43–5, 52, 54, 69, 76–7, 90–2, 94, 105–6, 210 *see also Jido Kwan*
Lee Sung Kook 8, 135–6
Lee Won Kuk 7, 39–4, 42–4, 48, 75–6, 210 *see also Ch'ŏngdo Kwan*
low kicks 117, 139

Mabuni Kenwa 5, 41, 87, 115
McCune-Reischauer system 3
majority score system 103–4
makiwara 70, 118
martial arts (definition) 145 *see also bugei; muyae; wuyi*
martial dances 66
Meiji Restoration 57, 146, 153–4, 158, 188
militarism in taekwondo 47, 50, 158–9
mixed martial arts (MMA) 109–10, 183, 192
modernists 1–2, 51, 191 *see also* sport taekwondo
Motobu Chōki 5, 38, 84–5, 87, 93–4, 115, 190
mudo 199–201 *see also budō; wudao*
Mudŏk Kwan (*Moo Duk Kwan*) 42–3, 72, 93
multiple points 99, 101–3, 128–9, 133
musul 199, 201 *see also bujutsu; wushu*
murals of Korean martial arts 13–14
muyae 199, 201 *see also bugei; wuyi*
Muye chepo 16–17, 67
Muye tobo t'ongji 16, 67 *see also Jixiaoxinshu*
mythology in martial arts 150, 188–9

Nakayama Masatoshi 85, 133
Nam T'ae-hŭi 6, 43, 47
Namwŏn'gosa 21, 27
national sport of Korea 52
National Sports Festival 92, 98
nationalism in Korea 44–8, 52, 55–6, 157–60, 167, 186–7, 189, 193
Nishiyama Hidetaka 6, 74, 77, 117, 132, 177–8
Nitobe Inazō 154
No Pyŏng-jik 40–1, 43–4 *see also Songmu Kwan*

Noble, William Arthur 21
non-contact/light-contact sparring 85, 88, 108–10

Odo Kwan (*Oh Do Kwan*) 45, 47
Okinawa 34–6, 57, 84, 155–6, 162–3 *see also* Ryūkyū islands
Okinawa-te 35, 76, 156 *see also te*; karate
Olympic Games 3, 9, 79, 98, 101–3, 106, 111, 165, 192 *see also* IOC
Olympic sport 4, 54, 79, 106, 162, 194
Ōyama Masutatsu 6, 44, 89 *see also* Kyokushin Kaikan

Paekcha-do 22
Pak Ch'ŏl-hŭi 6, 74–5, 208
P'algwae p'umsae 69, 76, 159–60, 210
paper and pencil scoring system 103–4
Park Chung Hee 24, 49, 51–3, 60, 111, 186
philosophy in taekwondo 156–61, 163–9, 190–5
power in sparring 118, 123–3, 128–9
protective (safety) equipment 101, 103, 108–10, 124, 164, 190 *see also bōgu*; *hogu*
Protector Scoring System (PSS) *see* electronic body protector
p'umsae 69, 76, 78–9, 160, 166, 181–2, 192–4, 210 *see also T'aegŭk forms*
punch 118, 127, 129–30, 176–9, 212
push-kick 108, 117, 130–2, 139, 212

qi see ki
quanfa see kwŏnbŏp

randori 181
Renbukan 88, 98 *see also Kanbukan*
Revised Romanization of Korean 3
Rhee Syngman 23, 40, 48
Romanization of Asian terms 3
roundhouse-kick 102, 116–18, 119–21, 128, 130, 137–9, 179–80, 183, 211
ryū (*ryu*) 68, 146 *see also kan*; *kwan*
Ryūkyū islands 34–5, 57, 150 *see also* Okinawa

samurai 38, 146–7, 150, 152–4, 157, 188
science in martial arts 154–5, 157, 177–8
scoring transparency 102–7
self-defense 1, 2, 4, 51, 70, 84, 147–51, 158, 163–5, 182, 189–3
self-improvement/self-cultivation 37, 146–8, 151, 188 *see also, budō*; *dao*; *do*

Shaolin Changquan see Solim Changkwŏn
Shaolin Monastery 13, 150
Shaolin fighting/monks 151
Shintōism 153
Shitō-ryū 41, 43
Shōrei-ryū 39, 68, 71, 208–10
Shōrin-ryū 39, 68, 71, 208–10
Shōtōkan 5, 39–40, 43, 46, 55, 74–6, 189 *see also Songmu Kwan*
Shōtō 40
shoubo 14–15, 44, 200 *see also subak*
Shūdōkan 41, 74
Shurite karate 35, 39, 41, 43, 74, 87, 190
side-kick 108, 115–17, 129–32, 139, 179–80, 211
side-rising-kick 116–17
Silla Dynasty 14–15 *see also hwarang*
Silla warriors 76–7
Sin Han-sŭng 24
snap-kick 116–17, 119–21, 131, 179
Solim Changkwŏn 72–3, 208
Son Duk Sung 7, 40, 43, 48, 68, 76, 89, 117, 210
Song Tŏk-ki 18, 20, 23, 25–6, 28, 74
Songmu Kwan 40, 43, 69 *see also Shōtōkan*
sparring 84–5, 116, 161, 175 *see also* full-contact sparring; non-contact/light-contact sparring
sparring/competition taekwondo *see* sport taekwondo
speed in sparring 119, 123–3, 128, 135, 137–9
spinning-back-kick 74, 117, 125, 133–4, 139, 211
sport taekwondo/taekwondo as a sport 4, 147–8, 164–6, 190–4 *see also* modernists
ssirŭm 15, 19–22, 67
stances in sparring 119, 176–7, 180
stalling fights 107
steps in sparring 119, 127–8, 134–5, 138–9, 180
sudden death rule 103
subak 14–15, 44 *see also shoubo*
subakdo 44
sumō 52
Suzuki D. T. 152–3

T'aegŭk 160
T'aegŭk forms (*p'umsae*) 69, 76, 78, 160, 179, 210 *see also p'umsae*
t'aegŭkkwon see taijiquan
T'aegŭkkwon form 73

Taikyoku forms 70–1, 208
t'aekkyŏn 13–14, 16–28, 47–9, 67, 73–4, 76–8, 187
t'akkyŏn 18
Taek'wae-do 18–20
taekwondo (invention of name) 48–9
taekwondo forms *see hyŏng*; *kata*; *p'umsae*
taekwondo in the military 47, 51
taekwondo literature 6–9, 72–8
Taekwondo Peace Corps 166
Taekwondo World Championships 77, 98, 101, 103, 126
taesudo 7 *see also* Korea Taesudo Association
Taiji see T'aegŭk
taijiquan 151
Taijiquan form *see T'aegŭkkwon* form
Tang Dynasty 35–6
Tang Soo Do Moo Duk Kwan Federation 53
tangsu 35, 37 *see also* karate
tangsudo 37, 44–5 *see also* karate-dō
tatami 162
te 35 *see also* karate
Thai-boxing 85, 110, 121–2
thrust-kick 116–17
tōdi see karate
Tokugawa (Edo) period 146–7, 153–4, 188
Tōyama Kanken 41–3, 90, 190 *see also* Shūdōkan
traditional taekwondo 4, 164–5, 190–4
traditional taekwondo technique 176–84
traditionalists 1–2, 51, 191
t'ul 69
turn-kick 137
turning kicks 102, 128 *compare to* turn-kick

Ultimate Fighting Championships (UFC) 109–10 *see also* mixed martial arts
under-kick 126–7, 131, 139, 212

video replay 105, 108

warrior ethos/spirit 38, 146–8, 157 *see also hwarang*; samurai
weight divisions 101–2
World Cultural Heritage 13, 26
World Para-Taekwondo Championships 166
World Taekwondo Academy (WTA) 3
World Taekwondo Federation (WTF) 4, 14, 53–4, 78, 80, 98–9, 101, 106–9, 160, 165–6, 194
World Taekwondo Poomsae Championships 79, 166
wudao 199, 200 *see also mudo*; *budō*
wushu 199, 200 *see also bujutsu*; *musul*
wuyi 199, 200 *see also bugei*; *muyae*

Yabu Kentsū 50
yaksŏk daeryŏn 85 *see also yaksoku kumite*
yaksoku kumite 84 *see also yaksŏk daeryŏn*
Yi Kyo-yun 7, 75, 117, 133, 209
YMCA Kwŏnbŏp Pu 41–3, 52, 74–5, 77–8, 90–1
Yun K'wae-pyŏng 41, 43, 87–8, 90, 93–4, 190 *see also Jido Kwan*
Yun Pyŏng-in 41–3, 53, 74–5, 90 *see also YMCA Kwŏnbŏp Pu*

Zen (Zen-Buddhism) 152, 155–7